T0198468

In the Interim

■ ■ ■ ■

In the Interim

Strategies for Interim Ministers and Congregations

2ND EDITION

BARBARA CHILD AND KEITH KRON

Editors

Skinner House Books
Boston

www.skinnerhouse.org

Printed in the United States

Cover design by David Brennan
Text design by Suzanne Morgan

print ISBN: 978-1-55896-793-9
eBook ISBN: 978-1-55896-794-6

6 5 4 3
25 24 23 22

Note on language usage: In the interest of transgender inclusivity, this volume
uses plural pronouns when referring to individuals as well as to groups of two
or more.

Library of Congress Cataloging-in-Publication Data

Names: Child, Barbara, 1938- editor. | Kron, Keith, editor.
Title: In the interim : strategies for interim ministers and congregations /
    Barbara Child and Keith Kron, editors.
Description: 2nd Edition. | Boston : Skinner House Books, 2017. | Includes
    bibliographical references and index.
Identifiers: LCCN 2017002570 (print) | LCCN 2017005202 (ebook) | ISBN
    9781558967939 (pbk. : alk. paper) | ISBN 9781558967946
Subjects: LCSH: Unitarian Universalist churches. | Interim clergy--Unitarian
    Universalist churches. | Change--Religious aspects--Unitarian Universalist
    churches.
Classification: LCC BX9841.3 .I5 2017 (print) | LCC BX9841.3 (ebook) | DDC
    253/.39132--dc23
LC record available at https://lccn.loc.gov/2017002570

Contents

■ ■ ▓ ■

Introduction

KEITH KRON

Many years ago, before I became a minister, I taught elementary school. On the last day of every school year, I presented my fourth graders with one final assignment: Write a letter of advice to my fourth-grade class for next year. One year, Tasha wrote this letter:

> Dear New 4th Grader,
> Welcome to this room. In Mr. Kron's class you will learn a lot about geography, do some cool science experiments, and you will get to read a lot of books. Mr. Kron will read to you every day. He will even read you *Winnie-the-Pooh*. You will really like Mr. Kron. You will really hate *Winnie-the-Pooh*.
> Love, Tasha

If only ministries ended with such gracious appraisals. The assignment was very popular with my students, I think because they needed some way to mark their own transitions, to reflect on where they had been and look toward the future.

Transitions are a part of life. Transitions in ministry are no less inevitable, and no congregation or minister can avoid them, nor should they try. Some of us do transition well; others need more practice. It is not a one-size-fits-all process.

One minister works well with one congregation but isn't as successful with another. Some congregations are better served by long-term ministries, others by shorter ones. I know a few congregations that thrive the most during the interim ministry. But every ministry ends. The new minister probably won't force the congregation to listen to *Winnie-the-Pooh*, but might insist on a new look at its structure, its social justice work, or its leadership development. Congregations need new and different ministries in order to adapt and stay relevant. Different generational needs require agility and flexibility.

To that end, ministry itself is changing. The long-term pastorate is less common and even less desired than it once was. Interim ministry was not a concept that existed thirty years ago but has evolved so that most of our congregations now do at least two years of interim work. Some congregations can manage with just a contract minister for particular pieces of ministry, such as preaching and pastoral care. Others know that they have chronic issues needing work and opt for a developmental ministry to focus on them. The Unitarian Universalist Association (UUA) is working to be responsive to the changing nature of congregational needs.

One of the brighter joys in my work as UUA director of ministerial transitions is seeing that more congregations now intentionally take the interim period to assess themselves and make their congregations richer, more vibrant places to be a Unitarian Universalist in the twenty-first century.

Now more than ever, we need good ministry and good interim ministry.

I once heard retired Starr King School for the Ministry professor Til Evans charge a minister, "In your ministry, you will be asked to be in a great variety of roles—preacher, teacher, counselor, scholar, activist, fundraiser, and much more. To be a good minister, my charge to you is this: Resist role, and just be present."

Her advice seems counterintuitive, but good ministry, being present, allows for more flexibility and openness than being overdirected. Sometimes simply asking the questions ("Why have you always done it this way? How would you like it to be?") causes more self-reflection and more change than any sermon could.

Psychologist Virgina Satir famously asserted, "People prefer the certainty of misery to the misery of uncertainty." Ministerial transitions can feel like an earthquake to some congregations. The congregation has slipped into a routine (even if chaos is the routine), but suddenly the world is no longer as it was. The minister is leaving. In these moments of the unknown, of transition, we need ministry the most.

Often, the congregation either tries to keep things exactly the same or breathes a sigh of relief now that "that minister" is gone and harkens back to a time when everything was right with the world. Often, the new interim minister finds the congregation trying to do both. Another common discovery for the interim is that certain things haven't been done in a long time. The website has not been updated, and the calendar reflects events from March of last year. Volunteers have not been recognized. The Board does not inform the congregation of decisions from their meetings.

What sold me on interim ministry was seeing an actual interim minister at work. Back in the late 1980s, I was a Board member in my home congregation. We'd lost our third settled minister in just over a decade. The longest had stayed four years. Twice we blamed the settled minister. Once we blamed bad luck.

We brought in an interim minister, the first we'd ever had. When he asked if we were a social club or a church, people got mad. He suggested that Board meetings shouldn't go until 1:00 a.m. He kept asking us why we did things the way we did. People got madder. He raised issues such as how we had treated ministers. He asked why we couldn't use the word *worship*. And he kept reminding us that this was what interim ministers were supposed to do.

The Board actually engaged in group learning. Together, we read Kennon Callahan's *Twelve Keys to an Effective Church*. Leadership implemented an executive committee of the Board that planned the agenda and limited meetings to no more than two hours. The leadership engaged in actual long-range planning.

When the new minister was called, the church worked in partnership with our new religious leader in ways we had never done before. For the first time, the church grew. We built a religious education wing that had been promised thirty years before. We added a second service. The church began to have an impact in the wider community.

The church would not have made this progress without the interim minister's special brand of ministry. He raised questions, let us get angry, and then connected us with the resources to answer those questions and gain clarity about who we wanted to be. I give him credit for helping my home congregation become the kind of place we had hoped for. The two settled ministers who followed were not only treated well but stayed—the first for over seven years and the second for more than a decade. Once a place of drama and chaos, the church stabilized, becoming a leading voice for liberal religion.

Interim ministry is hard, transformative work, and this book is for those who are called to it, and for congregations committed to making the most of the gifts of interim time. It's a time to explore the cultural geography of the church, do some really cool experiments, and get ready to make the next ministry a success, but the congregation will have to listen to some things they don't want to hear along the way. My co-editor Barbara and I hope this book will remind you of what you already know: If you wish for the world to change and be better, you have to start with yourself.

Make the most of this time. You'll be better for it.

About the Second Edition

In recent years, many congregations and ministers have come to a better sense of how best to navigate ministerial change and transition teams have begun to gain a better understanding of how their congregation's past influences who they are now and who they will become. As a result, Barbara and I decided we needed to include in this second edition new materials related specifically to these changes.

The advent of developmental ministry is one such change. It is explored in depth in this edition, along with other types of transitional ministry, in a new essay written by Nancy Bowen, the architect of developmental ministry. What happens if a congregation finds itself in transition without an interim minister and yet wanting to engage in productive assessment of its current circumstances? In another new essay in this edition, Barbara has written up her consulting experience with two congregations and what she has termed "jump-start transition work." Olivia Holmes has done jump-start transition work in tandem with a new interim minister, which enabled them to combine the excitement of a new interim minister with the experience of a retired interim minister still wishing to contribute to a congregation's healthy ministerial transition. This hybrid jump-start ministry is chronicled here in an additional new essay. I spoke with veteran interim ministers about how interim ministry is adapting to a quickly changing world. The interviews are combined into another new essay for further reflection. We have also updated terminology throughout the book and the resources section.

Barbara and I hope you find that, with these new essays and updates, this second edition of *In the Interim* serves you well. We fondly hope that this important field will continue to develop and there will eventually be enough new learnings for yet another new edition as the work continues.

PART I

The Idea

The History, Philosophy, and Impact of Interim Ministry

MARGARET KEIP

■ ■ ▦ ■

Images of paradise abound in creation stories and myths around the globe. Since humans began spinning stories, we've envisioned life beginning in hope and glory. And then something goes awry. In the Judeo-Christian heritage we share as Unitarian Universalists, the Bible tells a story set in a garden called Eden. There the first humans are enticed by knowledge, and in choosing it, are wrenched from paradise. It's a clever tale. Without awareness and self-awareness and compelling desire, the story would end there. Instead, all of life followed.

The insight captured in the loss of Eden echoes in our lives too. When you or I join a congregation, or when we join together with others to begin one, we invest it with deep hope. We hold close a vision of what it may be. And life intervenes. As the old saying goes, life is what happens while we are making other plans. Interim ministry intentionally focuses on what we do when life happens and the future breaks open.

Former transitions director for the Unitarian Universalist Association (UUA) John Weston writes, "When radical change is forced upon a congregation, often by the departure of a minister, the task is simple to name: it is to accept the change and move on to embrace the opportunities that change allows. This, naturally, is more easily said than done." Whatever the reason for a settled minister's departure—retirement, debilitating illness, death, a call to opportunity or obligation elsewhere, conflicts that fail to resolve, misconduct that destroys relationship—*life* has happened. Interim ministry engages with the downsides and upsides of life, of change. It builds a bridge from what *was* to *what will be*.

Let's step back a moment for a broader picture of our faith endeavor. Consider religions as offering frameworks that render life coherent and assure us that we *belong* to the human family, to the earth, to All That Is, however we name it. A religion that fits us helps us know we are at home in the universe. Religion seeks a cosmic view; it's a whole-picture enterprise.

Thus a religious community touches every aspect of our lives. It invites us to come together to grow more wholly, more fully, human; to become more truly who we are; to encounter the meaning of being alive. Religious leadership promotes this wholeness of being. Knowing that *whole, holy, heal*, and *healthy* are part of the same word family sheds warm light on our shared endeavors.

Historically, Judeo-Christian clergy were sometimes the only learned and literate people in their town. They preached and taught Scripture as the ultimate source of truth and sole guide to salvation. They kept official records of births and deaths and presided over these vital events. It was both a lofty and a solitary role.

And life continued to happen. The curiosity and yearning that triggered the mythic exile from Eden is inherently human, and irrepressible. Questions sought answers and yielded more questions, and the meteoric expansion of knowledge rendered singular authority obsolete. The more there was to know, the less of it could be mastered by one individual. Knowledge and skills diversified. Specialization became essential. Human community grew encyclopedic. Echoes of archaic authority linger when "Reverend" is attached to our names, but the role of ordained clergy is to share and shepherd this diversity. Ministry cannot be an individual responsibility when understood as nurturing and caring for the spirit, in partnership with Creation.

Parish ministry remains a generalist profession, involving multiple skill sets that have become specialties of their own, among them religious education, pastoral care, music and the arts, social service, higher education, and recently, interim ministry. In the past, primarily larger churches were assigned ministers to fill in between settled clergy. Smaller congregations—as most are—managed without a pastoral presence, simply arranging for pulpit supply and navigating the balance of parish life on their own during the transition between pastors. Judicatory guidance and aid was usually accessible but often out of mind, and congregations sometimes struggled when they most needed help. (For further discussion of the differences between large- and small-congregation interim ministry, see "Large Congregations" and "Small Congregations.")

The Development of Unitarian Universalist Interim Ministry

Dan Hotchkiss, UUA settlement director from 1990 until 1997, suspects that the Department of Ministry may have been pioneers in seeking to fill almost all full-time vacancies with full-time ministers on temporary assignment; this was already the norm when he arrived at the UUA. Congregations gained a little breathing room—time to accept and absorb the reality of significant change, renew, and give a new relationship a fresh start. These clergy usually were recently retired, with skills and wisdom honed in their own churches, or they were colleagues between settlements wanting a temporary placement. Some served simply as placeholders. The opportunity for temporary employment was a blessing for clergy, but care for congregations was the driving vision, and for this clarity and training were needed.

Training began in simple form, the Department of Ministry scheduling several days each August to convene ministers who would serve congregations in transition for an orientation to their role and to what their congregations would likely experience. Seasoned interims shared successes, missteps, and encouragement. Some colleagues serving in transition times valued their experiences in this role and discovered themselves uniquely suited for it. Interim ministry started to become a specialty that could be intentionally chosen.

Charles Gaines, who preceded Hotchkiss in the Settlement Office, took substantial steps to formalize an accreditation and empowerment process for UU clergy serving interim ministries. When Hotchkiss became settlement director, a cadre of seasoned interims was already available. During his tenure, the interim clergy created a three-person steering team to help organize and lead the summer orientations. Each member was chosen by colleagues and served a three-year staggered term.

Meanwhile, in ecumenical circles, others were examining the unsettled nature of ministerial transitions with keen attention—specifically, the Alban Institute's Loren B. Mead, who recognized these interim periods as unique opportunities to transform systems that were languishing or dysfunctional. One of Mead's many groundbreaking books, *Critical Moment of Ministry: A Change of Pastors*, pioneered the recognition of transitions between clergy as times of unique opportunity and foresaw transitional ministry as a specialized calling, generating a movement that gave birth to the Interim Ministry Network (IMN). His book rapidly became a resource for interim ministers of many denominations, including our own.

John Weston came aboard as UUA settlement director in 1999, following Hotchkiss and an interim period with Elizabeth Anastos, and then Peter Raible. Intent on continuing to improve the quality of interim ministry, Weston held extensive conversations with the steering team. More comprehensive training was wanted, but resources were limited. So the UUA decided to try using a training program developed by the IMN.

Training new interims continued during the summer of 1999. An annual spring seminar was added to the UUA calendar for clergy on the interim path. It provided a prime opportunity to bring in an IMN team in April 2000, to kick-start IMN training as a potential requirement for accredited interim ministry in the UUA. IMN basic training consisted of a year-long program, beginning with a Phase 1 training week, followed by a Phase 2 year of on-the-job mentoring, and concluding with Phase 3, a one-week follow-up a year later. About twenty of us graduated from the IMN training in April 2001. (Ecumenical opportunities for IMN training continue at various sites around the calendar.)

The experience proved invaluable, substantially advancing the repertoire of accredited interim ministers' knowledge and skills. It became a requirement for accreditation, in addition to the three years of interim experience, annual evaluation, and regular attendance at the spring seminars, where critical incident reports submitted for peer review also became a continuing practice.

There were now three levels of UU interim ministers: accredited interim minister (AIM), AIMit (an AIM-in-training), and ministers in transition who were not intending or in discernment about whether to pursue interim ministry as a career path. The last group often included newly fellowshipped ministers engaged in the search process and glad for an opportunity to serve a congregation short-term. Sometimes the focused challenges and joys of interim life fit so well that they chose this specialty as their own, or realized they would return to it when the "householder" stage of their lives was over—children had flown, and they could be more free to move.

The number of congregations in transition exceeded the number of intentional interim clergy available each year. And clergy who were geographically available to a given site or whose particular strengths fit that site's needs were fewer still. Connecting available clergy with congregations in transition required a substantial amount of Settlement Office time. What had been at most 20 percent of Dan Hotchkiss's workload doubled during Weston's tenure.

Weston began inviting district executives (DEs) to join in the spring seminars to expand the perspective of discussions. This proved to be immediately helpful: Anne Odin Heller, DE of the Pacific Northwest District, pointed out that interim ministries following either a lengthy tenure or a negotiated resignation were not preparing congregations to succeed with their next settled minister. Hapless churches were caught in their past rather than engaging their future. She voiced a vital need for a road map that would guide interim ministers toward what needed doing and how to do it. (For more about the hazards of congregations not being prepared to succeed with their next settled minister, see "The Temptation to Rush the Search.")

The *Janus Workbook* and the Tasks of Interim Ministry

Heller's challenge developed into the Janus Project, established with a grant from the Fund for Unitarian Universalism. Following the "brain trust" process she had used successfully in creating *Churchworks: A Well-Body Book for Congregations*, a group of nine UUA leaders gathered in retreat at Seabeck Conference Center in Washington State in January 2001.

They designed the *Janus Workbook* at that meeting, adopting its name from the Roman god of doorways, safeguarding the portal between the past and the future. It would provide an array of resources to aid interim ministers in their work with congregations—especially congregations following either a long ministry, the death of a minister, a negotiated resignation, or ministerial misconduct. Those attending this retreat committed to writing and compiling its contents, sorting them into sequential sections: looking back, standing in the present, and looking forward (the last section included saying good-bye to the interim and hello to the imminent future).

The *Janus Workbook* has been revised multiple times since then, with various interim ministers providing materials. It is the primary collection of resources that new interims are still urged to consult about a whole variety of matters.

The Janus team members focused on the developmental challenges facing a congregation in transition, guided by the five interim tasks identified by the IMN. The team described them in light of the project's goals:

- claiming and honoring the congregation's past, and healing its griefs and conflicts

- illuminating the congregation's unique identity: its strengths, its needs, and its challenges

- clarifying the multiple dimensions of leadership, both ordained and lay, and navigating the shifts in leadership that accompany times of transition

- renewing connections with available resources within and beyond the UUA

- enabling the congregation to renew its vision, strengthen its stewardship, prepare for new professional leadership, and engage its future with anticipation and zest.

It was an ambitious program to try to accomplish in a single year. An arriving interim needs to gain acquaintance, establish credibility, and grasp, as quickly as possible, a whole-picture understanding of the congregation. If the congregation was pursuing an immediate search for a new minister, intending to identify and call one by late spring, the year would already be growing short.

Some resilient congregations with healthy systems and committed leadership have followed through and achieved an enduring call. But people have a love-hate relationship with change. Especially at stress-filled times, folks often yearn to get through and beyond transition as rapidly as possible. If the interim minister is to help a congregation reap the benefits of working through the interim tasks, the first job is to get them to slow down, pay attention, and commit themselves to taking the time required.

If little to no change is achieved between settlements, the incoming minister may become an unintended interim, with shared dreams and hopes on hold, or may simply ignore the challenges as long as possible. This has happened—and still does—regrettably often.

Still, whatever shortcomings remain in the world of intentional interim ministry today, there has been steady improvement due to the gradual institutionalization of the interim program. For intentional interims, a few weeks of training proved insufficient to master their role and sustain excellence. AIMs yearned to strengthen their craft, and hone and expand their skills. They envisioned partnered mentoring, rigorous peer review, and maintaining standards in a mode similar to artisan and craft guilds of centuries past. The concept was given structure and fleshed out by the IM steering team, and adopted by AIMs collectively, giving birth to the Interim Ministry Guild on April 2, 2002.

However, the new group found it hard to maintain a reliable corps of expert and experienced AIMs. The peripatetic nature of the interim minister's life kept the pool fluid and small. Issues around home, families, and frequent moving presented obstacles. But as interim ministry becomes more and more recognized as a special ministerial calling, that pool is growing. The field of interim ministry is itself in transition, in accord with its transformational mission. The focus is shifting from existing congregational illnesses to ways to achieve congregational health. Other specialized short-term ministries are now taking form to address particular transformational needs—especially related to congregations of different sizes and with different challenges. (See material on such ministries in Part V of this book.)

Interim ministers experience life in microcosm. They arrive as newborns to a setting and learn fast, offering their skills and gifts even as learning continues. They leave without finishing everything, having done what they could in the time given. They relay a heartfelt farewell and let go. (For more on ending interim ministries, see "Bringing an Interim Ministry to a Successful Conclusion.") For me, the richness of each experience yields upwelling moments of joy and gratitude for the privilege of this work— until I'm overtaken by recurrent yearnings pulling me home.

This sketch of an interim ministry timespan parallels our individual lives. Humans too arrive, grow, learn, give who we are and what we have, and depart, and the world goes on. This essential truth about life explains why interim contracts are short-term and why an interim minister, keeping faith with that commitment, will not stay. Their skills, insights, and innovations are offered with no strings attached. Likewise, the congregation's preferences, decisions, and actions bind an interim minister only for the briefest time. They are not bound to each other long-term. Lest tendrils of connection entangle them, the maximum contract is two years.

Interim is always, conscientiously, attached to *minister* since we're serving the congregation yet not an ongoing part of it. Everyone must be aware that we'll be going our own ways. The congregation is trailblazing its way into its future with the present help of this hired guide—*present* as in "here and now"; *present* as in "freely given." Transition times are alive with opportunity—to discover, to explore, to practice, to try on ideas without necessarily having to commit to them first. And the freedom inherent in such fluid experience is transformative for a congregation.

Interim ministers, in turn, are afforded soul exercise. The opportunities transitions offer are real for us too. Encountering new situations, remarkable people, fresh challenges, and opportunities to learn something new in each setting, we may continue to deepen and grow our selves and become a little more truly who we yearn to be.

We carry who we are with us. The *Janus Workbook* was created as a kit to take along. At the conclusion of the workbook, John Weston reflects,

> From its tools, exercises, and admonitions emerge . . . the characteristics of effective interim ministry, and the beginnings of an interim pastoral theology. Interim ministry requires a consultant attitude. The congregation is a *you*, not a *we*. And always there is the implied *if*: *If* you want to become, in fact, the congregation you say you dream of being, these are the issues you need to attend to.

He emphasizes for interim clergy in the field the importance of trust, in both oneself and the congregation, and the essential quality of self-differentiation, as described by Edwin Friedman in *Generation to Generation: Family Process in Church and Synagogue*. Friedman illuminates family systems theory as it plays out in congregations, and teaches that the essence of religious leadership is to stay connected and to sustain a nonanxious presence in the midst of stressful situations. Agreeing with Friedman, Weston writes, "On the one hand, avoid getting tangled in the emotional processes of others. On the other hand, be emotionally available." It's paradoxical, growthful, and internally challenging, worthy work. "If your ministry needs validation," Weston advises, "stay away from interim ministry."

He concludes the *Janus Workbook* with these words:

> Interim ministry affirms so little—and so much! In this
> moment, under these conditions, with these people,
> with their history both noble and ignoble, the old veri-
> ties prevail: Truth is better than deception; secrecy avails
> not; compassion and forgiveness are sweet; generosity
> enlarges, while stinginess contracts; and life is worth liv-
> ing to the full. Say it is so!

We do indeed, through our deeds, say it is so—for ourselves
as interim clergy and for each congregation we serve in this role.
The adventure of this endeavor echoes the adventure of living
intentionally in faithful, faith-full community on the roller
coaster ride of life itself.

A Different Country

JUDITH WALKER-RIGGS

During a period of interim ministry, both new interim ministers and congregants will find themselves in a different country from the called ministry they have known. For instance, if a previous called minister was a leader in the community or in social action, the congregation may expect the interim minister to be the same. However, the interim minister's role—to guide the transition between the previous called minister and the new called minister—requires focusing inward on the congregation rather than looking outward to the community at large. The interim minister's attention will be fully engaged in having the congregation address interim tasks, such as coming to terms with its history and being able to articulate its present identity. (For more about reconciling congregational history and identifying congregational history, see "Coming to Terms with History" and "The Interim Minister as Systems Analyst," respectively.)

In addition, the interim minister will help the congregation prepare for change, decide what direction to take for the future, work together in a common purpose, and heal and develop trust if necessary. The interim time provides an invitation to the congregation to decide how the members themselves will do the work of the church in the world.

This period can be used to encourage members to become more active, to stand in for the minister at meetings, and to decide upon their own focus for community service and social action. For example, during a period of transition, one congregation decided to organize support for soldiers and families at a nearby military base, a lay-led program that continues well into their settled ministry.

During an interim period, congregants may discover other interests or abilities that have lain dormant because the previous called minister occupied large areas of congregational life. He may have loved teaching adult religious education courses and taught at least one every quarter. She may have been a poet who devoted considerable time to newsletter columns or poetic meditations during worship services. During the interim period, some congregants may step into teaching or writing roles and thus discover something new to enrich their lives.

Moreover, the congregation should not narrow its sights for future called ministry to candidates who share the previous minister's special interests. But how is the congregation to widen its sights?

The Transition Team

The good news is that there are travel guides for the expedition into this new and different country. With the assistance of the Board of Trustees, the interim minister may appoint a Transition Team. This group can give the interim invaluable information about the congregation's culture and circumstances, and can strategize with the interim to discover how to engage both the leadership and the rest of the congregation in interim tasks. The team can serve as both a planning group and a progress monitor.

A Transition Team is not the same as the Committee on Ministry that a congregation or minister may be familiar with, based on experience during called ministries. Committees on Ministry review the professional clergy in particular and the whole ministry of the church in general, monitoring how well they advance the church's mission and vision. Sometimes these committees serve as conflict managers or intermediaries between ministers and congregants who are dissatisfied with their ministry. In all cases, the goal of a Committee on Ministry is to maintain the equilibrium of the church as a peaceable, thriving body.

For this reason, an existing Committee on Ministry should disband or at least "go on vacation" during an interim period. There will likely be some purposeful disequilibrium created during the interim period. In fact, a peaceful, quiet interim period is one in which interim tasks are not completed, and needful changes do not happen. Moreover, if the previous ministry ended in a negotiated termination, the Committee on Ministry may have been functioning partly as a support group for the minister. If that is the case, members of the committee may not shift easily into the different roles and purposes of a Transition Team. The best members for a Transition Team are knowledgeable, engaged congregants who bring to the work no baggage from previous membership on the Committee on Ministry.

The Transition Team may be chosen by the Board according to the interim minister's instructions before the interim arrives, and certainly before the interim has been there long enough to know who would make good team members. Some interim ministers give the Transition Team the initial task of planning the interim minister's calendar for the first couple of weeks on site, including individual meetings with each Board member, committee chair, and staff member. Some interims prefer to wait until they arrive and then to consult in person with the Board so that interim and Board jointly appoint members of the team. Another typical early task of a Transition Team is scheduling house meetings to help the congregation get to know the interim and understand more about what to expect during the interim period.

Under the direction of the interim, the Transition Team may also lead projects designed to help carry out interim tasks. (For more about the specific interim tasks, see "The History, Philosophy, and Impact of Interim Ministry.") They might strategize with the interim about how to manage a "history wall," which provides people the opportunity to write and post notes about how significant events in the congregation's history have affected them. The history wall also invites people to read and reflect on what others have posted. Transition Team members might help the interim draft questions for focus groups or for use during an Appreciative Inquiry process. (Learn more about

Appreciative Inquiry in "Mining, Minding, and Making Stories" and "Coming to Terms with History.")

With training, team members can facilitate these group processes. Once such processes are concluded, the team can make valuable contributions to the interim work by assisting the interim minister in interpreting the gathered data. The team can articulate to their fellow congregants how the projects they undertake relate to the congregation's interim tasks. Having Transition Team members in such leadership roles conveys the message that interim tasks are the responsibility of the congregation, not just the interim minister.

Managing Anxiety

In one congregation, the interim minister sometimes added a third hymn to the order of service, which had traditionally included only two hymns. The president of the Board overheard a comment from one long-term member to another: "Last week two hymns, this week three hymns. What's going to become of us?" This scenario illustrates how change increases anxiety in people who are already anxious. It is natural for many congregants to be anxious when they don't know what is going to happen tomorrow with a new interim minister, much less who their next called minister will be.

Sometimes the Board will need to join the interim and the Transition Team in the vital work of encouraging congregational experimentation, especially if they have had one minister for many years and have long been doing things in a particular way, giving little thought to their traditions. The next called minister is almost certain to bring new ways of doing things, and a congregation open to change has much better odds for managing the transition well. When initiating an experiment, it can help to encourage the congregation to wait to express opinions about it until enough time has passed to give the change a chance. Couching a change as an experiment and asking congregants to comment at the end of three or six months rather than immediately can lessen the immediate resistance from those who feel that with any change, they are "losing their church." The Transition Team and Board should be prepared to manage congregational discomfort and anxiety as well as their own. Calming messages about change may be better received from a fellow congregant than from the interim, who may be perceived as "the one who started all this," even though the congregational leadership may fully support the changes.

Particular circumstances that heighten anxiety present special challenges. Perhaps before the settled minister resigned, the congregation was planning a capital campaign to finance renovations, or perhaps they had actually begun such an effort. "What now?" folks ask. If plans have been voted on and much of the money raised, the project might as well be finished. After all, it is by now truly a project of the congregation, not just of the departed minister. If planning has only begun, and most or all of the money is yet to be raised, some members can be expected to demand a rapid push forward. Our old friend anxiety may well underlie such demands. Since one of the transition tasks is to come to a new understanding about where the congregation is heading, it is premature to design when you don't yet know what activities you are designing for. The most helpful role for the interim in such circumstances is to help the congregation slow down. They need to discover who they are now and where they want to go before they start driving stakes in the ground and laying brick. Moreover, they may eventually realize that the next settled minister could have valuable opinions to contribute to the envisioned future.

Another contributor to anxiety—and the resulting wish for certainty and closure—is the predictable division that follows after controversy surrounding the previous minister has led to a negotiated termination. There may be an urge to endlessly discuss the past in an effort to find out "what really happened." However, all who were involved will never agree about "what really happened" because people will always have different points of view. A wiser approach is to work together in the present for the future of the church.

Congregations whose ministries have been terminated because of serious misbehavior, including broken sexual boundaries, need to focus on healing the damage as much as possible and rebuilding the ability to trust a new called minister. This particular form of healing and rebuilding ministry is called "after-pastoring." Sadly, ministerial misbehavior has happened often enough that there are interim ministers with special training and expertise as after-pastors. (For more about clergy misconduct, see "Congregations with a History of Misconduct.")

No matter the source of a congregation's anxiety, members may want to hurry up and dispel it. The interim minister's role, however, is to encourage them to substitute thoughtful reflection and deliberate decision making for thoughtless, reactive behavior.

For example, the Board may be disconcerted to discover that the monthly reports from the interim minister differ significantly from the reports they are used to. The previous minister may have used those reports to account for time spent on pastoral calls, sermon writing, and attendance at committee meetings. Interim ministers tend to report differently, sometimes to assess the Board's or congregation's progress on interim tasks, cataloging each task separately. These reports are likely also to point out concerns the interim has about what is or is not happening in congregational life. An anxious Board may resist such reports and exert pressure on the interim to report, as the previous minister did, on details of the interim's calendar for the previous month, even possibly including the exact number of pastoral calls made, meetings attended, and public appearances the interim has made on behalf of the church. That final number, of course, is likely to be zero if the interim is doing interim work rather than the familiar public work of a called minister. The Board and the interim can have an open and direct conversation about the nature of the monthly Board report, resulting in a valuable teaching opportunity when the interim explains why the reports differ significantly from the previous minister's. Once the Board understands why the interim's monthly reports differ from the typical called minister's reports, they can share that understanding and its implications with the congregation. The teaching is not just about monthly reports; it is about the difference between interim ministry as consultative ministry and called ministry as relational ministry.

Managing Relationships

One of the deepest, most subtle shifts in this different country takes place around relationships. Called ministry has intensely to do with relationships, forming deep knowledge and understanding of congregants, which grow over the years. Interim ministry is generally not about relationships with individual congregants. Indeed, some interims perform interim ministry for only a year or two before returning to called ministry because they miss the relationship component of ministry. Certainly, interim ministry can be a lonelier job than called ministry, but those who stay in this specialization find the challenges so exciting that, even without the individual personal relationships, they feel fulfilled.

Part of this work includes looking at the congregational system as a whole, work appropriate for a time of transition. Doing so requires some emotional distance to discern patterns of complexity and interdependence within the congregation: the many circular, familial, and interlocking relationships amid the whole. Just as when a fly hits a small spot in a spider's web, the whole web shivers and shakes, so in congregational life an action in one part of the congregational system affects all other parts of the system. The interim period is a good time to examine how the system as a whole works in a specific congregation and bring it into view so all can share in this new perspective.

I cannot stress enough that leadership and membership must come to understand the differences between called ministry and interim ministry. One way to increase this understanding is for the interim, the Transition Team, and the Board to talk about the differences explicitly and publicly.

If the leadership and membership do not come to understand the differences between interim and called ministry, the possibility for unintended hurt is immense. During one interim ministry, following a long and personal called ministry, the interim minister did not continue the former minister's practice of monthly home visits to the large number of elderly shut-in members. Not continuing the visiting practice was appropriate because the interim's obligation was to work with the congregation and Board on the interim tasks, and she did not have time to do her job and also make those visits. However, despite her urging, the Board did not consider it their job to find a way for the congregation to share the task of keeping in touch with these folks. Great damage was done to many vulnerable people by this absence of care.

This is not to say that interims are necessarily unfriendly or cold. But there is a difference between being friendly and becoming someone's friend. Some congregants may not understand why the interim, who was so friendly last month, is leaving this month with an explicit expectation of no further communication. It is easier for everyone if the unusual pattern of relationship in this different country is made plain throughout the interim period by the Board, the Transition Team, and the interim minister. They must also make plans for handling these relationship differences.

The desire to end the anxiety-filled interim time can be so strong that some members may demand that the interim stay and become the next called minister. This demand is fairly common as members witness signs of the interim's imminent departure. Unless the interim is properly prepared and professional, the demand can be seductive. Boards, Transition Teams, and interims should expect it and be prepared to address it directly with the congregation. They can explain that the Unitarian Universalist Association's (UUA) transitions director and the Interim Ministry Guild agree that interims will serve a congregation no longer than two years. Interims are ineligible for three years for candidacy for called ministry positions in churches where they have served as interim. Definitively saying no to the demand that the interim stay can alleviate congregants' anxiety by letting them know there is a plan, and it includes the interim leaving. (For more about ending an interim ministry, see "Bringing an Interim Ministry to a Successful Conclusion.")

People angry about losing the interim minister may blame the UUA's Transitions Office or their regional staff. It must be someone's fault that their beloved interim minister cannot stay. But these officers are responsible only to the extent that they have fostered what experience has shown to be best practice. In turn, the interim has entered into an agreement with the UUA that stipulates that the Transitions Office's services will be available to the interim in search of positions, and that the interim agrees not to stay in any congregation longer than two years. (Occasionally an interim has been extended to three years after the start of an interim period at the mutual agreement of congregational leadership, the minister, regional staff, and the Transitions Office when the work of the congregation will clearly not be finished in two years, though even in these cases, a congregation may be served with a new interim in the last year.) Ultimately, the people who have established that the interim minister will not stay are the interim and the congregation's Board. Interims are hired by the Board, not called by the congregation. The parties to the agreement determine its terms. In other words, it is not up to the congregation.

Helping the Interim Minister Adapt

The interim period is clearly a different country for congregants, and the interim minister helps them negotiate the terrain. However, interims also enter a different country when they arrive to serve a congregation, and they do this every year or two. They too need to prepare themselves for the experience. Nurturing close friendships at home and with interim colleagues can provide support, albeit from a distance. In this regard, the email list for interim ministers and the interim ministers' Facebook group called Wayside Pulpit are fine sources of support as well as ideas and suggestions for handling problematic situations. A query posted on the list or to the Facebook group typically elicits a variety of perspectives and answers. Interims also need to make frequent moving easy by making copies of all medical records to help a new doctor get up to speed; keeping careful tax records, particularly of professional expenditures; and logging the contents of every packed box.

Just as an interim will work to become aware of the needs of a congregation and to help meet those needs, it is important for the Board and Transition Team, as representatives of the congregation, to be intentional about helping the interim adapt to this new country. If the interim provides the Transition Team information about housing requirements, the team can scout good options for an apartment. Interims are more than a little grateful when a cadre of church members appears to help unload the rental truck. They are grateful too for recommendations of everything from dry cleaners and auto mechanics to dentists, hairdressers, and restaurants. One interim invited congregants to sign up in groups of four—the number of passengers that fit in the interim's car—to take Saturday or Sunday afternoon excursions to some of their favorite places in the area. Graciously welcoming the new minister is a fine way for congregants and interim alike to begin mutually guided tours of the new country that is interim ministry.

Good journeys, everyone!

PART II

Stories from the Field

Following the Interim

NATHAN DETERING

My daughter is an early riser. At 5:00 a.m. not long ago, I felt her hand tugging me awake. "Dad," she said, "my shins hurt. My knees hurt. It kind of feels like my bones are stretching." I may be a person of faith, but I am also an excellent worrier. So off to the pediatrician we went. The doctor listened patiently as I described my daughter's complaints, and then she smiled widely at both of us. "It's completely normal,' she said. "What you're describing are the classic symptoms of growing pains. Ever hear of those?" She then explained that when we are young, our bodies grow most not during our waking hours, but during the night, or what she called "the interim time." "That's why your legs hurt sometimes early in the morning," the doctor told my daughter. "Because all night your body has been working to grow, and sometimes all that growing hurts."

The doctor didn't know it, but she could also have been talking about the growth that happened during the two-year interim period in the congregation I have served as settled minister since 2003, Unitarian Universalist Area Church at First Parish in Sherborn, Massachusetts. Today, this congregation is able to say together its covenant, "Love is the Spirit of this Church," and actually mean it. But eleven years ago, just as the interim ministry was beginning, folks weren't so sure. The journey from then to now, from night to light, is due to many people—and a little luck—and began with the interim ministry. Even before my books were unpacked and my first sermon preached, I began hearing the stories.

First, I heard stories of an interim time in which people discovered that *the truth can be told and we won't die*. Unitarian Universalists love to say that we seek after the truth, but sometimes in our congregations, we love our secrets too, especially if we fear that talking about them will tear us apart. This is how it was at First Parish—that is, until the interim arrived and began speaking the truth. She gave a tough sermon challenging people to pledge more if they wanted their congregation to survive. She asked them what kind of message their then-shabby interior sent to newcomers. She asked what it would mean for them to move the real discussions about church finances from the parking lot to the boardroom. She named the times and places when people were not very nice to each other. She even had courage enough to disappoint a long-standing member or two who were not used to being disappointed. Sometimes it hurt to hear these truths, but she spoke in love, which is to say that she showed them how to stay in relationship even when hard things needed to be said. Much to the surprise of many, the relationships survived the truth telling, and so did the congregation. Growing pains, indeed!

I also heard of an interim time when people *rediscovered their pride*. Years of deficits and boot-strapped budgets taught the congregation lessons of survival and resilience. However, they also learned to think in terms of scarcity rather than abundance. The mantra "There's never enough . . . money, resources, volunteers, members" was heard and felt by many. Luckily, the interim minister brought with her fresh ears and fresh eyes, and with her fresh perspective, she discovered that the stories of scarcity were not nearly as true as people believed. Not only was the church not as poor as it thought, but she also reminded them that it had something to offer religiously to the people it served. They re-formed the youth group. They explored the positive impact of becoming a Welcoming Congregation. They celebrated the twenty-fifth anniversary of a merger with another congregation. They taught a class on how to welcome newcomers.

None of this was particularly complicated work, but not all transformations are, especially when a congregation all caught up in its survival remembers what it has to offer. By simply reconnecting the people to their congregation's worth and dignity, the interim minister helped them to see with fresh eyes and hear with fresh ears that they had reasons to be proud. Lo and behold! Along with this pride, more people began showing up for worship and programs. Coffee hour lasted longer. Board meetings grew shorter. There was more growth, and this time it wasn't all painful!

And that was not all. I also heard stories of an interim time when people were *encouraged to dream*. The people I met after the interim was over and my ministry began were energized for the present and hopeful for the future. But the stories I heard told me it had not always been this way.

Everyone agrees that something shifted halfway through the interim time when a respected lay leader spoke from her heart about what she saw as the congregation's frustrated potential. Motioning to the beautiful, historic sanctuary, this lay leader said to anyone who would listen, "You want red velvet ropes around that? You want this place to be a museum? Aren't we meant for something more?" The leader's questions were questions about mission and vision, and they drove straight to a choice facing First Parish to either be a faith and a church for those few on the inside, or to expand their vision for what was possible. The answer came as one person and then another and then another was heard to ask, "Who do we want to be? What do our communities need? What makes our congregation feel most alive?" In times of doubt, some asked the interim to chart the course for them. "You're the expert! We hired you! Tell us what you think!" But wisely she deferred. "When it comes to vision, your answers matter far more than mine," she told them. And in doing so, she empowered them to change and chart their own future instead of looking to someone from the outside to do it for them. More growing pains, more stretching. But something was happening. New life was happening. New possibilities were happening. And then the interim time was over.

Settled ministry came next. Excitement. Anticipation. Who would they get? There was talk of recruiting a seasoned professional to take First Parish "to the next level" after two years of hard preparation. And then the Search Committee found me—young (too young! some said), one year out of seminary, nearly brand-new to professional ministry. In the midst of some expressed doubt about my youth and inexperience, the interim offered an observation I am still indebted for. "It takes young ones to make old ones," she said, and people respected her enough by then to take her at her word.

Turns out we as minister and congregation found one another at the right time. Arriving to First Parish with zeal and vocation for ministry, but not many learned skills, I longed for a congregation that was ready to nourish its call to ministry at the same time I was seeking to nourish mine. But for this nourishment to happen, I needed to follow an interim ministry that had told the truth in love, and helped the congregation discover gifts and possibilities they didn't know they had. The interim period at First Parish was such a time, and the truth telling and gift discovery accomplished during those two years meant that the congregation and I didn't have to spend our first years of ministry together trying to "fix" each other. Instead, those first years were spent getting to know and love each other, and learning how to move the church from management to mission, from maintenance to vision.

Sometimes I hear colleagues and lay leaders from other congregations ask, "Why have an interim minister when there is so much desire to move on, get on, and get going?" I understand the impatience, but then I am reminded of what the doctor told my daughter, how our bodies grow most not in day time or waking time, but in the night time, what she called "the interim time." First Parish has been like that, growing in vitality and strength during the in-between time that was the sunset between one ministry and the dawn of another. Now in the full daylight of that settled ministry—which in 2010 saw First Parish recognized by the Unitarian Universalist Association as one of a handful of Breakthrough Congregations for the ways we have broken through barriers to achieve growth in both membership and congregational health—I have two words for the interim minister who served here with such strength and poise: *Thank you.*

Following Two Different
Interim Ministers

ALISON MILLER

■ ■ ▦ ■

When I was in search of a congregation to serve as settled minister, I sought a community open to change and ready to embark
upon a journey that would include building on tradition. I was
not interested in pouring my time, heart, and soul into a place
that was looking to just tend to the status quo. There was too
much at stake—namely, the potential for a community to grow
in numbers and deepen in spirit in ways that might lead more
people to find a home in our saving faith.

The two years of interim ministry with two different interim
ministers was a necessary step for the Morristown Unitarian
Fellowship to be open to the excitement, changes, and adventure a new ministry brings. I can easily see why I would have
said no to their offer to lead the congregation two years prior,
and why two years of interim ministry and all their hard work
allowed me to say yes without hesitation.

The previous settled minister served the congregation for
twenty-three years. While some members felt ready to move on,
many were still grieving the end of that long ministry. Because
there hadn't been an interim minister who worked with the
congregation prior to my predecessor's arrival, some were still
grieving the loss of the minister who came before him. As an
essential task, the interim minister in the first year led the con-

gregation through processing their grief, as well as other feelings, about the time with previous ministers. This helped the whole congregation move to a place of letting go that was absolutely necessary so we could form the strong relationship we now enjoy.

The First-Year Interim Minister

The minister who served Morristown in the first year of interim ministry brought with her the benefit of many years of experience as an interim. She was skilled at reflecting back to the leadership how the behaviors and organization of the congregation looked and felt to a wide variety of constituents: newcomers, long-time associates, people coming from other religious backgrounds, and others. Many congregants have said about year one, "In the first year, we looked at ourselves in a mirror and experienced the pain and discomfort of not liking everything we saw there." This self-reflection offered examples of both practices to be proud of and to continue, as well as practices to critique and change.

The first interim minister was in essence a diagnostician who named the ways that individuals and systems worked to help them achieve their stated goals and values, and the ways individuals and systems hindered or prevented them from their intended outcomes. For example, they wanted to be a community where honesty, compassion, and right relations were upheld, yet in congregational meetings, members questioned the transparency of the decision-making process, and several topics would lead to heated, unkind remarks. (For more about diagnosing systems in congregations, see "The Interim Minister as Systems Analyst.")

The Second-Year Interim Minister

A second year of interim ministry afforded the congregation an opportunity to go deeper with this process of self-reflection, as well as the time to experiment with and practice new behaviors and new forms of organization. Many congregants have said about year two, "In the second year, we began a process of letting go, healing, and finding ourselves receptive and ready to make changes." Concerns about members not treating one another with integrity and compassion led to the creation of a Committee on Ministry to foster right relations and also to monitor the well-being of different ministries. The second-year interim minister also brought with her a passion for good governance. Midway through the second year, the leadership introduced a new model of governance that allowed for greater communication and transparency around decision making. Several seeds of change were planted in the interim period that contributed to a healthier start for our shared ministry.

Attention to Staffing

When the interim ministers and the lay leadership examined the staffing structure, several important truths came to light. There was a convoluted reporting structure, which meant the staff and minister did not always function as a team serving the same goals and vision. During the interim period, the minister was made head of staff, and staff team meetings were held regularly. In addition, the interims assisted the Board with addressing whether they had the right staff roles and whether the current staff was a good match for the congregation's vision. This included the difficult work of letting a staff member go and the exciting work of creating a staffing plan. It became clear that the congregation's goals of growth would require an expansion of the staff, including a full-time administrator and a part-time music director. The leadership designed a fundraising plan to meet these goals. We successfully hired the administrator at the beginning of my first year of settled ministry and the music director at the beginning of my second year.

Attention to Worship

The interim ministers and the lay leadership examined the worship model and found that certain aspects needed to change. First, there was the issue of what to call "what we do together on Sunday mornings." When the congregation was founded in the 1950s, the members wanted a word that differentiated what we do from more traditional worship. They began calling it "Sunday Programs" and launched a lay-led Program Committee. However, during the interim period, it became clear that this language was not obvious to newcomers. Many would-be visitors didn't realize we had a big gathering on Sunday mornings. Changing the name of something central to what we do needed thoughtful discussion. In the end, the membership decided to change the terminology to "Sunday Services" and the "Sunday Services Committee."

Second, there was the issue of who was responsible for the worship services. Three totally separate groups were leading the services: The minister led services twice a month, the lay-led Sunday Services Committee led services twice a month, and a different group of volunteers led Morning Circles in July and August. These three groups did not meet together. Although this model led to some creative, powerful services over the years, it also led to a great deal of inconsistency. Many members shared that the inspiration they were looking for was missing at times. The Search Committee also conducted a survey of the membership and discovered that a majority of the congregation wanted more minister-led worship. It was time for change.

The interim minister began leading more services and created one coherent Sunday Services Committee to steer the worship life. The Sunday Services Committee continues to be the place where the minister, music director, religious educator, and lay-service leaders work together to create meaningful experiences on Sunday mornings. Our meetings focus on supporting the logistics of services, the training needs of leaders, and the development of diverse themes touching on theological or spiritual questions, social justice, the arts, and more.

Nowadays, I lead three services a month and the members lead one service a month from September through June. However, the lines are not so rigid. Members often have roles in my services, and they look to me for guidance in the shaping of their services. In July and August, we have a summer minister who leads half of the services. These changes have led to increased worship attendance throughout the year. Members also reflect that they are more likely to invite friends to come, being more confident that they will have a meaningful, uplifting experience. The work the interims did with our congregation around worship illustrates another reason why having two people serve as interims can be of great benefit. The first interim was a careful craftswoman in her shaping of the worship hour. Congregants have shared how she taught them the importance of having a trained worship leader offer a polished service with careful attention to the flow of one worship element into the next. Under her tenure, they began to appreciate the Sunday morning service as a sacred time very different from a lecture, play, or concert. The second interim had training in the fine arts and a passion for the visual aspects of worship. When she arrived, our sanctuary was bland, had no altar or focal point, and was in need of a paint job. Under her leadership, people learned how to dress up the room with visual aids to augment the theme or tone of a service by placing fabrics, flowers, hangings, images, and more. Worship was becoming a feast for all the senses.

Two Heads Are Better Than One

The two interims brought different styles, skills, passions, and insights to the congregation in all areas, not just worship. Interim ministry may be best served by the old adage "Two heads are better than one."

Two years and two ministers allowed for movement in many pivotal areas, including the staff team, worship and religious education, governance and leadership, and the creation of a Committee on Ministry, and allowed for a major identity shift from almost exclusively humanist toward theological pluralism.

Although some leaders admit that they once questioned the need for an interim minister, they always say that they were quick to see the light. The members and I both have fondness and gratitude in our hearts when we think upon all of the two interims' hard work helping the Morristown Unitarian Fellowship move down a path of reflection and renewal. This was absolutely a key ingredient in allowing for a vibrant shared ministry to follow and to flourish.

The past several years have yielded good fruits, and we have deepened together in spirit and grown in health and in number. Just this year, 2012, we were designated a Threshold Congregation by the Unitarian Universalist Association, affirming their sense that we are poised for significant additional growth and have the capacity to become a mentor to other congregations. The Threshold Program provides access once again to new resources and coaching. We embrace this additional opportunity for learning, self-reflection, and change with great enthusiasm for where this next leg of our journey will lead us.

Serving as a Lay Leader During Interim Ministry

ED ROCKMAN

After our minister of almost ten years resigned from her post at the Unitarian Universalist Church of the North Hills in Pittsburgh, we decided to participate in the interim ministry program from the Unitarian Universalist Association (UUA). Our participation in this program was truly transformative. Now, having completed the interim ministry and entered into settled ministry, we are a much stronger and more vibrant congregation, facing the future with optimism and enthusiasm.

At the end of our last settled ministry, we were faced with decisions about what our path forward would be. As a result of timing, we had a year of lay-led services after our minister left. A few wanted to continue as a fully lay-led congregation. Others wanted to move directly into search for a new settled minister. Fortunately, our leaders took the time to consult with denominational leaders and the congregation to present, discuss, and carefully consider the alternatives. At a formal congregational meeting, we voted overwhelmingly to proceed with interim ministry. We recognized that we needed time for introspection and for carefully looking at our needs and desires. We also recognized that, as a congregation, we were committed to returning to settled ministry.

We created an Interim Search Committee and soon selected an interim minister. One of her early requests, even before her arrival, was that we form a Transition Team to assist in her ministry. The Board did so. (For more information about Transition Teams, see "A Different Country.") At our first Transition Team meeting, I was elected chair and had the privilege and honor of serving in that role throughout her two-year ministry. It was one of the most rewarding experiences of my forty-plus years at our church.

During our initial meetings with the interim, we took these important actions:

- adopted a covenant between the minister and Transition Team members covering, among other things, the need to keep certain information within the group and to speak freely and listen attentively, and our commitment to cooperate and work together

- decided to have our efforts guided by the *Janus Workbook*, which is the Interim Ministry Guild's resource manual provided on the UUA Transitions Office's website (For more about the *Janus Workbook* and the Interim Ministry Guild, see "The History, Philosophy, and Impact of Interim Ministry" and the Resources.)

- set our tasks as honoring our past, looking at our strengths and limitations, strengthening our denominational ties, and preparing ourselves for the future

- decided to embark on a series of small group meetings with members of the congregation to exchange ideas and information with our interim minister.

At these meetings, which the interim structured and led, members were given the opportunity to discuss our history, concentrating on two questions: "What do you feel is good about the church?" and "What can be improved?" In effect, she held up a mirror to us as a congregation. That phrase, "holding up a mirror," symbolizes for me our interim ministry experience. At the conclusion of the last session, our interim created a two-page summary of what she had heard, noting our strengths and our limitations.

Our strengths included our religious education program, our physical space, and our welcoming nature. Our limitations were a bit more numerous and included our distrust of authority —both professional ministry and lay leadership—and a perceived intolerance of others' religious views.

The next steps were crucial in setting the path for success for the interim ministry. After the Transition Team discussed the interim's observations, we took the summary before the governing Board. We circulated it among our other leaders. Finally, we held an open session to discuss the observations with the entire congregation. We reached general consensus among the congregation that the observations were spot-on, and expressed a commitment to address our limitations going forward.

In her summary, the interim made the point, often repeated, that "we are the stories we tell." By that, she meant that what we say about ourselves reinforces and defines our identity. We recognized that it was important for us to look at the stories we tell to see that they faithfully represent the truth about ourselves. For example, one story some of us used to tell was that we were quite hard on ministers. Exploring that story helped us to see that we had had many good experiences with ministers. It also helped us to see that, in some cases, our ministers had not done right by us. Both helped us with the story we tell about ministry. (For further discussion of both positive and negative stories, see "Mining, Minding, and Making Stories" and "Small Congregations.")

Our church is a very different, much healthier place than it was before our interim ministry. We worked hard over that period to re-create our church as an institution. The Transition Team regularly encouraged our various constituencies to take actions aimed toward change. Here are some of our successes:

Coming to terms with our history. Because we challenged the stories we told about ourselves, our stories today are much better informed, broadly understood, and more honest about our past. Our self-esteem as a congregation is greatly improved as a result.

Discovering a new identity. We have made great progress in developing our concept of a religious "big tent," where we are much more tolerant of those who differ from us. We no longer tolerate the hostilities that had sometimes been displayed toward those with different or more traditional theological backgrounds, particularly Christians. We welcome all who are comfortable with the Unitarian Universalist principles of openness and free expression of ideas.

Empowering and equipping new leadership. We have made serving in leadership positions an honor and privilege instead of a duty and drudgery. With our interim's help, we rewrote our bylaws to reflect more trust in our Board and other leaders. We have instituted training programs and ways of recognizing and honoring our leaders. As one concrete example, in the past our Nominating Committee struggled to find people willing to serve on our Board. In our last nominating cycle, the committee received acceptances to each of its invitations to serve, with no rejections. We have also had successful stewardship programs in the past few years.

Renewing denominational linkages. We restored full Fair Share funding to both UUA and our district. We have been much more active in district affairs, including hosting district meetings and participating in webinars. (For more about congregations making broader connections, see "Strengthening Connections Beyond the Congregation.")

Preparing for new settled ministry. In past searches, we had always focused on the various talents needed for a minister. Our interim helped us to see that, while those attributes are important, it's the relationship between the minister and congregants that counts. We wanted a minister we could love as a congregation. That also meant that we, the congregation, must be open to developing such a relationship.

The second year of our interim ministry was also our year of search for a settled minister. The co-chair of the Search Committee had been one of our original Transition Team members, which helped a great deal with the search process. At the conclusion of the search, our congregation *unanimously* called our new settled minister. As I write this, he is completing eight months with us. From what I hear from members and friends, we are well on our way to the kind of loving relationship we yearned for.

At a recent service, our new minister talked about the state of our beloved community. He described us as a strong and vibrant church. He said that, during the search process, one of the things that impressed him the most was the way we described our interim ministry period. He really believed we had done the work that is so important during that time. I used to consider an interim minister as a placeholder between settled ministers. Now I understand that interim ministry is hard work but so very worthwhile!

Mining, Minding, and Making Stories

PAM BLEVINS HINKLE

■ ■ ▦ ■

Let me tell you a story. Like all good tales, it's filled with colorful characters, intricate relationships, a vivid backstory that reveals the roots of a struggle, and an attempt at transformation. It's the story of a congregation that uncovered its own rich anthology, from heroic journeys and intrepid adventures to leadership skirmishes and culture clashes. It's the story of an interim ministry's power to reveal stories, leverage stories, and create a fresh and inspiring story for the future.

Stories matter. Rachael Freed, founder of Life-Legacies and senior fellow at the University of Minnesota's Center for Spirituality and Healing, writes in the *Huffington Post,*

> Telling our stories is not an end in itself, but an attempt to release ourselves from them, to evolve and grow beyond them. We tell our stories *to transform* ourselves; to learn about our history and tell our experiences to transcend them; to use our stories to make a difference in our world; to broaden our perspective *to see* further than normal; *to act* beyond a story that may have imprisoned or enslaved us; *to live* more of our spiritual and earthly potential.

This rings true for individuals, institutions, and, most especially, faith communities, which are rooted in story. Seeking answers to life's big questions, we return again and again to the parables and poems of prophetic voices across the ages, seeking hope, guidance, and understanding.

As Unitarian Universalists, we draw stories from a deep and diverse well. While this diversity is a fundamental strength, it also casts a dark shadow that we often refuse to acknowledge. "We arrive out of many singular rooms," as Rev. Kenneth Patton writes, bringing a variety of life experiences and faith journeys. When we arrive at a UU church after a sometimes desperate search for community, we quite naturally gravitate to those like us. We join the Buddhist group, the humanist group, the pagan group, or another formal or informal social group where everyone seems to "think like I do." These groups offer comforting and important connections, but on their own, they may insulate us from the practice of living in diversity and blind us to the more complex and nuanced story of the congregation. We then begin to believe that our story is *the* story.

This brings me to the main character of this story, *the* Unitarian Universalist Church of Indianapolis (UUI) in central Indiana. In 2008, my church—the church where I dedicated my two daughters, the church that I served in multiple capacities (music director and chair or member of numerous committees), the church that I had called home since 1996—was lost.

The minister resigned after several years of bitter conflict over his ministry. The Board of Trustees immediately set about retaining the most qualified and experienced interim minister it could find, and not a minute too soon! In a few short months following the minister's departure, all remaining staff resigned, and dissatisfied congregants left to establish their own church.

The interim minister did something important when she arrived. She halted the frantic pace of our story. Eager to bandage the wounds and move on quickly, we were forming new committees and finding new ways to fret at every turn. This hurried rhythm left no space for us to reflect on the environment in which the conflict had brewed, or its devastating emotional impact upon the congregation. Our story needed to be interrupted.

The interim then set about listening to the many divergent stories of our faith community. House gatherings, one-on-one meetings, committee meetings, and a series of events around our thirtieth anniversary mined the many individual stories to reveal shared and opposing tales as well as new stories and voices missing from the larger narrative.

At the same time, workshops on a variety of topics helped congregants reflect on their own personal stories, in and outside of church, and how this connected to the congregation's past and future story. The Smart Church workshop on conflict and anxiety in congregations had a profound effect on me. I was introduced to the concept of triangulation, in which two people talk *about* a third person rather than *to* that person. (I realized that I was enabling this destructive dynamic in my own family. The next day I contacted those family members to say I would no longer participate in these conversations. Interim ministry can also teach us about our own lives.) (For more about triangulation, see "Working with Staff.") The workshop also helped me recognize the inevitability, perhaps even desirability, of conflict as we seek right relations amidst needful diversity.

The interim saw that our congregation's story was deeply connected to the stories of other UU congregations in central Indiana. Over four decades, there were split-ups and split-offs, with only sporadic and superficial attempts at cooperation. Did this make sense for one of the few liberal religious voices in the region? Certainly not!

She proposed a process that would bring these congregations together to focus on the larger UU mission in central Indiana, while helping UUI address the interim tasks and reclaim an external, community-focused vision. She gathered seventeen representatives (including me) from six congregations, and suggested that each undertake a strength-based process of self-discovery known as Appreciative Inquiry (AI). (For more about congregations making broader connections, see "Strengthening Connections Beyond the Congregation.") This is a practice that seeks to "energize the creative best in people and their organizations." As the Center for Appreciative Inquiry puts it, "Its assumption is simple: Every human system has something that works right—things that give it life when it is vital, effective, and successful." (For more about Appreciative Inquiry, see "Coming to Terms with History.")

After the interchurch task force designed a shared framework, each congregation assembled its community independently. Congregants paired off to interview each other as they answered four questions designed to reveal the congregation's strengths and dreams for the future. The listener simply took notes. This deceptively simply activity was powerful for two reasons: The interview pairs created new personal connections, and the process forced us to practice listening without interruption, commentary, or judgment.

The interchurch task force then met to identify the common "energy centers" and design a day-long, AI-based program for all the congregations. This extraordinary day called the Greater Good Gathering (G3) was attended by over one hundred central Indiana UUs from six congregations. After some inspiring singing and preaching, we again paired off for one-on-one interviews, and then split up into five facilitated groups to brainstorm projects of mutual interest. Champions, poster-makers, note-takers, and cheerleaders for each project huddled together to create over two dozen "provocative proposals" for the whole gathering.

This process resulted in a few wonderful initiatives, but I want to follow one inspiring thread. Through the AI process, we learned that music and art were highly valued in each congregation. During the G3 brainstorming, a UU-style revival was proposed to celebrate the creative arts and the big tent philosophy of Unitarian Universalism.

Although the first meeting was poorly attended, the idea caught fire at the second meeting, and soon over twenty people had been recruited to the planning team, representing seven congregations: All Souls Unitarian Church (Indianapolis), First UU Congregation (Terre Haute), Heartland UU Church (Zionsville), Oaklandon Universalist Church (Indianapolis), UU Church (Lafayette), UU Church of Indianapolis, and UU Church of Kokomo. Funding was secured from UUI's Beacon Fund as well as the UUA's Fund for Unitarian Universalism.

On September 18, 2010, nearly four hundred people (including ninety-five youth) gathered at the HUUsier PalUUza on the UUI campus to celebrate, create, and worship together. Participants hailed from UU congregations in eleven states, ten UU congregations in Indiana, and local folks from five Christian denominations. The eight-hour, intergenerational extravaganza included hands-on activities, ranging from community painting and cairn-building to rhythm and chant circles; a youth-led worship service; a rock concert; a collaborative art exhibit; a community meal; and a raucous and celebratory evening service that featured firebrand preaching from Rev. Meg Barnhouse, Rev. Bill Breeden, and Rev. Stephen Sinclair, punctuated by energetic gospel-style singing by a forty-member choir representing ten congregations.

It was a day that underscored the vitality of our faith as well as the promise of our collaborative power. Together, we had transcended our old stories of division and found common ground. Together, we had written a new and triumphal account, a chapter that revealed the magic of shared vision.

And it all began with understanding our stories—the individual stories of founding members and new members, the church's birth story, the tales of treasured church events, the stories of betrayal and hurt, and the intertwined narratives of our sister congregations. These stories told us about ourselves, told us what we do and do not value, told us how our actions align with our principles, told us where we find joy, told us how we dream together, and more. When we practiced listening to these stories, we began to recognize that our congregational narrative was not one but many stories. It was a multidimensional tome filled with wildly different characters and vivid, twisting plot lines. Recognizing and valuing these stories is a critical first step in transforming the rhetoric of diversity into meaningful practice.

The interim ministry period is an opportunity to mine these varied stories, to pay attention to their meaning, to discard ones that no longer serve, and to write a new story that can sustain a future vision. The interim minister facilitates this process, often acting as the archetypal trickster, the shape-shifter who catalyzes transformation—sometimes the hero, sometimes the villain—always sacred and intentional. No matter the circumstances of a particular congregation, whether healthy or conflicted, and regardless of the process undertaken, the interim ministry period will illuminate your congregation's stories in ways that strengthen its future and help a congregation engage new challenges and exciting possibilities.

PART III

The Work

Coming to Terms with History

DAVID KEYES

Loren Mead from the Alban Institute writes in *Critical Moment of Ministry: A Change of Pastors*, "Every congregation lives in dialogue with its past. Every congregation is strengthened immeasurably by its history, but every congregation has also been deeply wounded by its past. It is both the heir and the victim of its story." Effective transition ministry begins with a long look in the rearview mirror, where we must read the admonition: "Objects may be closer than they appear."

A study of the congregation's past should easily reveal points of pride: the burning of the mortgage for the religious education wing; celebrating the forty-fifth anniversary of dear old Dr. Longview's ministry; the way everyone rallied round after a fire damaged the sanctuary. Identifying these milestones is a necessary step for the interim minister when joining the system, which is built on such points of pride. "Joining the system" means that the interim minister must not only respect the blood, sweat, and tears of those who have built the church, but must also effectively communicate to the congregation that the interim is doing exactly that. When the interim constructs and leads a worship service honoring Dr. Longview, the congregation knows that their interim minister has joined them in seeing the value of their heritage.

What is unseen, like nine-tenths of an iceberg, is the shadow side of the congregation's history, the milestones that some consider millstones. These points of shame and discomfort are hidden under carpets or in closets, or are buried in the churchyard.

While most of the members may have arrived since Dr. Longview retired, his sins live on. If the interim is fortunate, they are minor and easily, even humorously, named. "I know many of you remember when your beloved former minister forgot to spring ahead for daylight savings time and showed up to find an empty church. I wish I could have seen the look on his face."

Not at all humorous, however, are actions by former ministers or church leaders that damaged human beings, or that sent the church spiraling downward, leaving behind Mead's "deeply wounded." The hurt and pain linger. The sickness infects future generations. We might all want to suppose that such negative things are rare in our congregation's past, or in the one we are serving, but it is best to assume they are not. With a frequency higher than expected, the interim ministry will uncover an incident or incidents of sexual misconduct, betrayals of trust, breaches of confidentiality, abuses of power, misappropriation of funds, or derelictions of duty. (For more about ministerial and other misconduct, see "Congregations with a History of Misconduct.")

In my interim ministries, it is common for congregants to line up during my first weeks to tell me about one or more past unfortunate circumstances. These comments always offer valuable insights, but they are by no means always credible. A member's assurance that Rev. Ms. Dimples robbed the church blind may turn out to reveal nothing more than a disagreement about the use of the minister's discretionary fund. Real and damaging skeletons are likely to be more securely locked away.

First Unitarian, a mid-sized congregation in the Midwest, is noted for honoring its nineteenth-century founder and for celebrating many events that occurred before the Second World War. Newer members are mystified by the hushed atmosphere, the invulnerability of the incompetent administrator, and the failure of the church to keep a settled minister for more than five or six years. Any suggestion by the interim that hidden secrets may be at the root of their problems is greeted by angry denial by lay leaders. What damaging misconduct awaits discovery here! The extent to which past misdeeds continue to hobble a church exactly corresponds to the vigorousness with which members deny that anything happened, or if it did, that it lingers in any way.

In another part of this same Midwestern city, a much healthier and much larger congregation prepares to celebrate an anniversary. Guided by the interim, the Transition Team mounts butcher paper around the interior of the church, and draws a timeline along the top, representing the last fifty years. Congregants write recollections on big sticky notes and affix them at appropriate points. From the pulpit, the minister urges both candor and circumspection in this joint history project; those who are afraid that their public recollections would upset others are urged to make an appointment to share privately with the minister. In a spirit of community and mutual respect, much is learned, much is revealed. (For more information about the importance of congregations' stories, see "Mining, Minding, and Making Stories" and "Small Congregations.")

Common Dysfunctions

To adapt Tolstoy's dictum, while healthy churches all seem to be healthy in the same way, troubled congregations each have distinctive sorts of troubles. Some churches stagnate and are on a numb autopilot. Others are in denial about their issues, while still others either had a long pastorate or had a minister stay longer than liked and were negotiated out of being the minister.

The stagnant church. Landmark UU Church in Southern California has several hundred members, has just completed a spacious new wing, is nationally known for innovative programs, and counts among its leaders top executives of major corporations. The dynamic minister of Landmark has just been lured away to head a respected nonprofit.

The interim minister will soon discover that Landmark gladly suffers from "satisfaction stagnation," a kind of stasis that will require the interim to quickly join the system, adapt to the church culture, and concentrate on consensus building around any growth or change. Members will respond favorably to frequent laudatory references to past ministers and past accomplishments, and will be savvy enough to know how to preserve what they value from any attempts to introduce significant change. Service in such a church will allow the interim minister to concentrate on sermon preparation, golf, and tennis. Real life, however, is rarely this simple, and health is a relative term.

Do all churches need to take advantage of the opportunity to significantly change during a ministerial transition? Research and experience tell us that this is a time to discover a new identity. That discovery will best be made when the congregation has examined its *old* identity and compared it to present reality. In the case of Landmark Church the congregation took great pride and comfort in being an elite gathering of people from similar backgrounds and of like minds. What some called elitism appeared to the interim minister to drive away those who sought a more open and accepting church. This was especially true of young families, who often had less education and lower incomes than those who sustained and led Landmark. This attitude seemed to be a major cause of the near-collapse of the religious education program.

A candid review of Landmark's history would have revealed what first attracted the young families of lower social status (very intentional work in their neighborhoods by a departed associate minister). Yet Landmark's leaders were too satisfied to embrace the self-examination that might have led to a change and to service to a broader community.

The church in denial. An even greater challenge is the church afflicted with both satisfaction stagnation and deep, disabling dysfunctions. Landmark Church can do good but very limited work during the interim (strategic planning and leadership development), but truly has much to be satisfied about. Inevitably, Landmark inspires wannabe congregations that think of themselves as just as healthy, just as satisfied with "the way we've always done things." Such self-deception is common and keeps the church stuck, constantly searching for treasures they never quite find and would never find.

First Church, in the elite suburbs of an Iron Belt city, claims to be a six-hundred-member church, and thinks of itself as a healthy, leading congregation that needs nothing more than a competent replacement for a minister of fifteen years' tenure, gently pushed into retirement. Leaders at First Church even doubt that they need interim ministry; things are going so well that they can simply have the associate minister fill in for a year. Because of the church's reputation, these leaders are confident that dozens of exceptional ministers will be knocking at the door. Besides, they've heard that interim ministers are change agents, and there is nothing at First Church that needs to change.

But unlike at the genuinely healthy Landmark, a review of markers and a probe of reality at First Church reveals a pattern of declining attendance and giving over the past decade, a staff with extremely low morale, a church school relying on outdated curriculum, a rogue youth group, and a seventeen-member Board of Trustees that attempts hands-on management of staff, programs, and facilities.

When, after fits and starts over three years, First Church finally hires an accredited interim minister, the actual membership stands barely above four hundred, and church school classes have been combined because enrollment no longer supports age-appropriate classes.

First Church has been the Church of Denial, and its grief at its lost reputation and lost membership will be considerable. The interim minister's challenge will be to rebuild self-confidence while helping the church tell the truth about its neglect of systems, programs, and governance.

Interim ministry following a long pastorate. Dowdy Universalist is a 230-member church in the Northeast. Their retiring minister has served them for thirty-two years, building the church up to more than 500 members at one point in the 1980s, a time that many at Dowdy remember fondly and to which they long to return.

Several long-time pillars of Dowdy have confided to the interim that "Rev. Lovejoy just stayed a bit too long." But the facts point to his "retiring in place" considerably longer than a decade ago. Religious education, worship, staffing, and governance all smack of the way things were done forty years ago. Fortunately, declines in membership and stewardship have convinced lay leaders at Dowdy to take emergency action. The interim will accomplish much by honoring Rev. Lovejoy and staying in close touch with him, even as organizational development moves the church ahead three decades in two years.

The effective interim keeps ministers emeriti informed of major decision points, activities, and changes in the church; it is so much better for them to learn from their successor than to be surprised and thus feel dishonored, or to hear of changes through the grapevine—and many retired ministers have excellent grapevines. Ministers emeriti frequently retain active followings in the church, and even when they are scrupulous in staying out of church affairs, their opinions are often sought and cited. The effective transition specialist will have a productive alliance with the past minister(s), even if that alliance is largely private.

Following a negotiated resignation. It is surprising how many departures are negotiated, even when unacknowledged, and the congregation assumes that their minister simply got a better offer. I always assume that the minister I follow was somehow pushed or shoved out, sometimes subtly, sometimes in a very messy way. And I am always delighted when I find that was not the case.

At Central Community UU Congregation (CCUUC), the 105 members seem mystified by the sudden departure of their minister, who had been with them for only four years. The Board's application for interim ministry refers to "questionable work habits of the previous minister that made some feel she might be better suited for another position."

As the interim digs for the details, it becomes apparent that the questionable work habits may have included excessive use of alcohol, evidenced both while driving children to an off-campus activity and, on one unfortunate Sunday, in the pulpit.

Because Rev. Smiley was much loved by the younger families in the church, many seem angry that she might have been forced out; they refuse to believe that she had a drinking problem and warn the interim not to bring it up. Longer-term members, including those who quietly urged the departure, feel alienated and unfairly shunned by younger members. As is often the case following a forced resignation, an excellent opportunity now presents itself for a healing ritual.

Healing Rituals

A formal healing ritual can have a powerful effect on a troubled congregation. Howard Dana, early in his ministry at Harrisburg, Pennsylvania, originated this idea for Unitarian Universalist congregations.

Plenty of advance publicity about the ritual is needed, including a sermon or two. The congregation needs to understand that a safe space will be created for the responsible sharing of hurt, grief, and anger. Stories may be told and feelings expressed as long as participants remember to honor the feelings of others.

Ideally, the ritual will last for two hours or more to allow time to move from the awkwardness of raw anger or grief to healing and wholeness. A lay leader working with the interim may begin with introductory words; participants sing a song. Seated in a circle around a table, they are invited to come forward as they are so moved to light a candle and speak their truth. After more singing and a time of meditation, participants write their grudges or anger on flash paper. One by one, they come to the bowl holding the flaming candles, announce what they are letting go of, and ignite their flash paper.

Supporters and detractors will likely relate several sides of the story of Rev. Smiley. Those who suspected she was unfit for ministry will hear from those who loved her and felt she transformed their lives. Those who loved their former pastor will hear about the anger felt by those she seemed to snub or ignore. If all are sharing responsibly, using "I" statements, and speaking more from their hearts than their heads, the congregation may seem, during the ritual, to melt into a beautiful pool of mutual love and respect. In some cases, of course, repeating the ritual may be necessary to accommodate those unable to attend, or in need of more healing.

Now, with the raw edges off, it may be time to lead the congregation in an Appreciative Inquiry process.

Appreciative Inquiry

Providing an opportunity for congregants to get in touch with their positive feelings about their church, and from those feelings to cast a vision for the future, is vital transition work that can be done in a variety of ways.

Appreciative inquiry (AI) is now a recognized academic discipline generating PhD theses and a library of technical tomes, but it can be as simple a process as sitting down for an hour or two with a few parishioners willing to respond to some questions. These include:

- What was it that first brought you to this church?

- Tell about a time when the church was important to you.

- What was your most moving moment here?

- How would it feel to arrive at Middle UU one day and discover that the church was gone?

- Imagine coming to this church in five, ten, twenty years. Tell about what you see and what you feel on those visits.

Responses to questions such as these can be collected by a Transition Team, handed off to a writing team, and developed into "provocative proposals"—a technical AI term for vision statements that stretch the congregation to develop plans as big as their dreams.

While small congregations may want to do simple, home-grown exercises like the one above, larger churches and those with ample resources may want to bring in AI consultants with the expertise and cachet to truly make the congregation sit up and take notice. The point is to involve as many congregants as possible in remembering the power of the blessings the church has brought them, and from their hearts, to project those blessings onto those who will come after them. In this way, the past is being used to build the future, which is really what this task is all about. (For more about the AI process and using the past as a resource, see "Mining, Minding, and Making Stories.")

Congregants sometimes resist AI, especially in times of stress and conflict. They may say, "You are only giving me a chance to say positive things, and I want to complain and solve some of the problems around here!"

Yes, AI is a positive exercise, does not seek to solve problems, and will frustrate those who want to vent, which accounts for much of its charm and success. By keeping the focus on what's right with the church and putting problems in a "parking lot" for later consideration, congregants seem to have direct experience of the spirit and power that will propel them toward greater service.

The churches described above are mostly composites, constructed from actual situations but at least minimally disguised. A host of real churches can be confidently cited for their success with Appreciative Inquiry:

- At Unity Church-Unitarian in Saint Paul, Minnesota, AI led the way for the transformation of church governance that has spread the Unity model to dozens of other churches. The provocative proposals produced objectives that one leader says have taken Unity from a church with sixty people "really involved" to a church with hundreds of congregants participating in ministry teams.

- At the eight-hundred-member UU Congregation of Atlanta, AI is cited for giving a fresh vision to a church that had trouble letting go of a long-term ministry, turning congregants' vision from the rearview mirror to plans for innovative initiatives, including more spirited worship and a day care center for low-income families.

- At First UU, a mid-sized church in Houston, Texas, AI helped heal a badly divided congregation, creating nonthreatening opportunities for members to listen to one another's stories, and then to unite around a fresh vision.

In some congregations, interim ministers report little noticeable impact from Appreciative Inquiry. Of course, no process will produce the same results every time. Yet the tremendous success of AI in so many places, and the growth of professional interest in the method, point to its effectiveness when it is done with the firm intention that it will be done well, will be a priority for the church, and will yield guideposts for the congregation for years to come.

Useful Tools

Coming to terms with history and past ministries is possible only when the best information about the congregation is available, and when it is used. Much of this information will be anecdotal, but some can be extracted from data collected over the years.

Reviewing membership and participation numbers with church leaders at an interim ministry start-up retreat can be effective. A regional staff member or consultant can help interpret data and ensure that the numbers are extracted and ready for review. When charted, a roller-coaster effect will usually be noted. Many churches grow in membership and participation until they exceed the comfort level of members, then drop back, build back up, drop back, and so forth. Seeing this or other patterns overlaid with a history of ministry and major events in the life of the congregation can be revelatory for leaders.

Giving congregants an opportunity to construct a timeline is one way to support a congregation in telling its story. The graphic timeline, highly visible in the hallways or the sanctuary, is especially effective because it provides a visual image of hope. ("If the church has been here through all those years and all those ups and downs, I guess we can have confidence in the future.")

There are plenty of other tools. Video interviews with senior members can be shown to various church gatherings. Sermons can creatively highlight the history of the congregation. I once molded into a sermon a longtime member's "discovered" diary describing the strengths and foibles of several previous ministers. Likewise, liturgical dramas, religious education curricula, and other means to tell the core stories of the church provide opportunities to share its history.

While the tasks of interim ministry are not necessarily undertaken in any particular order, coming to terms with history and past ministries really does seem to come first. All congregations in transition suffer some sense of loss, some grief. They must be given an opportunity to process that grief, even if it seems minor.

The best description I know for the good work that interim ministers can do comes, of course, from the sage Loren Mead. He is largely responsible for transforming so many lives by transforming our understanding of the great strides that can be made in the interim. In *The Once and Future Church*, he writes,

> Coming to terms with the past means the congregation comes to a place where it is able to look at its past, lay to rest its ghosts, value its heroes and heroines, honor its special story, forgive itself for its faults, and gain energy for a new stage of its journey.

The Interim Minister
as Systems Analyst

RICHARD A. NUGENT

■ ▨ ▨ ■

Interim ministry is, first and foremost, *ministry* in the interim. It is about ministering to the whole of the congregation—the children, youth, and adults its programs serve—but it is also much more. Interim ministry is about inviting the present congregation to envision the congregation of tomorrow. It is about looking at the health of the congregation as a whole as well as each of its component parts. It is about rediscovering the significant historical events and prophetic stances of the past. It is about coming to understand the emotions (grief, sadness, anger, disappointment, among others) associated with the end of the previous ministry and navigating the anxiety of looking ahead to the future ministry.

Within the individual church, all ministry occurs somewhere along a continuum between meeting the needs of individual congregants and supporting major congregational programs and initiatives. Ministers, lay leaders, and other congregants decide how much energy and resources to devote to each point along the continuum. Congregational leaders may devote an hour or two during the annual leadership retreat to strategic planning, but too much work and not enough resources keep it from being a congregational priority. Settled ministry tends to focus more on pastoral care to the adults, youth, and children whose hopes, needs, challenges, and talents reside within the congregation and beyond its doors. In significant contrast to settled ministry, interim ministry focuses on pastoral care to the *institutional systems* within the congregation.

Ministry in the interim offers a unique opportunity to step back and reflect on the congregation and its ministry. I call this phenomenon the Brigadoon effect, recalling the play in which a mythical town of that name in the Scottish Highlands emerges from the mist once every hundred years but only for one day. In interim ministry, the congregation emerges for a brief time, not from the mist but from the ordinary, day-to-day work of settled ministry, to see itself with new clarity.

There is no one right way to do the interim minister's work. Each congregational situation is as unique as individual interim ministers' gifts of discernment. Ministry in the interim is as much art as science. Though skilled interims do bring various tools to help them, the lay leaders and congregants do the work. Some interims are particularly adept at facilitating workshops; some do more of the work from the pulpit on Sundays. Some concentrate their efforts on working with leadership in retreats and meetings. Some use analytical tools, such as questionnaires and surveys. Some work more as storytellers and ritual artists. But in one way or another, the skilled interim minister conveys to the congregation that they themselves must perform the interim tasks. The interim may be an organizational development consultant, coach, mentor, cheerleader, facilitator, guide, but is not a fixer who does the work while the congregation sits back and lets it happen or resists at every turn. Through it all, the interim's finger is on the pulse of the interacting systems that are the stuff of congregational life.

Components of a Congregational System

The skilled interim understands that a congregational system is really a collection of intersecting and overlapping subsystems. Some function harmoniously while others compete with each other for resources that are perceived to be, or actually are, limited. The primary work of the interim is to discover and evaluate the various subsystems and their interactions and to suggest how each advances or hinders the congregation's mission. In effect, the interim holds a mirror up to the congregation so they can collectively make informed decisions about their future.

By analyzing these systems and subsystems, the interim can help the congregation—especially its staff and lay leaders—determine the work they need to do to best prepare for the next chapter in their organizational history.

To get an overview of the kind of analysis an interim performs, think of a congregational system as distinct groups of people within the congregation, some intersecting or overlapping, engaged in a variety of activities that, taken together, comprise the life of the church. These groups include the choir, religious education teachers, the Finance Committee, social justice activists, the youth group, ushers, the founders, the meditation group, aging singles, and the Board. While smaller interest or identity groups help individuals develop deeper bonds with other like-minded congregants, these groups sometimes become the primary relational focus of their members rather than the broader congregational community. When that happens, there is a danger that the priorities of the small group may drive the larger agenda of the congregation rather than the reverse—a sure route to internal conflict that can easily derail the congregation and its ministry. Understanding such organizational traits is essential but often gets lost in the day-to-day work of settled ministry. Interim ministry affords congregational leaders the time and opportunity to step back and get a balcony view. Doing so helps guide their decision making.

While examining the subsystems, the interim might well ask, or invite leadership and congregants generally to ask, a set of questions about each of the major components of the congregation's system. These questions have no right or wrong answers. They are not questions that the interim or anyone else should be expected to answer without considerable observation and reflection. Instead, they offer a way into observation and reflection for the interim and congregants as they operate together as systems analysts.

Newcomers. What happens when newcomers appear on Sunday morning? Is there an official greeter to welcome them, show them where the sanctuary and bathrooms are, and invite them to stay after the service for coffee? Is there a whole team of greeters? Do any of these greeters have a hidden agenda that sabotages the work of the congregation? Better yet, do many members keep their eyes out for newcomers and welcome them in personal ways? Does anyone offer to accompany a newcomer into the sanctuary, or invite a newcomer to come back for some activity other than Sunday service? Are new families shown the classrooms and introduced to the religious education staff? Are newcomers invited to sign a guest book/card and put on a name tag? Does anyone call or write to them during the following week? Or are they typically left standing alone by the bulletin board during coffee hour, holding the distinctively colored visitor's coffee mug, while members chat with their old friends or perhaps attend to congregational business? Is it easy to wander away without much notice being taken?

Membership. How does a newcomer become a member? Is there an easily discovered path to membership? Is the membership book left out for anyone to sign any time, perhaps mistakenly thinking they are signing a visitors' guest book? Are there frequent classes for prospective members on Unitarian Universalism and the particular congregation? What role does the minister usually take in such classes? Is much asked of members, because of either bylaw or congregational culture, or is membership viewed casually? Are new members celebrated during a worship service? Is there a mentoring program or some other systematic way to assimilate new members into the congregation? Do they fill out a "needs and gifts" questionnaire? If so, does anybody follow up on it, or does it go into a file somewhere, never to be seen again? When a member resigns or simply drifts away, is there any systematic follow-up to find out why? When a member or family moves away, is there a formal leave-taking ceremony during a Sunday service where they are given a remembrance gift?

Caring. Is there a Caring Committee or its equivalent that participates in the pastoral ministry by such practices as sending cards to the ill, arranging for rides for the incapacitated, and providing refreshments for receptions after memorial services? How attentive generally are members to each other? Do they keep in touch to know when someone is ill, in grief, or otherwise in need? Are there more formal support systems, particularly in larger congregations, where informal networks may not be sufficient to keep people from falling through the cracks?

Worship. What is the meaning of worship to the gathered community? Are theological differences celebrated, or does the congregation practice the theological version of "don't ask, don't tell"? Is the congregation primarily committed to one style of music, or does the music vary widely to best accommodate the service's theme? Do the various components of worship seamlessly blend together, or does the Sunday service lurch from one element to the next? Are there worship associates, trained by the minister, who take part in planning and celebrating worship? Is there a Sunday Services Committee or Program Committee who are not trained but nonetheless take significant parts, including conducting services when the minister is out of the pulpit? What role does the minister take, or not take, in authorizing and being responsible for worship whether or not present? Does the same style and quality of worship prevail year round, or are summer services different, or differently led? Or does the congregation not even gather every Sunday during the summer?

Religious education. Is religious education readily available to people of all ages, or limited primarily to children and youth? Who teaches the classes, and what kind of training do they have? Are teachers new to Unitarian Universalism themselves or are they long-term members well versed in the history, polity, and theology of Unitarian Universalism? What role does the religious educator take? What role does the minister take? Are the youth connected in a meaningful way to district or regional youth programming? Are district, regional, and Unitarian Universalist Association (UUA) resources for lifespan religious education used, such as the Our Whole Lives sex education curricula for different age groups? Is there a safe-congregation policy in place and understood congregation-wide to protect people of all ages, not only those in religious education classes, from sexual or other forms of abuse? Are children and youth incorporated meaningfully into Sunday worship so that worship addresses their needs as well as the needs of adults?

Theological grounding and spiritual deepening. Are there systematic efforts beyond offerings labeled "religious education courses" to make sure that active participants in the church, whether members or not, learn about Unitarian Universalism, including beliefs, history, and polity? Are longer-term members given the opportunity to develop a more nuanced understanding of their faith? How do they obtain it? What opportunities do individuals have to deepen their spirituality and to question how best to respond to challenging life issues? Do covenant groups or other forms of small-group ministry thrive in the congregation with significant numbers participating?

Congregation's self-identification. Do the members see the congregation primarily as a religious community or as a social club, advocacy group, or oasis for like-minded political liberals? Although, of course, some individual members may see the congregation as each of these, which view is shown to be dominant because it governs how members act and treat newcomers? Is there a broadly shared vision for the congregation's ministry, are there multiple competing visions, or is the congregation drifting in the wilderness, lacking a clear vision? Is the congregation forward looking, satisfied with the present, or longing for a ministry from the distant past? Does the congregation strike a good balance between ministering to the needs of its current members and reaching out to the larger community, including welcoming newcomers? Do members see themselves as engaged in a shared ministry, or are they a collection of essentially independent subgroups that relate only to their subgroup rather than to the congregation as a whole?

Finances. Are financial resources available to fund desired programs, or are there major unmet needs? Is the dominant financial narrative one of abundance or scarcity? Is the congregation paying its bills by spending down an endowment? How knowledgeable is the typical member about congregational financing? What are the expectations of members with respect to pledging? Do the bylaws specify making a pledge and contribution of record as conditions of membership? What percentage of the membership make an annual pledge of financial support of a specified amount? How many members are included in each quartile of pledge income? Is stewardship a year-round program rather than an annual month-long blitz? Are canvassers trained, and does each year's stewardship campaign have specific and manageable goals? If the stewardship campaign does not yield enough pledge income to fund the proposed budget, is the first response to think about where to find the additional needed income, or to decide what to cut? How adequate are the financial reserves, and under what circumstances can they be spent to advance the congregation's mission?

Staffing. Does the congregation employ sufficient professional and administrative staff to support its programs adequately? Are all the paid staff, not just the minister or other religious professionals, compensated according to the UUA's fair compensation standards? If not, why not? If surplus funding does happen to be available, is it used to compensate existing staff more fairly or to hire more staff? Are job responsibilities clearly delineated, and are adequate resources provided to enable staff to do their jobs well? Are performance goals and objectives for each year agreed upon by employees and their supervisors, with regular evaluations based upon those goals and objectives? Are employees rewarded for jobs well done? Are there rewards for jobs well done by volunteers, such as recognition in the newsletter, special "Volunteer of the Month" parking space, and annual volunteer recognition dinners? Is the minister understood to be the chief of staff, with this role specified by letter of agreement if not by bylaw, or do committees attempt to supervise paid employees while at the same time acting as their support groups? Does the minister have a Ministerial Relations Committee that either protects the minister from disgruntled complainants or serves as an energetic complaint bureau—in either instance, encouraging dysfunctional triangles rather than direct communication? Do other professional staff have their own support committees, or does the congregation have one Committee on Ministry that monitors how well all of the congregation's ministries are carrying out its mission? (For more about staffing, see "Working with Staff.")

Physical plant. Is the physical plant adequate to meet the needs of the congregation and to advance the congregation's larger mission? Are buildings and grounds attractive and well maintained, or is there substantial deferred maintenance? Are the kitchen facilities adequate to meet the social needs of the congregation? Is there a fully equipped nursery and toddler space? Is there a "crying room" where someone with a crying child can see and hear what is happening in the sanctuary without disrupting the Sunday service? Are the classrooms and meeting rooms warm and inviting, or have the upholstery, rugs, art, and other displays seen better days?

Governance. How are major and minor decisions made? Who makes them? Is the governance model appropriate for the size of the congregation, its staffing, and its mission? Does the congregation clearly understand the distinction between the policy-making province of the Board and its committees on the one hand, and the ministerial province of the minister and others sharing in ministerial functions on the other? Are individuals easily recruited to serve in key leadership positions, or is recruitment an annual struggle? Are some leaders entrenched in positions they have held for many years? Are there term limits for any positions other than Board members? Are there one-person committees? Are there far too many committees, boards, and councils, producing an over-complicated and unwieldy governance structure? Are there short-term task force opportunities available for people who would like to serve in some way but have limited time? Do some people hold multiple leadership positions at once? Are former leaders frequently recycled? Are relatively new members whisked onto the Board without having served in other positions that are reasonable precursors to Board membership? Is there any in-house leadership training, or are leaders encouraged to take advantage of district or regional training?

Operations. Are the combined lay leadership, volunteer pool, finances, and staffing sufficient to achieve established goals, or are resources inadequately allocated to certain programs? How much authority do ministers, other religious professionals, and administrative staff have with respect to program and use of time and resources? What kind of accountability are lay leaders, volunteers, and staff held to? Is it a given that all in positions of leadership, paid or not, will write an annual report? Are there planning meetings in advance of each church year for people in charge of various operations to coordinate their efforts and calendars?

Communications. How effective are the various avenues used to convey information to the congregation? Is the congregation's website attractive, informative, and likely to appeal to people in search of a congregation, or is it clearly the work of an amateur and filled with obsolete information? Is the congregation's sign, or wayside pulpit, easily visible and kept current and in good repair? Is there a weekly email newsletter as well as a monthly one? Are they read? If not, why not? Is anyone in charge of policies about what information goes into the newsletters? Are the same announcements run issue after issue? What about announcements in the Sunday bulletin or spoken announcements at Sunday services? Are there policies to govern them? Are announcements monitored? Who makes spoken announcements? Are there email lists? What use does the congregation make of social media? Are the tools available used to advantage for outreach, or is there so little control that they are allowed to do harm?

Congregation's emotional health. Is the congregation collectively grieving the loss of its beloved former minister, or is it rife with internal divisions occasioned by the circumstances of that minister's leaving or other differences? Is the congregation anxious about its future, or have the members seen so many ministers come and go that they take one more ministerial transition in stride? Is the atmosphere on Sunday morning stormy or calm, sunny or dismal? Is the congregation the type of organization that existing members would want to join if they walked through the doors for the first time?

The unspoken story. Are there secrets from the past, such as betrayal of trust by a previous minister or lay leader, that continue to affect the present? What sacred cows or elephants in the room might severely limit the future if they are not brought into view and addressed? Does the congregation say it wants to grow but behave in ways that sabotage growth? Are newcomers welcomed, but only if they mirror the people who are already members? How welcoming is the congregation actually to people who are different theologically, politically, or ethnically? Would the members prefer to stay the same rather than engage in changes that growth would require? (For more about engaging with congregational history, see "Coming to Terms with History.")

Connection to the larger faith. Do most members see themselves as part of a larger faith community, or does their identity with Unitarian Universalism actually end at the church's property line? Are they engaged in significant numbers with denominational organizations such as the Unitarian Universalist Service Committee? Does the congregation have a Partner Church in Transylvania, the Khasi Hills, the Philippines, or elsewhere abroad? Do they take visible part in denominational initiatives such as Standing on the Side of Love? How many members attend district, regional, or national annual assemblies? Does the congregation contribute its fair share to the district or the UUA's Annual Program Fund? Have they done the work to earn certification as a Green Sanctuary or as a Welcoming Congregation to bisexual, gay, lesbian, and transgender persons? Have they been a teaching congregation, supervising a ministerial candidate's internship? If they have not made these connections with the UUA, why not? (For more about making broader connections, see "Strengthening Connections Beyond the Congregation.")

So Many Questions, But to What End?

Like individuals whose unique needs are addressed by congregations, each congregation within the UUA has its own distinct traits. Some follow a traditional Sunday liturgy, while others thrive on experimentation each week. The liberal values of some stand in stark contrast to predominantly conservative values found in their communities, while many alternative progressive religious congregations may be found in other locales. Some congregations focus on spiritual deepening, while others primarily identify with social action. Of course, each informs and sustains the other. The nearest other Unitarian Universalist congregation may be less than a mile away or hundreds of miles away.

Effective interim ministry begins with the interim minister listening to the stories of the gathered community and learning about the history, traditions, and challenges of the congregation. The interim may come with a toolbox of techniques, but not with predetermined conclusions. Like Brigadoon, magic occurs in the deepening relationships forged during this special time.

In each generation, Unitarian Universalism has sustained itself and evolved because of our openness to question our own dogmas and explore new ways of being religious. Congregations sustain themselves and evolve, in large measure, by questioning their own dogmas and exploring new ways of being religious. Interim ministry is most effective when the questions posed by the interim and explored by the congregational leaders and members challenge them to find new ways of living our faith in their shared religious community.

Interim ministry is a gift to Unitarian Universalism and to each congregation that experiences skillful ministry in the time between settled ministers. It is a gift to Unitarian Universalism because it affords congregations an opportunity to strengthen their connections to the broader faith. It is a gift to individual congregations because it gives them an opportunity to rediscover, to reinterpret, to reclaim, and to reimagine their own vision of what constitutes contemporary Unitarian Universalism in their community, and ultimately to recommit to it. It is a gift to individual Unitarian Universalists because belonging to a revitalized congregation offers individuals so many more opportunities to learn about life, to deepen their own spirituality, to advance progressive values, and to serve others both in the congregation and beyond its doors.

Working with Staff

HEATHER LYNN HANSON

■ ■ ▨ ■

The work of the interim minister requires a great deal of coordination and support. During the interim period, the work with the congregation will be largely dependent on the cooperation and support of the staff, whether paid or volunteer. Therefore, the interim will spend considerable time working with staff members and leadership so they understand the process and can apply their skills to support the activities required in the interim period. The interim interval is also an opportunity for staff members to hone individual and team skills in service to the mission and goals of the congregation.

Staff Levels

Staff members may either be hired or may volunteer to work on a regularly scheduled basis (not ad hoc), usually one-fourth time or greater. Key or senior staffers have responsibilities that include a certain level of independent judgment and decision-making authority. Each job description should include both general expectations and specific responsibilities.

Depending on the size and resources of a church, key staff positions might include administrator (office manager or business manager), religious education director, music director, volunteer coordinator, programs coordinator, and other positions. Senior staff comprises the professional team of which the minister is direct head. In smaller congregations, anyone who is authorized to make decisions about work priorities and resource allocation would probably be included on the staff team.

Support staff members' work is directed and supervised by a key staff member. For example, office assistants, receptionist, bookkeeper, and custodial staff may report to the church administrator. People in transient or minimal part-time positions, such as groundskeepers or child care assistants, may be church members, and are generally supervised by one of the senior staff.

Some factors to consider regarding staffing arrangements can be addressed in three categories:

Members as paid staff. Since the 1980s, church organization experts have recommended that churches not hire their own members to fill regular staff positions, for two reasons in particular. The first involves their relationship to the minister. The minister as supervisor cannot also be a pastoral presence or a mediator for staff members because the supervisory relationship is necessarily different, involving evaluations and possible disagreements. In effect, hired members lose their pastor, even if there should be need for personal counseling or cause for dismissal.

The second reason is that staff's relationships with fellow congregants must be neutral. Information the staff member is privy to must be handled with confidentiality. Chitchat with old friends about one's work situation too easily becomes a time to vent frustrations or inadvertently reveal confidential information. Maintaining professional boundaries puts a strain on the quality of church friendships. (For more about the difficulties of members as staff, see "Changes in Leadership.")

However, when a church is hiring for a part-time key staff position, an applicant who already is in sympathy with the values and principles of the denomination is more likely to affirm and promote the values of the church in conversations with members and inquirers.

Volunteer staff. Most small congregations have one or more important positions filled by quarter- to half-time volunteers, who are also part of the staff team. They should adhere to the same expectations and protocols as paid staff, and honor the code of confidentiality and other staff guidelines. They also should have appropriate job descriptions and supervision, including opportunities for goal setting and evaluation of their work.

Part-time staff. The smaller the congregation in terms of membership and budget, the more likely key staff members will work half-time or less. Part-timers frequently hold a second job outside of the church's regular office hours. Pulling staff together for meetings to exchange information or even to cross paths in the hallway other than on Sundays may be difficult. Many part-timers may have only partial commitment to the mission and values of a congregation. The interim minister must try to schedule short regular meetings that are relevant and honor the part-timers' time restrictions. Accommodating everyone's disparate schedules may not be feasible, but arranging a separate meeting to keep a key staff member up to speed can become a time sink if not wisely managed.

Informing the Interim Minister

Because churches vary widely in size, resources, organization, and culture, understanding the roles of leaders, volunteers, and paid staff requires that the interim learn about the local situation as quickly as possible. Prior to arrival, the interim will gather information about the church, including the staff. Conversations with the regional staff and the search team, plus documents from the team, will inform the interim what has been expected of each staff member and if there were staff issues connected with the departure of the former minister.

On site, the interim will determine how best to support and supervise the current staff, and what goals for improvements should be considered during the interim period. They should review key staff members' tenure, job description, supervision, and evaluation documents, which reveal expectations and satisfaction. If volunteers hold key positions, similar questions may be asked. The interim will also query their recruitment, training, and supervision. As soon as possible, the interim will talk with the staff as a group and may interview each staff member individually. These meetings and interviews will help the interim understand the dynamics between the staff and the larger congregation.

Staff members can be invaluable resources for the interim. Along with their specific job competencies, their own history with the congregation provides valuable insight into congregational culture.

Supervisory Objectives

Supervision of both employees and volunteer staff involves three general objectives: administration, education, and support. Balancing these involves applying best practices.

Administration. The interim expects staff to be accountable for their specific tasks and the requirements of the larger organization. The whole staff needs to know and follow established policies and procedures in a timely manner. Digital communiqués can keep everyone informed, but regularly scheduled meetings allow members to ask questions and better understand their roles. The interim will work to create a team that serves the congregation, utilizing their various gifts and perspectives. Staff may have valuable suggestions that simplify or clarify administrative procedures, programming complexities, or scheduling problems, and they can often resolve difficult issues by respectful and creative problem solving.

Education. Staff meetings allow the whole group to exchange important information, receive training, build morale, convey appreciation, understand the transition process, and in turn learn how to respond to anxious behaviors of church members. The interim may encourage staff members to expand professional skills and expand their knowledge of church history and programs. As the ministerial search process progresses, staff members need to understand how their responsibilities may, or may not, be affected during each stage, especially preparing for and assisting during candidating week and beyond. Education can create a strong, resilient, knowledgeable staff, able to accommodate the transitions the congregation must go through with the arrival of the next minister.

Staff made up of mostly part-time employees will benefit from education during staff retreats or occasional meetings dedicated to increasing staff knowledge. Work time for these meetings must be allocated and scheduled well in advance. Terms of employment should include required periodic paid training time for every key staff member.

Support. During the early weeks of the transition, it is not unusual for staff to be nervous about the new boss. Grief, anger, or relief over the former minister's departure is not uncommon. Some staff members may be anxious about their jobs. Uncertainty often increases competitive behaviors, such as jockeying for attention, resources, or priorities, or undermining colleagues' programs or other aspects of the church. In early staff meetings, the interim minister will convey what kind of support the staff can expect from their new chief, and the interim's expectations and vision for the staff and for the congregation. It is also wise to help staff understand and respond effectively to congregants uncomfortable about the transition. Congregants' anxiety is often expressed by an increased level of complaining and fault finding, so staff can help calm fears during the transition. The interim will model a non-anxious and respectful presence, giving staff time to ask questions, and discouraging any rehash of the departure or habits of the prior minister and other staff or leaders.

Supervisory Roles

Effective supervision requires a clarity of roles, particularly among the Board, the Personnel Committee, and the minister.

The role of the Board. The Board of Trustees is the fiduciary agent for the congregation, responsible for contracts and, in many cases, for hiring and dismissing staff. The Board's work with the staff should always reflect the vision and mission of the congregation, so leadership and staff may need education and support to understand that the financial resources of the membership must further the purpose and vision of this unique congregation, not please a donor or provide someone employment. Evaluations of staff progress, and of Board-set goals, should be based on the overarching direction and dreams that motivate and inspire the whole congregation.

In very small congregations, a Board or subset of the Board might conduct new staff searches and supervise employees. In larger congregations, a personnel task force can be assembled to develop job descriptions and bring recommendations for appropriate staffing. The interim should be involved in discussing the functions and job skills required for program-related staff and other relevant positions, selecting senior staff members, and serving as their supervisor, whether de facto, designated by Board policy, or specified in the bylaws.

The role of the Personnel Committee. Establishing a Personnel Committee is the responsibility of the Board of Trustees, and may be delegated through bylaws or Board action. However, establishing it as a standing committee is normally not encouraged. Instead, it should function as a task force or advisory group. It should be formed when particular personnel tasks are to be undertaken, such as writing job descriptions, advertising, and screening applicants. However, the Personnel Committee does not make final hiring decisions, nor administer the evaluation of staff. The interim may need to help clarify these roles and take appropriate leadership in hiring and evaluation of staff, setting the pattern for the coming settled ministry.

The role of the minister. Unless the bylaws state otherwise, the Board delegates supervision. As a rule, the minister, whether interim or settled, is the head of staff, as the person most likely to be aware of the employees' work as it impacts the dynamics of the congregation. This responsibility can be complicated and fraught with tension. An employee may be used to having little attention focused on their work or accustomed to informal supervision by a committee or committee chair, but not by the minister. The employee may assume that the interim has limited expertise in what the position covers (e.g., a youth program coordinator or office administrator) and is therefore not qualified to supervise.

A common mistake made by small congregations is appointing a committee to search for and recommend the hiring of a key staff member, and then acting as both advisory committee and supervising task force. Besides creating blurred and confusing responsibilities, this can result in power struggles between the staff member and the committee chair. For example, the director of religious education and the Religious Education Committee chair might argue about who selects children's curricula or has authority over the religious educator's work schedule and time off. Instead, the Search Task Force should be separate from the Advisory Committee (or if the same people serve on each, they need to understand their new responsibilities and wear their appropriate hats). Supervision of the staff person is delegated to the minister, whose perspective includes the total ministry of the church and whose role includes straightening out such staffing challenges.

The interim should work with all senior staff to clearly delineate job responsibilities and create job descriptions that become the basis for future evaluations and goal setting. The interim also educates and advocates with the congregational leadership to better understand what is needed for each key staff person to do the work well. This could include training expenses, supplies or equipment, and understanding appropriate work boundaries and time expectations. Often understanding the scope and nature of an employee's work requires significant education of the church leadership. It is particularly vital for lay members to understand appropriate expectations of part-time employees who may do some work from home via phone and Internet, where logged working hours are less obvious to Board members than outcomes and results.

As chief of staff, the minister, and therefore the interim, oversees supervision of all staff. Supervision in any organization is intended to empower its workforce to further the mission and goals of the organization. In churches, the manner of supervision must reflect and model the values held by the congregation, including the attitude of respect and care for individuals, held in creative tension with the spirit and vision of the religious community. The interim seeks to develop relationships with staff that are mutually respectful, trustworthy, and accountable. Because the interim comes with a time-limited agenda into an unfamiliar congregation, this process is an ongoing sifting of the observations and opinions of others, weighing of various factors, adapting one's own inquiries and observations, and creatively applying general principles for building trust while asserting authority.

Within the broad context of ministry and the interim tasks, the interim minister may do the following: direct or request staff actions or priorities; review and revise job descriptions; assess church staff performance and goals; provide or recommend training and other resources to develop staff understandings and skills relevant to their service to the congregation and its mission; and keep records and documents of staff performance to support evaluations and recommendations to the Board of Trustees. If the prior minister was not doing these things, the interim will need to ensure that Board members, staff members, and the congregation itself understand the scope and purpose of these activities.

Staff Meetings

Meetings with staff members may occur in a variety of formats. Congregations with a large staff may have daily meetings on the fly with the interim and key staff members, a weekly senior staff meeting, and monthly or quarterly meetings with all staff.

In smaller congregations, especially those with fewer than three hundred members, the relational aspect of the religious community tends to dominate people's assumptions about staffing. Church members tend to think of employees as part of the church community, whether or not they are members. The interim and other leaders must balance the need for accountability with the desire for compassion and collaboration without blurring the lines of responsibility.

Information exchange and conversation within the staff meeting is valuable, but staff should not be permitted to complain about other staff or congregants. The interim may need to coach employees and other leaders to appropriately bring requests for change or to responsibly report apparent transgressions. The interim should conscientiously model those standards as well.

The interim may need to meet privately with individual staff members to avoid embarrassing employees when offering encouragement, advice, or feedback. Periodic reviews and renewals of goals are also usually done in one-on-one meetings. In private meetings with any staff member, the interim should model the desired attitudes and standards of accountability, respect, and confidentiality.

In turn, individual staff members may want access to the minister from time to time to plan or clarify a work assignment, discuss how to interpret a policy, lay groundwork for a project, or just get some encouragement. Even if part of the conversation includes correcting an error or misconception, this private time with a staff member is valuable for building validation and mutual trust, conveyed by the minister's respectful presence, full attention, and thoughtful responses. If the interim realizes that a discussion will require more time than anticipated or is feeling pressure from other demands, the meeting may need to be postponed. Both minister and staff member should remain respectful of each other's needs but agree to follow up and address the concern(s) as soon as possible.

Staff members sometimes have personal issues that interfere with their work performance. The interim may offer professional advice; however, giving professional guidance to an employee is not the same as providing pastoral counseling. It might be tempting to give the same attention that might be afforded a church member, but the minister's time should not be absorbed by an employee whose personal problems interfere with the ability to function effectively in the workplace. A staff member with extensive personal problems or mental or personality dysfunction should be referred to qualified professional support outside the congregation. Some churches have a policy of personal time off for health issues.

As supervisor, the interim will record consultations with the staff member, the effort made by the employee to follow through on therapy or counseling, and any evidence of change, such as events that indicate improved or deteriorating job performance.

If the employee is a church member, their "loss of the pastoral relationship as a member" must be clarified; that explanation should occur before the job is even offered.

Goal Setting and Evaluations

In the interim period, staff evaluations may be new or may be done formally for the first time. Key staff may be especially sensitive about who is doing the evaluating and what is being evaluated —they are the ones most likely to be directly supervised by the interim and they may be worried for their jobs. Evaluations should be done based on goals and expectations that were made clear to the employees in the previous six months or year. Yearly goals should be specific, achievable, measurable or observable, and relevant to both the employee and the church mission.

Each year, employees and volunteers should review their job descriptions with the interim, to discuss what is still relevant and reflect on what has been satisfying; what requires support, adjustment, or reassignment; and what may need to be added or enhanced in some way. Then, in light of the church's mission and goals, they should set professional goals for the coming year. These goals could include learning a new technique; changing a set of procedures; accomplishing a routine activity more efficiently; or consolidating, organizing, or creating information. For example, an administrator might plan to develop job cue cards for custodians and report their usefulness in training new hires. A religious educator might learn how to coach classroom teachers and journal about the results. A music director might plan a choir exchange with another church or coach volunteers to develop a summer children's music program.

Three goals for the year that require some stretch, yet are attainable, should be recorded on the staff member's goals document for the year. Mid-year (or with new employees, every three months), the interim will confer with staff members on their progress—what is going well, and what needs more attention, resources, or a change in priority. The gist of that conversation should be added to the goals document, and be initialed and dated. At year's end, the staff member and interim will engage in a more extensive review of what has been gained, learned, or set aside. These reviews become the foundation for the next year's goals. If mid-year discussions have been candid, and concerns have been addressed, the year-end review should be a time for satisfaction, appreciation, and pride. Staff members should feel a sense of accomplishment, and the interim can celebrate improvements with the Board and the congregation.

Team Building

In many churches, key staff members who are specialists in their field may think that their responsibilities are somehow separate or isolated from those of other staff members. This perspective, which can engender understandable pride in their work, can also include feelings of privilege or protectiveness of their arena. Each specialist may have an advisory committee but no professional peers in the church. The resulting gathered key staff function more like an array of independent silos of competent influence than a real team. In contrast, a well-functioning staff team seeks to understand how each one's job contributes to the larger goals of the church. As senior staff, their individual experiences in the church can be brought to bear on thinking jointly about the big picture and brainstorming on problems outside their own arenas. The interim guides them in thinking more broadly and appreciating one another's diverse perspectives.

The team, including the interim, must develop a level of trust and vulnerability with each other so that disagreements can be both candid and productive. As people feel free to express divergent opinions about a topic, their commitment to coworkers and to the larger congregation grows. Many conflicts between individual staff members can be addressed by looking first at the level of trust between them. The interim can work with staff, or bring in a facilitator, to work on that basic level of mutual confidence.

The staff team will benefit from creating their own "covenant of right relations," which should become part of their regular self-evaluation as they assess their work together. Although examples from other churches' staff teams are available, a truly valuable and valid covenant will arise from discussion and shared concerns expressed by everyone who will rely upon it. The team might discover that what they want from one another is not supported by their current communication skills. For example, giving and receiving constructive criticism may need to be the topic of a staff workshop. Learning how to recognize and avoid triangulation will enhance people's sense of respect and confidence in handling uncomfortable situations among staff and with congregants.

Ideally, everything the interim does and says should model healthy ministry and healthy staff relations. The interim keeps the goal of building trust, not only within staff but also among lay leaders and congregants. There is always the risk of lost tempers, regrettable speech that cannot be retracted, and vulnerable and apologetic moments. Here are some guidelines the interim can follow to help minimize difficulties:

- *Tell the truth, even when it may be hard to receive.* Truth gives others the option to make informed choices. Being "kind" by padding the message masks the importance of one's concern. Giving and receiving criticism effectively is a necessary art of leadership. For example: A staff member had been hired to do office computer work, at which she excelled. However, when she answered the phone, she was abrupt, often grouchy, and perceived as rude. To avoid hurting her feelings, in five years of evaluations, she had never been told by senior staff or the minister how detrimental her phone presence was. When the interim finally gave her a truthful evaluation, she was crushed and angry, both at the messenger and at the years of deception. To maintain her position, she was required to take telephone presence training, paid for by the church, which she agreed to do. Her working arrangements were changed to reduce the need to respond to the phone as often.

- *Avoid triangulation at all costs.* It's natural for community members to exchange information and concerns by talking about people when they're not present. However, it is destructive when one or more of these parties avoids responsibility for the consequences of this communication for the absent person. This is called triangulation—indirect communication to a third party rather than direct communication between the persons involved. Grievances and complaints need to be heard, but people should not dodge respectful and responsible relationships. Those with a concern should go directly to the person with whom they have disagreement or misunderstanding. When criticisms and complaints come from congregants or other staff, the minister will listen. The minister will not become the messenger for a congregant but will teach the complainant how to handle the situation responsibly. The complainant may need to practice what to say to the person.

- *Create staff and minister trust by being reliable and trustworthy.* An experienced minster once said, "I will support the staff and insist that they support you. Staff members should always know that I've 'got their back'; I will never publicly blame them for anything, nor criticize anything they have done. Likewise, they do not blame me or explain unpopular decisions or policies by saying, 'The minister made me do it.'" If a complaint is made about the actions of a staff member, the minister will likely get the staff member's perception in private and then work with staff to change what needs to be changed, but should never do so in front of congregants.

- *Document problems.* When there are concerns about or problems with congregants or staff, the interim should document what occurred that day, including how the interim responded, and bring it to the attention of the offender as soon as possible, with a request for a change in behavior. If a pattern begins to emerge, the interim will have a record to identify repeated behaviors. It may give insight into alternative ways of approaching the issue, or validate the need to bring in outside help, particularly if a marked change in the person's health or cognitive ability is seen. These notes may become part of a staff member's personnel record, or may be discarded if the situation is resolved and no further incidents occur. They also provide the legal paper trail needed if a staff member must be dismissed.

- *Document the positive.* Note observations about situations handled well by any staff member. They provide supportive feedback on the spot and at evaluation time, and should be added to personnel records and, if appropriate, mentioned in the interim's notes to the Board.

Paving the Way for the Next Minister

As the interim prepares to depart, records regarding staff, such as goals, evaluations, and candid notes of appreciation and/or discipline, should be brought up-to-date. A brief narrative of works in progress toward staff personnel goals will be helpful to the incoming minister. Appreciation and thanks for staff members given during the interim's farewell remarks are especially appropriate, indicating particular ways in which sometimes "invisible" staff members have served the congregation by contributing to the interim process and the health and vitality of the church. (For more about the departure of the interim minister, see "Bringing an Interim Ministry to a Successful Conclusion.")

The goal of every interim is to loosen the soil, remove some of the rocks and weeds, and plant healthy seeds in the staffing garden. Although interims are advised to leave a small footprint, the next minister will appreciate the fruits of a staff that has been thoughtfully tended. The challenge in the midst of our work is to always remember these words, attributed to Oscar Romero:

> We cannot do everything, and there is a sense of liberation in realizing that. This enables us to do something, and to do it very well. It may be incomplete, but it is a beginning, a step along the way, an opportunity for the Lord's grace to enter and do the rest.
>
> We may never see the end results, but that is the difference between the master builder and the worker.
>
> We are workers, not master builders; ministers, not messiahs. We are prophets of a future not our own. Amen.

Changes in Leadership

ANDREA LA SONDE ANASTOS

About three years ago, I picked up the phone to hear the voice of a young colleague, new to interim ministry. With some concern, Carolyn said, "I understood there would be changes in leadership during the transition, but the chair of the Interviewing Committee just called to tell me that the church secretary has already resigned, the choir director *and* his wife (who is the Board president) are both stepping down at the end of the month, and the religious education director says that he will wait to meet me before he decides whether to remain—although I am not supposed to know that. Is this normal? The Interviewing Committee is wondering if First Parish should skip the interim time and go straight into the search process."

The only thing I could think to say was, "You are a lucky woman."

Carolyn laughed, but it was clear that she was still uneasy. As we talked, she thought back to her training and wondered aloud if perhaps the most anxious, burned out, and fearful members of the leadership team and staff had actually paved the way for one of the most essential interim tasks before she even walked through the door. I agreed with her assessment, but I also acknowledged that these resignations could be unsettling and might even appear like a crisis to the remaining leadership. However, we both concluded that there was a substantial upside: The congregation and Carolyn, as interim minister, could focus their energy on discovering and nurturing new personnel resources rather than persuading disgruntled, burned-out, or—possibly—incompetent staff to resign.

Resignations and leadership shifts seem routine in venues other than churches. In the corporate world, for instance, new CEOs in healthy organizations on their first day of work frequently find a neat pile of resignation letters on the desk from every person in the company who reports directly to them. This gives the new leaders the time and flexibility to build a team with the skills and emotional energy required to move the organization into its new vision. A couple of weeks after arrival, the CEO accepts the necessary resignations and tears up the others.

Obviously, there are substantial differences between the goals of the corporate world and the alternative vision of community that is the purpose of religious congregations. However, churches often shoot themselves in the foot when they dismiss wholesale the best practices of "worldly" organizations. Unfortunately, in the name of tolerance and inclusivity, many congregations create structures and invite behaviors that are designed less for the good of the whole than to placate the most anxious, immature, and critical members, or to protect the least competent staff. Therefore, the necessary work of changing leadership effectively and smoothly during the intentional interim time can be one of the most challenging tasks of transition. However, it can also be a path to new and life-giving practices.

Interim times in congregations begin with a highly visible and emotionally laden leadership shift as a former minister retires, moves to another position, experiences a negotiated termination, or dies, and a transitional minister enters the community. However, for the purposes of this essay, discussion of changes in leadership will focus on shifts in the other three categories of leaders in the church: paid staff (clerical, janitorial, and administrative positions), unpaid staff (anyone who functions in any position, from choir director to receptionist, but receives no financial remuneration from the congregation), and appointed and elected volunteer positions. In light of the initial ministerial shift, the congregation may strongly oppose these further changes, perceiving them as unnecessary or undesirable.

Resistance to Chaos

At its best, intentional interim time is an amazing vortex of creativity and chaos. It infuses a congregation with fresh air, encourages outside-of-the-box ideas, unlocking previously under-utilized personnel resources, and invites the community to experience new perspectives and visions. However, for many people, chaos elicits more fear than excitement and, therefore, systemic resistance can be high. Other factors can also impede normal and healthy process of leadership change. These include:

- fear that engaging wholeheartedly in *any* adaptive change will be perceived as a vote of no confidence in the past ministry or ministries

- a widespread sense of shame/guilt that "maybe we did it wrong" if any aspect of church life shifts substantively

- a culture of permanent ownership rather than temporary stewardship of church roles and functions

- a belief in entitlement on the part of lay leaders ("I've been a member for thirty-five years; it's my turn to be president of the Board!")

- fear of offending or upsetting elected leaders, their families, and allies

- fear of offending or upsetting church members who are paid staff, their families, and allies.

It is easy to understand why those elected to councils and boards might prefer not to rock the boat. This also explains why Carolyn and First Parish were far from alone in experiencing what seemed like a mass exodus from important staff and elected positions. And since the desire to avoid conflict is wired deep in the human psyche, it is normal to notice these responses, regardless of church size, configuration, or history.

So whether you are a council or Board member about to enter a period of intentional transition, an interim minister about to take up a new position, a staff member (paid or volunteer) whose mandate might shift in the next few months, or a member of a transition team tasked with helping the congregation navigate the rapids of change, you will be well served to understand the rationale for engaging in leadership change. Understanding such change also makes it possible to appreciate its benefits and to stay steady amid the natural anxieties we all experience in the face of potential upheaval.

Benefits of Leadership Change

Any system—from an individual human being to a nation—becomes exhausted and susceptible to dis-ease (dysfunction) without steady renewal and a regular realignment of goals, emphases, and resources. The best personal exercise regimens for our bodies include a balance of aerobics, weight training, and stretching. Likewise, institutional bodies need variety in their functioning, or some muscles will be damaged from overuse while others waste away from under-use. Times of transition provide ideal opportunities for an intentional switch from tired or worn-out resources to fresh ones. Changes in the church's exercise routine (worship, programs, governance) are equally beneficial. Not coincidentally, research teaches us that both of these shifts lay down new pathways in the brain, revitalizing ideas and possibilities, and suggesting previously inconceivable options.

"Changes in leadership" refers not only to moving tired or entrenched leaders out and new, untapped members into decision-making positions but also to assessing the inherent need and value of each position. Larger churches may have a helpful organizational chart to reference, but if not, a thoughtful look at the committee structure (in most churches still found in the bylaws) and the staff configuration will usually reveal whether a congregation is appropriately staffed for its mission and vision. There might be obvious signals that something is amiss, but sometimes deeper digging is necessary to reveal unproductive accretions in leadership.

Church leadership can be broadly divided into four categories: the ordained minister(s), elected and appointed lay positions, paid staff, and unpaid staff. (See also "Working with Staff.") Established leaders imprint a position and an organization with their personal style. In congregations, this is particularly true of long-term pastors (although long-serving directors of religious education, church secretaries, and music directors can have a similar impact). The impact of charismatic clergy may be so powerful that the minister and the congregation become almost synonymous; however, even a quiet or retiring minister will leave a profound imprint. Therefore, the loss of this person contributes to feelings of dislocation in the system. Emotional dislocation is a prime reason behind the "cult of the former minister," which can serve as a roadblock to forward movement, making it harder to prepare for the call of a new minister, and harder for the new minister to assimilate fruitfully. (See also "Predictable Roadblocks.")

During the natural process of a minister becoming established, a relatively small group of people (both volunteer and paid) emerges as the central functionaries of the congregation. This group usually self-selects because they resonate with the minister's style and personality, and feel a sense of loyalty to their leadership. Losing that pastoral presence puts emotional and psychological stress on the central leadership group. For some of these folks, the stress is a low-level situational anxiety that happens whenever human beings need to adjust to new ideas and practices. This kind of stress normally runs a predictable course. Eventually, this group will accept the new minister. For others, however, the stress experience is much more intense and challenges the identity that has formed around their place and role in the former administration. (For more about congregants' anxiety, see "A Different Country.")

Being enmeshed in role identity—and the reluctance to relinquishing it—can be especially noticeable in churches—one of the few institutions in which people who otherwise feel powerless can exercise substantial authority. Sadly, churches also too often allow inappropriate behaviors, such as turf warfare, emotional blackmail, and outright incompetence, to flourish under the rubric of nonjudgmental compassion.

Thoughtful, intentional, and (often) widespread change in across-the-board leadership is a healthy response to all levels of anxiety, and a wise corrective to non-covenantal behavior. Some leadership change can happen through personnel shifts, while other change needs a shift in structure (i.e., policies, procedures, staffing). These changes should include:

- addressing institutional paralysis—in anything from fiscal priorities to programs to worship style—that results from one group having power for a long time

- giving permission for long-serving leaders and managers, including unpaid staff, to rest and recuperate from grief and loss, exhaustion, and/or burnout

- engaging previously marginalized or peripheral members, bringing those at the margins into the center and those at the center outward; this movement should be natural in any system, as reflexive as inhaling and exhaling

- correcting unproductive or unhealthy patterns and relationships that have become institutionalized, including:

  - policies, procedures, and structures that are no longer effective for mission

  - behaviors such as power grabbing and turf warfare that have become normalized

  - protected incompetence in staff or elected leaders

- renewing the commitment to discipleship (covenant behavior) in the congregation where it has been replaced by expectations of professional service

- creating opportunities for members and staff to explore un- or under-utilized strengths and skills.

Change Need Not Equal Crisis

Carolyn and First Parish were not unique in experiencing an exodus of staff and elected leaders prior to, or shortly following, an interim's arrival. It is rarely a sign of crisis. It requires some thoughtful consultation with those who leave to determine whether there is a pastoral issue that needs addressing. But a vast majority of the time, it is the best thing that could happen to the community, because it leaves in its wake breathing space in which to explore potential and possibility. Indeed, as the situation unfolded, First Parish experienced several immediate benefits of leadership change.

Alice, the church secretary, had never successfully mastered a computer despite extensive training, paid for by the church. The former minister had compensated behind the scenes for her lack of skills, but Alice suspected that a new head of staff would expect her work to be professionally competent without the coaching she had come to depend on. Retirement became an attractive option, and removed an underperforming staff member from the organization.

Bob, the choir director, and Joe, the organist, had been in conflict for years. Out of loyalty to the former minister, they had tried to get along, but Bob was tired of the constant stress. He also resented that, in spite of his professional training in music, his position was uncompensated while Joe's was paid. Bob finally felt free from the burden of his loyalty and saw the interim time as a perfect opportunity to use his skills in a different forum.

Jason, the religious educator, was worried that a new minister would resist his lively and unconventional style, and micromanage him into misery. In fact, Carolyn found him to be a self-motivated, highly effective, energetic, and thoughtful team player, deeply committed to lifelong learning and continually excited by new opportunities. Her positive response and affirmation encouraged him to stay.

And the president of the Board? I'm saving that story for later.

Carolyn's primary task in the midst of these early shifts was to keep reminding the Board and the congregation that they were in a time of *change*, not a time of *crisis*. The Board vice president stepped smoothly into place, a temp agency supplied a trained secretary on a week-to-week contract, and Joe agreed to double as choir director for three months. However, as paid staff, he was unwilling to volunteer the additional time. This became an opportunity for the congregation to decide how important it was to have a professional choir director with appropriate compensation and accountability.

Carolyn's decision to ask Joe to temporarily cover as choir director is not the only one that would have worked at First Parish. But it prevented a rushed, anxiety-driven decision and gave the congregation three months to consider its priorities around the shape and relative cost of the music program. Carolyn asked the Transition Team (intentionally constituted of long-term and new members) to help design a process to gather the hopes and visions of the whole congregation around a series of open-ended questions. Their responses would be used to propose future staffing.

She also used the pulpit to reclaim past history and to frame the future of the congregation as an opportunity. She provided church members with a language of potential to replace the language of crisis. She likened the journey to a relay race in which runners with different strengths are strategically used to ensure that the team finishes successfully. Leaders who were skilled at maintaining a steady pace during the long pastorate just finished, for instance, need to pass the baton to those skilled at sprinting, who have high energy to prepare for the intensity of major change. One pace or skill is not better than another, but each is necessary in its time for the congregation to reach its common goal.

Carolyn faced some entrenched resistance. She was following a sixteen-year ministry, so familiar patterns were well established, including the committee structure and decision-making practices. Because the bylaws had not been reviewed in fifteen years, wisdom around internal governance had not adapted to new realities. Three of the vestigial structures that most hindered changes in leadership were the Personnel Committee, the Religious Education Director's Support Group, and the Organist's Support Group. The latter two had begun as task forces in response to a staff conflict twenty years earlier. (We will look at the disadvantages of advocacy groups later in this essay.)

Originally, the Personnel Committee was an advisory group to the senior minister, instituted to ensure that hiring and employment practices complied with new laws. Since the committee was perceived as "needing" experts in human resources (HR), no provisions were made for term limits. Over time, the chair became firmly entrenched and his power went largely unchallenged. Gradually, his expectation that "his" committee would be consulted on all hiring and staffing decisions, as well as handle all evaluations (even though they did not supervise any of the staff) became fact.

Carolyn's contract, negotiated with the Board, established her as head of staff. This position gave her both the responsibility for effective administration and the authority to accomplish the task, including the authority to hire and fire. This practice was new to First Parish and was perceived as a direct threat to the power of the Personnel Committee chair. When Carolyn firmly refused to submit her decision about Joe to the agenda of the Personnel Committee, the chair resigned *and* withdrew his pledge, thereby breaking covenant relationship.

The Board accepted the resignation and, as required by the bylaws, appointed a new chair until the next annual meeting of the congregation. With Carolyn's coaching, the Board selected a leader with HR experience, someone relatively new to the congregation, with fresh ideas about how the committee could make practical and valuable contributions to the congregation and to the work of the senior minister. The new chair invited the whole Personnel Committee into a process of re-examining its mandate and considering how it could be rewritten in order to best support the current mission of the church.

This became part of a larger conversation at First Parish as the members looked at streamlining an outdated leadership structure with one adapted to twenty-first-century realities. They noted that the way they had always done it no longer worked well because the number of empty committee positions increased with every annual meeting.

Continuity

Those fateful words "We've always done it this way" can sometimes express an appropriate resistance to reinventing the wheel, but more often they function as a stopper to life-giving change.

Most church organizational charts are designed to insure an uninterrupted continuity of corporate memory. Traditional (three-year, staggered) committee structures establish a slow turnover in order to maintain the rich history of the congregation's learning curves, accomplishments, grief/loss, and dead ends. However, when continuity itself becomes an idol, it slides into unhealthy stasis. The desire to maintain what was functional in some past era becomes a straitjacket in a newer one. As the familiar James Russell Lowell hymn says, "New occasions teach new duties / Time makes ancient good uncouth."

A culture of deliberate planned transfer of leadership insures healthy continuity by avoiding conflicted, erratic, anxious, or resistant shifts—all of which result in a selective or wholesale *loss* of corporate memory. Planned transfer may involve deliberately nurturing successors, but more commonly takes place as a result of a term-limits policy. Although most church bylaws include such limits, they tend to fall by the wayside in practice. The perception or reality of an "in-group" gathered around the minister trumps wise practices, and often limits not only the pool of those invited, but also the pool of those *willing*, to serve in leadership roles.

Leadership transfer is imperative for adaptive change, but such change cannot happen without fundamental shifts in the current culture and without accompanying psychological stress. Tired, burned-out, and/or entitled leaders are especially prone to receiving and escalating congregational anxiety during adaptive transitions. Self-blame/shame/guilt (in burned-out, tired leaders) or anger (in entitled leaders) is pervasive among those who act out congregational anxiety. The longer their tenure and the more fully they were associated with the previous ministry, the greater their guilt or entitlement, and the more easily they are co-opted by the most anxious or disaffected. It is both a practical and a pastoral necessity to release such leaders from their work for their own refreshment, as well as for the good of the congregation. A wise interim elder once quipped, "Accept every resignation you are offered. Immediately . . . or sooner, if you can."

In the midst of these stresses, one of the best resources for interims and lay leaders is the pool of former leaders who have experienced more than one adaptive transition. The wisdom of parishioners still active in their seventies, eighties, and even nineties but no longer in elected positions can help counter the anxiety effect in the community to a profound degree. Because they have lived through historical as well as congregational adaptive change, they can authentically affirm the ability of the community to pass through further change without imploding or exploding. Seek them out and use their wisdom, their spiritual maturity, and their capital in the system.

Appointed and Elected Lay Positions

One 250-year-old congregation with whom I consulted a decade ago had 140 active members and 42 committees and task forces listed in the bylaws! In their love for one another, they had no difficulty creating positions to lift up the gifts of their members, but they were totally unable to disband anything for fear of hurting someone's feelings, or someone's child's feelings, or someone's grandchild's feelings. While few congregations provide such hyperbolic examples, the vast majority are caught in a similar pattern of leadership overload.

An interim time is ideal for rebalancing committee, task force, or ministry structure to bring it into line with current functional needs. If the church is particularly blessed, an initial wave of resignations will spawn more resignations, and the existing structure may be largely vacated. This is not a crisis, but an opportunity. This makes it considerably easier to look at positions without having to deal with personalities. Helpful assessment questions include:

- When was this position/committee/role instituted? For what purpose? Or in response to what need?

- Is this purpose/need still a priority for the congregation?

- What would happen if we left this position/committee/role unfilled for a year?

- Is this position/committee/role duplicated anywhere else?

Answers to these questions invite the community to look outside the box of familiar patterns to determine whether they are being wise stewards of the communal resources of time and talent.

This process also goes a long way toward addressing the perennial concern expressed, most often in small churches, about finding adequate new leadership. The usual suspects are frequently asked to serve again and again, because they are the folks who are willing to participate in the old structures. Streamlining the structure, adjusting term limits to reflect task and function, and aligning leadership requirements with vision and mission are all natural invitations to people who are not willing to engage in traditional patterns of commitment that are meaningless to them or impractical in their lives. It is surprising how many folks step forward in response to thoughtful change, who are willing to invest their time, talent, and treasure in the realigned community.

Paid and Unpaid Staff

Staffing is another area in which positions that once had purpose or practicality can devolve into vestigial organs. A full-time religious education director makes sense when the congregation boasts one hundred or more active children; it does not when twenty show up on a good day. But a full-time religious education position is often maintained by a parish church, even in a retirement community, in the mistaken belief that the church is "staffing for growth." A pastoral visitor to share the load of hospice, home, and hospital visits or a staff person with gifts in elder programming would be a more appropriate and useful position.

When the minister is head of staff, vestigial positions tend to get eliminated quickly, replaced by positions that support the congregation's vision, mission, and reality. The ability to be flexible and nimble is one of the best reasons to move intentionally toward minister as head of staff. Also, the person who supervises and evaluates staff, and is accountable for pastoral and program effectiveness, has the authority to act to ensure professional competence and appropriate use of personnel resources.

With two staff positions (one paid, one unpaid) open before she arrived, Carolyn had a natural opportunity to ask direct and searching questions about whether First Parish was appropriately staffed for its mission and vision. She also had the opportunity to look at policies around hiring church members into staff positions.

Church-members-as-staff can be the cause of virtually limitless problems and conflict for the members, the congregation, any nonmember staff persons, and the minister. The benefits are far more difficult to identify. In his article "Is It Wise to Hire Members?" the Alban Institute's Dan Hotchkiss identifies two benefits frequently cited for hiring a church member:

- We are hiring someone who already understands the system.

- No one else applied. (This is more common in smaller communities.)

And sometimes there is a third:

- It's church policy to hire internal candidates first.

Consider these reasons carefully. Is it useful to reinforce the systemic status quo rather than to actively seek fresh perspectives? Might it be counterproductive to hire no more than a warm body to fill a chair? Is it useful to ask the head of staff to "prove" that the internal candidate (someone with whom they have a pastoral relationship) is not adequate so that a more qualified external candidate can be hired?

The inherent problems are numerous. They include:

- the emotional and psychological difficulty of switching from fellow pew-sitter to professional staff member; friendships (and marital-partner relationships) become problematic as confidentiality determines what can and can't be shared or discussed

- the imperative to exercise objectivity around people (including parishioners one does not like), policies (including those with which one disagrees), and mission (ditto)

- the perception (or reality) of conflict of interest, especially if a spouse or partner is in an elected/appointed position with crossover agendas (such as the Board president and choir director at First Parish)

- the loss of a pastoral presence to the staff member, since the minister as supervisor cannot be the minister as pastor—the two roles are nearly always mutually exclusive

- the virtual impossibility of the minister supervising a member without sparking internal church conflict, since the member often calls on friends in the congregation for support when they disagree with the supervisor. This invariably divides the congregation into sides and involves the minister in time-consuming and ineffective "supervision by congregational opinion."

And from the perspective of the staff person:

- the hurt, anger, and resentment when cuts are proposed to their salary or benefits by "friends" who are trying to balance the budget. The emotional fallout is present even when salary and/or benefits are reinstated.

Few can successfully transition from congregant to staff (and the exceptions prove the rule). Even when a person can make the change, their spouse or partner may not be able to cope with it. Pillow talk is always a danger.

A colleague recently shared the story of a hiring process in which she received applications from two internal (church member) candidates. Since the congregation did not have a written policy about *not* hiring church members, she decided to interview both as a courtesy, along with three of the eight external candidates. Best practices suggest that any hiring process be confidential, so no names were released to the congregation. However, immediately following the first set of interviews, the minister learned that the spouse of Sue, one of the internal candidates, had announced to a number of people at a church social event that his wife was in the running for the job. The information circulated quickly, not only breaking the confidentiality of the process (which had been explained to all candidates), but also raising expectations among Sue's friends and causing anxiety for those who thought she was unqualified.

In fact, Sue had already been eliminated from consideration since her experience did not suit the position. But the ensuing furor would have eliminated her anyway. As my colleague observed, "Sue was humiliated for weeks when someone else got the job. No one should even have known that she had applied. But thank heavens, I learned that Tom is a blabber. The position for which I was hiring required handling all sorts of confidential information. One slip would have been reason for Sue's dismissal—and it wouldn't have mattered whether *she* slipped or Tom did."

Streamlining Leadership Structures

Every congregation is different; there is no one-size-fits-all program that can address every issue of leadership change. We have
discussed two possibilities already: deliberate changes within an
extant volunteer structure (including the use of term limits to
routinely engage the broadest pool of candidates), and changes
in staffing to reflect the current mission and vision of the congregation (overseen by the minister as head of staff). We've
hinted at a third: reassessing the current structure to determine
whether it effectively uses volunteer time and talent.

Let's look again at the Personnel Committee at First Parish.
Both Carolyn and the new chair noted that although its original mandate required that only one or two HR professionals be
consulted when the head of staff had questions about current
practice, its original structure was determined by a decades-old
committee pattern. Therefore, it comprised six members who
thought their task was to be the devil's advocate for the minister's suggestions for hiring or evaluation. In other words, the
way the congregation had always done it kept the congregation
in cumbersome patterns that required a lot of time and unspoken insider information.

Because the chair had routinely exercised such powerful
authority over staff, two staff "support" committees—one for
the organist and one for the religious education director—
had been created to serve as advocates and protectors, especially
at evaluation and budget times. However well-intended, advocacy committees under any name are unnecessary and virtually
guarantee that the staff will function in a pathological model of
relationship.

As head of staff, the minister's responsibility is to ensure that
all staff positions, paid and unpaid, are held to standards of
accountability and competence, and are treated according to best
HR practices. For the staff to be effective as individuals as well as
a team, the relationship within the staff needs to be one of trust.
This is unlikely, if not impossible, when some staff have protec-
tive allies constantly second-guessing the head of staff and challenging her or his authority to act on behalf of the congregation.

Further, it undermines any contract between the staff to speak with one voice. Finally, these groups too often act to stop healthy adaptive and structural change, especially regarding "their" staff member. It is not unheard of for advocacy groups for two different staff members to bring budgeting and staffing decisions to a complete halt, splitting the congregation and damaging everyone by leaving only losers as all sides try to win.

Carolyn was blessed to have received the resignation of the two staff who were members of the congregation (the choir director and the secretary), but also one of the two remaining paid staff (the religious education director) confessed that he did not need "one more committee meeting every month." He preferred to focus his energy on working with the Religious Education Committee, which served as an effective advocate for the program, and the minister. When Carolyn pressed further, he confirmed that he would actually prefer not to have an "RE Relations Committee."

Carolyn then opened conversations with the organist about his committee. During the discussion, Joe realized that he also had effective advocates for the music *program*—which was his primary concern—on the Worship Team. He observed that his own relations committee was always looking for problems, and he frequently left the meeting feeling slightly depressed. He commented, "I think they are looking for problems because there really is no other reason for them to keep meeting. But I don't think that is helpful for them or for me. It really is a waste of time, isn't it?"

When First Parish concluded its bylaw discussions about nine months after Carolyn arrived, they decided to disband both advocacy groups and to streamline the Personnel Committee. Those two changes released twelve leaders to take rest and refreshment and/or to move into areas where they felt passionate about giving their time.

Realigning the lay volunteer structure can have an enormous impact on the whole shape of leadership in the twenty-first century. Leaders are freed from attending "planning meetings" so that they can share their gifts in a flexible and life-giving way. Individuals can move easily from place to place as needed.

They can try working in one area of interest for a period of time and then move on to something else if that proves an unfruitful match. This kind of flexibility is almost impossible under structures that solidify all actions into a committee structure.

Freeing Leaders to Serve in New Ways

Finally, we can learn something from the story of Meg, the Board president at First Parish. She confessed to Carolyn that she had taken the position only because "I had said no twice before, and it was my turn, I guess." She hated running meetings and hated "feeling responsible for everyone's happiness." About four months after Carolyn arrived, Meg asked to meet. She said, "I was reading another church's newsletter. They have a program called LOFT (Living Our Faith Together). Could I resign as president and start one of those here?" Meg's enthusiasm was infectious. She agreed to find a co-leader and take full responsibility. She explained that it would not be a committee, but would include just those who wanted to participate in each month's project. She anticipated that people would come on board when they were interested and not participate when they were too busy or didn't feel a call to that month's idea.

Within three months, the program was going strong. Meg's high-profile resignation to do something more meaningful gave others permission to look more closely at their own leadership. As more people expressed to the Nominating Committee their intention to resign at the next annual meeting, the Bylaws Task Force interpreted the news as an opportunity to reassess business-as-usual thinking.

Naturally, there was some resistance. Some folks could not conceive of a church functioning any way other than in the familiar patterns. But friends talked to friends and, in most instances, the loudest voices of resistance were willing to come on board and "try it out" for a while. The Bylaws Task Force wisely presented a three-year draft proposal so that state legal requirements were met, but nothing was set in stone.

Carolyn, as head of staff, used the personnel consultants (not the Personnel Committee) to help write a job description for the secretary position and, likewise, used their savvy to adver-tise the position in the right places. She asked one of the con-sultants to sit in on the interviews, which led to her hiring a woman who was a member of another church—someone who understood churches but was not entwined in First Parish's relational system.

When she called me to debrief at the end of her time with the congregation, Carolyn reflected that the initial "crisis" had been a massive blessing. And she wasn't the only one who felt that way. A number of laypeople had noted at her going-away party that leadership at First Parish felt fresh, exciting, and visionary for the first time in their experience.

Non-anxious leadership provided a gateway for more hope, positive change, and new possibility.

Strengthening Connections Beyond the Congregation

ROBERTA FINKELSTEIN

The departure of a minister brings dramatic changes to a congregation. Whether the ministry was beloved or conflicted, long-term or short-term, a change in ministry means changes in the way members of a congregation relate to each other and to the larger community. It means changes in the way decisions are made and the way information is communicated.

Much of the work during an intentional interim is focused internally on questions of identity, governance, and leadership development. But as the system opens itself to new ways of doing and being, myriad opportunities also present themselves for a congregation to look beyond its walls. New relationships can be established with nearby congregations, regional staff, and community organizations. Relationships that have been neglected or lost can be renewed. These connections beyond the congregation bring an infusion of new energy, new ideas, and a rededication to our Unitarian Universalist social justice principles. A sense of belonging to the local community and the larger Unitarian Universalist movement offers stability and inspiration to a congregation experiencing change.

During the interim period, a congregation may ask, "What is the ideal balance between the independence so beloved by Unitarian Universalists and an interdependence that supports

growth and transformation?" Congregations that define independence as intentionally avoiding being in relationship with
other congregations and with the larger movement often find
themselves challenged to grow and adapt. They reinvent wheels
rather than learn from the experience of others. They repeat patterns of ineffective decision making, are frequently frustrated by
the failure of their plans, and find themselves in ruts that stymie
growth. Working with an interim minister is a perfect time to
break out of a pattern of isolation and discover new energy and
new ways of being that lead to the hoped-for future.

For example, during an interim a congregation might look
at long-established membership practices to determine their
effectiveness in welcoming visitors and whether they provide
a sufficiently structured path to membership. One step in that
process could be to find out what other Unitarian Universalist congregations, especially those experiencing vitality and
growth, are doing in this area. This research will likely indicate
that to achieve success in this area, the congregation must be
clear about the expectations of membership. This kind of clarity and direct communication can create anxiety among Unitarian Universalists who cling to a vision of congregational life
based on the "rugged individual" model. They might object to
stating clear expectations, insisting that so-called best practices are an imposition from outside and that the strength of
the congregation lies in its independence. But if the leadership
points to neighboring congregations, rather than an outside
expert, as the source of these new ideas, they are more likely
to convince the naysayers of the wisdom of trying a different
approach.

Of course, ministerial transitions are not the only times of
change that offer opportunities for congregational self-assessment and self-improvement. Congregations faced with a natural
disaster can also be shaken out of their usual ways of doing
and being, and can teach congregations in ministerial transition from the vantage point of their own experience. Take the
Unitarian Universalist congregations in greater New Orleans
after Hurricane Katrina, for example. For years these three congregations had little to do with each other. Hurricane Katrina

changed that. In a personal correspondence, Jim VanderWeele, minister of Community Church Unitarian Universalist, wrote,

> The members of three New Orleans-area congregations were jolted to a new reality in the aftermath of Katrina. In the midst of our personal hurt we easily saw the pain and trials felt by those around us, particularly the Unitarian Universalists around us. Perhaps it helped that evacuees from First Church and Community Church went to Baton Rouge where members of the Unitarian Church there provided housing. We met each other at Sunday worship. We gathered for teary-eyed Wednesday evening discussions. We knew that the North Shore Unitarian Universalist Society was receiving help from Unitarian Universalists in Houston. Volunteers had come to remove fallen trees and repair their roof. Several months later we met with representatives from the UUA to discuss our hopes for the revival of our faith in New Orleans. These discussions led to a new cluster, the Greater New Orleans Unitarian Universalists. We dedicated ourselves to supporting each other as we worked toward recovery and today we continue to expand the connection that began when the wind and the water shattered our previous reservations about the other two UU congregations in our area.

Why should a congregation take seriously the suggestion that they develop stronger lateral connections during an interim? Perhaps Melanie Morel Sullivan, minister of First Unitarian Universalist Church of New Orleans, says it best: "If advice on lateral relationships from the three New Orleans-area UU congregations could be summed up in one phrase, it would be 'Don't wait for a hurricane!'"

A change in ministry may be unsettling, but it isn't a hurricane. It is an opportunity to reach out for new relationships and new ideas. An interim ministry is a time to re-evaluate all aspects of congregational life, from governance to mission to external relationships. Congregations that choose to do this work—developing collegial relationships with nearby congregations, involving themselves more deeply in district and regional activities, strengthening their relationship to the Unitarian Universalist Association—will reap benefits in terms of a stronger Unitarian Universalist identity, greater commitment to mission, renewed energy for the leadership, and easy access to tools, resources, and best practices.

In the early weeks of every interim ministry, I tell the congregation that their goal for the interim time is to answer three questions: Who were we? Who are we? Who do we wish to be? Answering these questions is the core work of the interim period and is essential to the successful settlement of the next minister. The search and settlement process is about understanding and articulating the identity, practices, strengths, and hopes and dreams of the congregation in such a way that a potential minister will understand how their personal strengths and visions fit best with those of the congregation.

The process of discerning identity, strengths, and vision is enhanced in interactions with people and organizations outside the congregation. An American Baptist congregation in Virginia decided that their goal for the year was to better understand their identity as American Baptists. They did this by inviting a series of ministers and lay leaders from neighboring congregations in other denominations to present programs about their faith communities, and then engaged in conversation with them. Through these dialogues with others, they were able to arrive at a better understanding of themselves.

You might say that every interim congregation has the same goal as that Baptist congregation in Virginia: to better understand its identity as a local Unitarian Universalist congregation in relationship to its community and to the larger movement. Having a strong identity allows for the development of structures that support adaptation to the changes that inevitably come with new ministerial leadership. It also enables the congregation to live out its mission more successfully. And of course a congregation with strong relationships to the larger movement presents an attractive portfolio to potential ministerial candidates.

It may be tempting, when faced with all of the challenges of a change in ministers, to pull back from engagement with the denomination and community, and focus inward. But an intentional decision to look outward and strengthen rather than neglect relationships beyond the local congregation can reap great benefit. Particularly when this decision is made with the support of an interim minister, a congregation in transition can learn so much from lateral relationships—about itself and about new and exciting ways to assert itself as a progressive force in the community.

Historical Perspective

The tension between independence (whether for individuals or for congregations) and interdependence is embedded in our religious DNA. Throughout history we have struggled with this dynamic. Even a brief historical review reveals the narrative arc of Unitarian Universalism as one seeking the balance between individualism and connectedness, between autonomy and organizational effectiveness. "Individual freedom of belief exists," writes William Schulz in the fourth edition of *The UU Pocket Guide*, "in dynamic tension with the insights of our history and the wisdom of our communities." That narrative arc runs through the history of our movement as a whole as well as through the history of each local congregation. During a time of transition, congregations benefit from a renewed understanding of that struggle as it has played out in their particular context. They also benefit from a re-evaluation of where they fall on the spectrum between individualism and connectedness.

Our religious tradition is proud to affirm the inherent worth and dignity of every person. This radical assertion—that humans are born with the capacity for good rather than cursed by original sin—led to the separation of Unitarians from other liberal Christians in the nineteenth century. Too often today, we make the mistake of thinking that contemporary Unitarian Universalism is based entirely on the affirmation of the individual. A more complete and nuanced understanding of our faith would cause us to acknowledge that individuals thrive on relationships that make us whole. We are, each and every one of us, worthy. But we are better together. Our personal faith journeys are richer and deeper when we find companions for those journeys. That is why we seek out and join congregations. As individuals, we need the encouragement and synergy that comes from companionship. But groups of individuals also need the encouragement and enlightenment that comes from being in relationship with other groups engaged in the work of progressive religion.

A community of faith needs the synergy of lateral relationships to live out its mission in the larger community. Congregational work for justice and human rights is more effective when we work in concert with others. Lay leaders are enriched when they share ideas and best practices online and in regional gatherings. In relationship with others we create a Unitarian Universalism that is more vibrant than any individual or single congregation could hope to experience in isolation.

This is particularly true during a time of transition. Many congregations rely on their minister to maintain contact with the larger movement; they assume that their minister will keep them in touch with the Unitarian Universalist Association, the regional staff, and nearby UU congregations. When the minister departs, lay leadership can learn first-hand what is going on in the larger Unitarian Universalist world. The opening up of the system that happens during a ministerial transition makes new relationships possible; there is an openness to new ways of learning from others and relating to people and organizations outside of the congregational cocoon.

When we understand the value of relatedness, we understand what it means to be a voluntary association. Theologian James Luther Adams wrote extensively about the nature of voluntary association in our movement. In essays collected in *The Prophethood of All Believers*, he traces the history of the free church and the voluntary association back to the earliest Christian communities. Those courageous early Christians chose to come together, despite the dangers, in order to nurture each other in their faith development. They were a believers' church rather than a state church. The believers' church, gathered voluntarily, reappeared during the Reformation. At that time, a group called the Anabaptists called for a church gathered on the basis of their like-minded approach to religion. This threatened the commonly held assumption that the religion of the ruler should be the religion of the ruled, and the patriarchal assumption that the religion of the father should be the religion of the children. It took courage to answer that call.

Those brave radicals of long ago bequeathed to us the practice of voluntary association, of covenant as the basis for religious community, and the vision of the free church as the agent for transformation in the larger community. That is the vision that came to our shores along with the Puritans who landed in Massachusetts. In 1648, they produced the Cambridge Platform, a document crafted to bring unity to a somewhat fractured group that would need to work together in order to survive and thrive on American soil. Building on principles articulated in the Radical Reformation, this document established the doctrine of congregationalism—the form of church governance that recognizes the sovereignty of the local congregation. It also affirmed the importance of the relationship among congregations. In *Congregational Polity: A Historical Survey of Unitarian and Universalist Practice*, Conrad Wright states that in the Cambridge Platform, "the autonomy of the local church was carefully protected. Yet it is not a proper understanding of congregationalism to leave it at that. Congregationalism meant, and should still mean, not the autonomy of the local church, but the community of autonomous churches."

Historically, in congregational polity two things are important: the sovereignty of the local congregation *and* the community of those sovereign local congregations. Lateral relationships were just as important as local autonomy. Our Unitarian Universalist congregations are healthiest and strongest when the members make a mutual commitment to each other, when they covenant together. We are healthiest and strongest when we pay attention to the reality that we are part of a larger association. Just as the interim period is a time to reflect upon and renew the covenant between and among members, it is also a time to reflect upon and renew the covenant between the congregation and the larger movement. To remember and strengthen that covenant is to strengthen the congregation's ability to live out its mission.

Freedom and Structure

"It has been a chronic problem for both Unitarians and Universalists to reconcile their love of individual freedom and autonomy with the necessity of church structures," Harry Scholefield
and Paul Sawyer point out in the fourth edition of *The UU Pocket
Guide*. Church structure is one of the essential foci of intentional interim ministry. Experienced interims find that in congregations that have enjoyed a long-term ministry, inattention
to infrastructure is not uncommon. Congregations that have
grown and thrived often outgrow their organizational structure without realizing it. An interim ministry can help structure
catch up to function. Congregational effectiveness suffers when
structures and resources are inadequate. It may be counterintuitive, but one of the best ways to revitalize the infrastructure of
a congregation is by revitalizing connections to other institutions, bringing lay leaders together to share ideas, best practices, and stories of success and inspiration. When lay leaders
come together and learn from each other, they are empowered
to go home to their own congregations and apply that learning
to the particular organizational challenges they face.

During the years of conversation between the American
Unitarian Association and the Universalist Church of America
which led to the creation of the Unitarian Universalist Association (UUA), this issue of organizational effectiveness was
often addressed. They referred to the rights of congregations to
self-governance while holding up the vision of a merged organization that would provide resources to those congregations
that would enhance congregational effectiveness. In *Redeeming
Time: Endowing Your Church with the Power of Covenant*, Walter
Herz urges us to continue to pay attention to the need for effective Unitarian Universalist congregations. Embracing freedom
does not excuse us from exercising institutional effectiveness
and responsibility. Herz writes, "We are individual overachiev-
ers and institutional underachievers."

The interim period is an ideal time to bring issues of institutional effectiveness to the fore and rebalance the tension between
individualism and institutionalism. After all, the great hope is

that this period will culminate in a successful search for a new minister who will be able to walk with the congregation into the future they seek. The congregation must offer that minister the opportunity to work within an effective structure of staff and lay leadership who will support that forward movement.

Freedom and structure complement one another. Combining freedom with the structure of community enhances both, allowing high levels of creativity, innovation, and effectiveness. Think about jazz—an amazing array of freewheeling improvisation occurs within a highly structured form. Having structure in our relationships enables us to experience congregational life, and denominational life, in a safe and affirming manner. This is true for individuals as part of a congregation and for congregations as part of the larger movement.

During the interim self-assessment, many congregations discover that they have neglected important lateral relationships. The energy of the transition may bring a congregation back into right relationship with neighbors, community organizations, and Unitarian Universalism as a whole. By re-engaging with the larger movement, a congregation in transition may discover synergies they hadn't previously imagined.

Resources and Opportunities

Congregations in transition are learning organizations. They can take advantage of lateral relationships and resources from the UUA as they work on identity, focusing their mission, governance structures, and methods of communication. Everything they learn will enhance their standing with ministerial candidates.

Effective electronic communication serves both learning and lateral connections. Webinars, Skype consultations, and electronic search packets are good ways to maintain lateral connections while decreasing travel and paper use. Several years ago, a district executive initiated a series of monthly webinars on various topics of interest, including one on Committees on Ministry. Leaders and staff in congregations around the district gathered around a computer screen to observe the presentation, ask questions, and interact with other leaders. One of the participating congregations, in its second year of interim ministry, was actively involved in the search process. They realized that their understanding of the way a Committee on Ministry could and should function was something that would make them more attractive to ministerial candidates. They made sure that the Search Committee was aware of the fact that the Board and leadership were in learning mode on this subject and were prepared to work with their new minister to create an effective Committee on Ministry.

Several years later, their former interim minister was serving another congregation trying to transition from a complicated system of multiple Ministerial Relations Committees to a comprehensive Committee on Ministry. The minister pointed them to that webinar. They watched it, and then reached out to congregations that had learned from this process. The result was a well-organized plan for educating their congregation about this new approach and implementing the new system in anticipation of calling a new settled minister.

Perhaps the most obvious area in which congregational cooperation yields better results is social justice. There are two reasons why congregations should sustain their focus on social justice during the interim period.

First, the UUA's Standing on the Side of Love (SSL) campaign, which champions a commitment to human rights, marriage equality, and immigration reform, has inspired the passions of many of our ministers who seek to serve congregations that will support their work on these issues. A commitment to SSL and other social justice programs enhances the résumé of a congregation in the eyes of many candidates.

The materials generated by SSL have been used by congregations, clusters, and districts to further civil union and marriage equality legislation as well as legislation aimed at reforming our inhumane and ineffective immigration policies. Given the complexity of these issues, individual congregations would have difficulty advocating effectively without readily available research materials and language to use in their advocacy.

Second, even during an interim period, when inward reflection is emphasized, maintaining a focus on mission-based, outward-looking activities keeps the congregation in balance and aware of its core purpose in the world. In addition, this period is a perfect time to collaborate with other congregations, interfaith groups, community organizations, and the UUA to make social justice work still more effective and visible.

A congregation that welcomes the interim period as a time to explore new ways of being will reap many benefits, including stronger and mutually beneficial relationships with nearby congregations and community organizations as well as more fruitful interactions with the larger movement of Unitarian Universalism. Enhanced lateral relationships developed during this time lay the groundwork not only for a successful search for a new minister, but for a successful long-term relationship between minister and congregation, based on a common understanding of mission, furthered through the right balance of inward and outward focus.

The Interim Minister's Role in Ministerial Search

EVAN KEELY AND LISA PRESLEY

■ ▨ ▦ ■

The simultaneity of the work of interim ministry with a ministerial search is in no way merely coincidental; the interim tasks and the search for a new minister complement one another. Ideally, the Search Committee is not selected until after the interim minister has engaged the congregation in significant work coming to terms with its history and articulating its present identity, including strengths, challenges, and needs. The interim and congregational leaders, including the Search Committee, are well situated to disabuse the congregation they serve of the misconception that the purpose of interim ministry is exclusively to prepare the congregation for a new settled minister. It is not. The purpose of interim ministry is to enable, encourage, and empower the congregation to move into the future with a renewed zeal for the church's mission. The congregation can build upon and reinvigorate its strengths, constructively addressing impediments to vitality, to make the most of the opportunities presented during transition so that the congregation can move toward greater emotional agility, organizational maturity, and spiritual strength. A congregation prepared to enter into a dynamic and transformative relationship with a new settled minister is a *result* of the fulfillment of the interim ministry's key purpose, rather than a primary goal in and of itself.

The Search Committee's task—to find a ministerial candidate to present to the congregation—is part of a broader and deeper transformational process of congregational self-assessment, renewal, and recommitment. The committee and the interim, working as partners, guide the congregation through self-examination. Dusting off past ideas about the congregation's identity and future, looking for a clone of the previous minister or that minister's opposite, or just moving through the process like a cog in a machine, will result in losing a major opportunity for growth.

To reap the real benefits of the combined interim and search period, a steady healthy partnership of interim minister, Search Committee, and congregation must be created and sustained, while the congregation does its deep work to discern its desired future. The congregation, and especially the Search Committee, need to avoid viewing the loss of the previous minister as a technical problem to be fixed and instead strive to do what Ronald Heifitz describes as "adaptive work" in *The Practice of Adaptive Leadership: Tools and Tactics for Changing Your Organization and the World.*

Technical problem solving involves applying known solutions to solve problems. If X breaks, you replace X, and then everything returns to working the way it did before. In search terms, it would mean listing the qualities of the previous minister, going to the minister store, reading the ingredients on the minister boxes, choosing the one with the most similar features, adding a bit more hard-drive capacity perhaps, a remote starter or a back-up battery, then taking it back and installing it right out of the box. The new version might work, but what new possibilities did the congregation lose by looking only for the familiar?

On the other hand, adaptive work invites the congregation members to check their bearings, to see if they are still the same people with the same dreams they had when the last minister arrived, to discover where their longings and imagination lead them now, and to chart that course. The congregation may reaffirm a path similar to the old one, but often it will discover new passions or variations simply by daring to ask questions. Rather than settling for the technical fix, the congregation does the adaptive work of seeking answers in the realm of the unknown. It attempts to discover what the congregation wants to say yes to and what it wants to say "not now" to, knowing that the yes might be something the congregation has never done before or describes a place it isn't sure yet how to reach. But without the needed adaptive work, the Search Committee may not be able to discern the appropriate ministers to consider from among the pool of contenders.

The Search Committee is not left to venture into its work alone. A regional transitions coach, representing the district or region and ultimately the Unitarian Universalist Association (UUA), is particularly helpful regarding the search process, strategy, and best practices. Some transitions coaches facilitate search committee retreats as well. The UUA Office of Church Staff Finances, typically through a district or regional compensation consultant, provides support and wise counsel to the congregational Board and the committee about ministerial compensation. The regional field staff can offer the committee advice and practical help in the form of references for ministers in their district or region. They also provide perspectives on congregations to both the transitions coach and ministers in search. Field staff may link search committees with consultants available to facilitate retreats. They offer support for part-time ministry searches. In some districts or regions, they serve as mentors to search committees. Finally, the UUA Transitions Office is available for consultation, articulating best practices through a variety of resource documents online and providing the technical platform for the search process. The director of the office provides oversight and training for transitions coaches as well.

If they are wise, all of these resource people maintain good collaboration with each other as well as with the search committees they serve. By sharing information about the process, they can better assist the congregation. The interim minister, of course, being on site, is the resident expert on the search process, and has several significant roles to play.

Preparing the Congregation for the Search

Even before a Search Committee is selected, the interim minister helps the congregation understand both its history and its dreams for the future; as a result, the Search Committee will know how to focus the search. The interim can also help everyone understand best ministerial practices, ministerial leadership, and shared ministry of the clergy and the laity. The interim who is willing to be a truth-teller as well as companion during this period of discernment does a great service to the congregation and its future ministry.

When educating the congregation about the search process, the interim should emphasize dynamic financial stewardship so that the congregation can offer fair and competitive compensation not only to the next called minister but to all of the paid staff. The interim can also lead the congregation in exploring the meanings of professional ministry, including helping the congregation think deeply about healthy expectations for ministers. After all, the next minister will not duplicate the habits, strengths, idiosyncrasies, and shortcomings of the previous minister.

Although it is the regional transitions coach's role to educate the congregation about the selection of the standard seven-member Search Committee, the interim can facilitate the selection process by explaining who can best serve on the committee. Committee members need to be able to take a "balcony" view of congregational life rather than being so devoted to one aspect that they cannot see the entire picture. Congregations are much more than the sum of music, worship, religious growth and learning, social justice, and pastoral care. Instead, these components come together synergistically in a constellation unique to each congregation. Search Committee members need to have the interests of the congregation as a whole at heart; they should not be representatives of perceived constituencies. Moreover, both nominators and prospective nominees need to understand not only the nature of search committee service but also that the search year will typically require up to four hundred hours of a committee member's time. It does not help anyone to select for the committee a member who simply cannot give the required time.

The best people to serve on the committee know their own point of view, but their view of the whole is not blocked by their own perspective. They understand management of the congregation not only on a micro level but also at the macro, visionary level. They are excited about possibilities rather than fearful of change. They are willing to put the congregation's interests above their own. They are well respected and trusted by the congregation at large, not having been part of any recent congregational conflicts. They work well with others. They can be expected not to wall themselves off during their search work but to stay present and active in the congregation, watching how it is changing and growing during the interim time. They are people who can be counted on to communicate about their process and progress regularly to the congregation, while being able to maintain the confidentiality of the ministers they are considering.

Once the Search Committee has been selected, the interim minister can heighten everyone's understanding and appreciation of the ministerial search ahead by leading a ritual with the whole congregation during worship that commissions the committee and thanks them for their willingness to take on this demanding and important ministry.

Confidentiality and Communication

Once the Search Committee is at work, the interim's teaching role continues but with a different focus. The committee may experience pressure from other congregants whose anxiety levels rise because of the necessary confidentiality involved in the search process. Congregants may pepper committee members with questions about which ministers they have been in contact with and what they are like. The interim must articulate the difference between confidentiality and secrecy.

Confidentiality is the appropriate handling of sensitive information, the untimely or indiscreet disclosure of which has the potential to do harm. Secrecy is concealment intended for gain at others' expense. Congregants may not initially understand that ministers in search who are in dialogue with the Search

Committee may not wish to reveal to the congregation currently being served that those conversations are taking place, particularly if they are simply exploring possibilities but have not yet informed the congregations they are currently serving. By explaining to congregants the appropriateness of confidentiality, the interim and the committee enhance the power of the message that no congregation operates in a vacuum, and that every ministerial search takes place in a wider context of national and even global relationships within a community of faith.

The interim should make it clear to both the Search Committee and the congregation that ministers in dialogue with the committee are likely to contact the interim. Indeed, the committee might well regard with suspicion any minister in search who does not contact the interim. This is entirely appropriate; it is intended to assist ministers in search to make informed and mature decisions about whether to pursue a relationship with the congregation. The interim can remind the congregation that before serving there, the interim spoke extensively to the congregation's previous ministers as well as other clergy, denominational staff, and lay leaders acquainted with the congregation—and that this web of relationships that has bound our faith community together in mutual support is one of our hallmarks. Some interims consider it their duty to tell the Search Committee which ministers in search have called them, and some do not. In any case, the interim's answers to searching ministers' questions need not be completely identical to the committee's responses, although a wide disparity may raise a red flag. For instance, if the Search Committee declares, "Our religious education program is terrific!" and the interim reports, "This church's religious education program is really dysfunctional," the committee should be made aware of the disparity. Ideally, the interim and the committee will make congruent statements, and when they do not, each should be prepared to articulate an understanding of the other's point of view in conversation with ministers in search.

Coaching the Search Committee

After systematically learning the congregation's wants and needs, the Search Committee's next major tasks are to prepare the Congregational Record to go online and to assemble the search packet to share with selected ministers. They need to present the congregation clearly, accurately, and as favorably as possible without misleading. The interim can show them how to openly and honestly frame both delightful and difficult episodes in the congregation's history. It is easy to talk about marvelous things that have happened and their vibrant sense of the congregation. But how are they to speak of the fight that led to a division? How do they refer to the not-happy ending with the previous minister or staff member? How do they understand and convey other trust-breaking episodes? How do they talk about the work done in the past and during the interim time that has helped resolve old issues? These are important questions to answer, and the Search Committee can rehearse possible answers with the interim, who has a personal history of being in search and so can offer a perspective on how ministers might view these answers.

Any responsible Search Committee will share their draft Congregational Record and search packet with their interim, not just with their regional transitions coach, as required by the settlement process. The interim can offer perspectives on how this congregation is different from others and can point out features that committee members haven't noticed because they are too close to it. The interim can help them understand that not all ministers are alike or seek the same kind of congregation. In short, the interim can provide insight into how both the committee and the congregation might appear to ministers.

The interim can also encourage the committee to recruit ministers actively by inviting them to enter the UUA's settlement system; the committee need not wait passively, hoping ministers will register an interest in them. The interim cannot ethically recommend specific individuals to the committee, just as it is never appropriate for the interim to discuss individual prospective candidates with the committee.

As a professional religious leader, the interim has a broad understanding of ethical and practical issues related to compensation and employment expectations in congregations, and can help the Board, the Search Committee, and the negotiating team as they navigate the complexities of creating a compensation package and a proposed letter of agreement.

The interim can encourage the Search Committee to accept the UUA's advice to schedule the Beyond Categorical Thinking program, designed to help a congregation understand and get beyond prejudices or presuppositions about categories of ministers based on race and color, ability challenges, or sexual orientation and gender identity. The program typically includes an initial meeting with the Search Committee and Board, a worship service, and a workshop for the entire congregation. The program not only helps with the congregation's anti-oppression work, but also challenges everyone to recognize rarely spoken assumptions that could affect the choice of a minister: "He's from the Midwest, so he will be mild mannered." "She's an older minister, so she will have less energy." "He has young children, and we want to attract young families, so he could be a good minister for us." The Beyond Categorical Thinking program can open up new areas for reflection and discussion. The interim can partner with the Search Committee in fostering that dialogue and make sure it continues long after the workshop has ended.

The interim minister can play a valuable role as interview coach. While many on the Search Committee may have had interview experience, few are likely to have interviewed a minister, or been interviewed by one. The interim can gently but persistently remind the committee that interviewing is always a two-way street, and also that when they speak to ministers, they need to be honest about their concerns.

The interim should offer the committee the opportunity for a mock interview. In most cases, the interim should be the interviewee, although some search committees may wish to role-play with someone less familiar to them. In this case the interim can help them find a suitable mock interviewee, typically a nearby colleague who is not in search. The interim should coach the committee members to consider their questions carefully, pondering why they want to ask each question and what values each question reflects. Holding the mock interview via telephone or Skype rather than in person can be helpful. The committee will learn whether their speaker phone system and locale actually work well and will appreciate how hard it is for a minister having to distinguish several voices on the telephone and connect each with a particular individual.

The interim can steer the committee away from sweeping questions such as "Tell us about your theology" that have been addressed in ministerial records and packets, and possibly during reference checks. These kinds of broad questions communicate a lack of genuine interest in the minister. The committee can be guided to ask more meaningful questions such as: "We noticed in several of your sermons that you believe the divine is present in acts of compassion. Can you tell us more about what this means for you?" Such an approach is likely to lead to a deeper understanding between interviewers and interviewee, and also to clearly communicate respect and interest.

During the mock interview, the interim can also put some hard questions to the committee to give them practice answering such questions. In fact, the mock interviewee should ask questions more challenging than those likely to be posed by actual ministers in search to prepare the committee for the uncomfortable, awkward moments that can arise in intense questioning. For example, the minister may ask about the resignation of a previous minister, especially if that minister left under difficult circumstances such as a negotiated resignation. Ministers who inquire about such matters are trying to find out how a congregation handles conflict and what issues may remain to be worked on. Asking about these matters is a sign of trust and respect; the minister wants to know who the congregants truly are in all their complexity. The most valuable part of the mock interview might well be the indispensible debriefing that happens afterward.

The Interim Minister as the Search Committee's Pastor

While it is extremely helpful if the congregation has been well taught in advance about what is and is not the work of the Search Committee, the interim should protect the committee from unreasonable expectations by others. Sometimes the Board or others attempt to assign responsibilities to the committee that could be seen as tangentially related to its discernment about the congregation's future ministry, but that in fact distract them from their specific work. The Board's invitation to the Search Committee to take a turn as Sunday greeters or hosts at coffee hour probably reflects their thinking that their presence will help the congregation recognize the committee as a group; it will keep the committee visible and provide easy opportunities for congregants to ask questions. However, the proper tasks of the Search Committee are themselves so time-consuming and focused that it is no service to them or to the church to ask them to take on other responsibilities, either individually or as a group. Moreover, committee members should not be expected to serve on other committees or task forces. In fact, even before selecting the committee, the interim should clarify that anyone who is going to serve as a member needs to step down from other leadership positions in the church. The interim may need to run interference to protect the committee as a group and as individuals from anyone else's creeping mission.

If the Search Committee finds itself in some internal conflict, the interim can provide pastoral support, help them figure out how to work well together, and suggest processes to resolve the conflict without supplanting the committee's own decisions and wisdom. Conflict within a search committee is not inevitable but is frequent enough in a venture in which the stakes are high that the interim should maintain a pastoral connection and check in with the committee as they move through the crucial stages of the search. With such a connection already established, if conflict does develop, the committee will more likely feel comfortable turning to the interim for help.

Search committees often feel that their task is to find the "right match" for their congregation, and it is not uncommon for them to liken the process to a courtship: getting acquainted, dating, engagement, and getting married. However, this analogy is not helpful, and an interim can provide profound pastoral care to the committee by challenging this notion. Few people get married with the intention of breaking up after a decade or so, but a minister-congregation relationship is rarely "till death do us part." Interim ministers and denomination staff do well to coach congregants not to use the phrase "permanent minister" in their search process, for no minister is permanent. Indeed, the average length of settled ministry in Unitarian Universalist congregations is around nine years. The search for a partnership intended to be ended by nothing short of death or extreme duress is a very different endeavor than the search for a relationship that is, by definition, transitory.

Moreover, the idea of a right match is imbued with romantic yearnings that are not constructive in a ministerial search. A congregation's choice of a minister should not be a coldly rational decision; the emotional dynamics of the decision are actually very important, including the recognition of the ever-present intangible elements in any instance of mutual esteem. Nevertheless, if the congregation feels its duty is to "fall in love" with the minister, or if they expect the minister's regard for the congregation to be distinguished from day one by an unalloyed, breathless adoration, miserable disappointment and frustration will ensue. A more meaningful, mature approach on the part of search committees and ministers alike is to avoid the language of the right match, which implies the preposterous and destructive notion that there is one minister out there who is "just right" for the congregation. The interim can instead encourage the Search Committee to think of the new minister and the congregation as walking together, with the potential consequences and benefits of the choices that companions make.

When Setbacks Occur

It is safe to assume that all congregations in search hope that their effort will unfold according to plan and end with an enthusiastically offered and joyously accepted call that will usher in a new era of vitality in the congregation. Although this does indeed happen, everyone involved in the process needs to remain mindful that it is not the only possible outcome.

Search Committee members may eventually find themselves in circumstances that will call for particular courage, circumstances in which the interim's pastoral role will be most needed. The committee may not find a minister available that year whom they agree to present to the congregation as a candidate. The minister they have selected may withdraw from the search process or choose to candidate elsewhere. Or, after having become the candidate, the minister may withdraw from candidacy. Or the candidating week may end without a call, or with an unaccepted call.

Withdrawal of an offered candidacy is rare, but it has happened. After announcing the candidate to the congregation, the Search Committee may discover information that makes them reconsider their decision. Since congregations often put aside their own misgivings and trust the committee, the committee members must either remain fully committed to their chosen candidate or withdraw the candidacy if they have serious concerns.

Candidating week can result in no accepted call for one of two reasons. Either the congregation votes positively in insufficient numbers to match the plurality required by their bylaws, or the candidate, having received an affirmative vote, chooses to decline for whatever reason, expressed or not.

If a search process does not result in an accepted call, the congregation's, and especially the Search Committee's, disappointment level is likely to require significant pastoral care. The committee, feeling the weight of the responsibility assumed for the congregation, may experience heightened disappointment, anger, a sense of failure, or even betrayal when the outcome doesn't follow the predicted or hoped-for plan. The interim can help by reminding everyone that there are worse outcomes than not finding a minister in the time frame originally anticipated. The cost to the congregation is much greater when the Search Committee settles for a candidate about whom they are not truly enthusiastic instead of extending the search through another cycle. Choosing the "wrong" person to be minister leaves repercussions that can last for many years, whereas the pain of an additional period of interim ministry and search can help the congregation be even more ready for their next called minister.

Interim ministers and denominational staff can strive to eradicate the concept of a "failed search." Perhaps after two years of interim ministry, the Search Committee did not find a suitable candidate; or the Search Committee offered candidacy to a minister who didn't accept; or candidating week ended with an 82 percent vote to call, which the minister and many others felt was insufficient. These outcomes are likely to be disappointing. However, they are not failures. They are signs that the process is unfolding as it was intended. There are many ways a healthy, conscientious search can unfold.

Given what is at stake, it *should* be difficult for a minister and a congregation to come into a confident agreement to walk together, just as it should be difficult to learn to fly a passenger jet, to perform heart surgery, or to play a Beethoven piano sonata. The elaborate phases and steps of the search process exist for good reasons. If the process has been fair, honest, thorough, and hopeful, it was a success, regardless of the outcome. Ironically, if there is such a thing as a failed search, although it is not likely to be described that way, it would be the search that concludes with a minister being called whose ministry ends years later on an unhappy note because of some issues that remained unresolved from before the start of the search.

In any case, if the Search Committee's year of search does not conclude with a minister being called, decisions will need to be made about whether this committee steps down or continues, and whether, if a new committee is to be selected, the selection process will be the same or different from the previous one. Coaching on these matters, like coaching earlier if a Search Committee member dies or moves away, is the province of the regional transitions coach, not the interim minister.

The Third-Year Interim

It is not unusual for a longer-than-intended search to continue while the congregation forms a new relationship with a new interim minister. This outcome may occur if, after two years of interim ministry, the search process has not concluded with an accepted call. Unitarian Universalist interims, according to standard letters of agreement mandated by the UUA Transitions Office, do not serve one congregation longer than two years. A longer period of service could start to feel like an "unintended settlement." A new interim minister in the third interim year may take some adjusting to. There may be new challenges, but the opportunities include having a new perspective and entering a new partnership that can enhance the congregation's agility in dealing with change.

The Search Committee that selects a third-year interim minister to recommend to the Board for hiring is not the same committee that conducted the search for a minister to present as a candidate for the settled ministry. Search committees for interim ministers are typically much smaller than the standard seven-member settled minister search committees. They are often a small group with as few as three members. They may all be Board members, or they may be appointed by the Board. The Search Committee seeking a third-year interim minister should search for one whose interests, skills, and personality seem particularly well suited to help the congregation manage the disappointments of the recent search experience and take advantage of the learning opportunities it presented.

The interim minister, in short, has a complicated role to play with respect to the congregation's search for its next called minister. The interim who works cooperatively with both the Search Committee and the MSR does the congregation an enormous service.

Bringing an Interim Ministry to a Successful Conclusion

FRAN DEW AND MARTHA L. MUNSON

■ ▦ ▥ ■

Interim ministers arrive at each congregation they serve antici-pating their leaving from the beginning. They arrive antici-pating that they will leave a congregation changed through the work they do, especially with the leadership, on specific goals. How different their ministry is, start to finish, from that of settled ministers! The latter not only plan to stay for an indeterminate but considerable length of time but also arrive with ministerial goals yet to be established. Interim ministry, by design, is short-term—a year or two at most with the same interim minister. Congregants may not know what to expect during the interim period, but they know it is temporary. Interims and congregants share the goal that, by the end of the interim period, the congregation will be prepared to welcome a newly called minister with enthusiasm for their newly envi-sioned future.

Ministers entering interim ministry must fully understand and accept the fact that theirs is a ministry of leaving. This means understanding that they come into a congregation know-ing that with the first hello, they are also preparing to say good-bye to people they may have come to love and who may have come to love them. They must come to terms with their own feelings about leaving from beginning to end. The ability to do this is rarely a gift a minister naturally possesses; more often it is a discipline that must be practiced and mastered.

Part of the interim's work is to earn the trust of the leadership so they may together facilitate the changes that need to be made. The interim models good boundaries, self-differentiation, and clarity about the role of a minister, laying the groundwork for the success of the next called minister. At the end of the interim period, the congregation will understand what a minister does and does not do. Leaders will understand better their leadership roles and that the minister does not do or even lead everything. The interim will be trusted to undertake ministerial responsibilities and appreciated for doing them well. In fact, trust and appreciation are likely to be signs of how well the interim time is proceeding and harbingers of the success of the next settled minister.

An interim who masters the art of leaving does more than simply model best practices for ministers leaving congregations. In Harry Freebairn's article "Hello and Goodbye, Easter," psychologist John Hughes is quoted, "Saying 'Hello' and 'Goodbye' are two major tasks all humans need to, and often fail to, accomplish." In this sense, the interim minister has an opportunity to model invaluable and difficult life skills for the congregation.

The Previous Minister's Departure as a Model

The interim minister inevitably finds teaching material in the circumstances of the previous minister's leaving. Ideally, the previous minister was straightforward and clear about the reasons for leaving so congregants understood that it was not because of something they did or did not do. However, most ministers receive little or no training on how best to leave a ministry. It is sometimes said that they tend to leave too early or too late but rarely on time.

If the previous minister's leave-taking was difficult, the interim may need to teach the congregation about leaving well by using the stories they tell of the previous minister's departure, showing them the pitfalls of making assumptions or leaping to conclusions. At the very least, congregants should in time be able to contrast the previous minister's difficult leaving with the interim minister's leaving well.

When speaking of any minister's departure, the word *termination* is not helpful. It suggests the end of a job rather than a ministry. Using this business term fails to account for the complicated relationship of minister and congregants. The congregation, with the help of the interim, will work through lingering issues. In thinking ahead to their own departure, the interim can reflect on what matters to emphasize to this particular congregation. Peeling back layers to reveal tensions, factions, or secrets around the departure of the previous settled minister will help the interim shape their own graceful departure.

Ministerial departure affects congregants in various ways. No minister is completely beloved or hated. Whether the previous minister's departure was because the minister took another settlement; retired; negotiated a resignation; left the ministry; or left due to illness, disability, or even death; multiple stories will be, or will need to be, told by people in the congregation.

The easiest departure for the interim to address may be the previous minister's leaving for another settlement, although it is important to learn more. Were there dynamics in the congregation that prompted the minister to seek another settlement? Was it simply time because the minister and congregation had no more gifts to offer one another? Has the congregation accepted this reality without blaming? In the latter case, the congregants can relatively easily process their degrees of relief or regret about the change.

Negotiated resignations require more heavy lifting. The "why" may not be clear to the congregation; real clarity may not be possible in some cases because of confidentiality in personnel matters. The process of getting to the negotiated resignation may have seriously fractured the congregation. Financial fallout, for example, can affect the budget not only during the transition but well into the future.

If the previous minister left to take up a different profession, the interim may need to teach about the unfortunate tendency to assign all-or-nothing blame. Some congregants may say, "It's our fault because we were too rough." Others may insist, "She should never have entered the ministry in the first place." Ministers who leave for health reasons may have stories told about them that are over-simplified in order to blame someone else for their leaving. Sometimes the Unitarian Universalist Association is blamed for credentialing someone "in bad shape." Sometimes the minister gets romanticized as "the perfect minister," prompting disproportionate blame to be placed on anyone else who might be held responsible for the minister's leaving.

How congregants construct the story of the previous settled minister's leaving will be instructive and will offer important keys to understanding the history of the congregation. Whatever the stories, there will be a need to create space to tell them and for the emotions they bring forth. It will be important to hold this space open for a time, with discrepancies and contradictions unresolved and unresolveable. Then the congregation must move forward to embrace a new future instead of constantly looking back. (For further discussion of congregational stories, see "Mining, Minding, and Making Stories" and "Coming to Terms with History.")

When the Ministerial Search Begins

When the Search Committee is selected, the congregation's energies are likely to begin to turn, but they must not turn too swiftly. The leaders and congregation will still be working on the changes they identified earlier, but some will long for the stability of a settled minister. In part, this is a good thing, but the interim adventure must not be ended before the congregation has achieved clarity about both its present identity and its vision for the future to build a strong foundation from which to call a new minister. If they are ready, members ought to be feeling lighter, with griefs and conflicts resolved. They ought to be able to articulate with pride what they have accomplished during the interim period and who they are now. They ought to be quick to appreciate, celebrate, and thank those who have undertaken leadership in the congregation. They ought to understand that each person's contribution to the good of the whole is important. They ought to value stewardship of time, talent, and treasure.

Once the search process begins, the interim needs to begin intentionally setting the stage for leave-taking. It starts with writing a letter for the congregation's search packet about the interim work being done, a visible reminder that this work is preparatory for the next phase of the congregation's life. Ideally, the letter will reflect a spirit of collegiality, showing that the interim is working on behalf of both the congregation and the next settled minister's ministry with the congregation.

Ministers considering whether they might want to candidate for ministry with the congregation are likely to call the interim to get an impression of what it would be like to serve there. The interim serves the congregation well by graciously accepting those calls, speaking candidly with the ministers in search, and answering questions as fully as possible.

The time between pre-candidating weekends and candidating week is when the interim minister begins in earnest to model departing with grace. If the interim knows the candidate personally, the Search Committee may seek to have the interim join them in their efforts to garner enthusiasm among the congregation for meeting the candidate. The interim needs to decline these invitations. It is not the interim's role to endorse, any more than it would be to criticize, the candidate.

The interim can be a valuable resource for the candidate, offering to answer questions that arise and asking what might help make this important week go smoothly. Candidating week offers the interim the opportunity to be a perfect host-in-absentia for a colleague, preparing the office to become the candidate's office for the week. The interim can also prepare the staff to be helpful and accommodating by making certain the phone system, computer network, and copy machine are in good working order. The interim needs to instruct the staff so they clearly understand that if the candidate wants to interview them, they do not have license to interview the candidate as well. Gracious interims make themselves available by phone or email for assistance to the candidate during candidating week if requested and let the candidate know that they are on call in case of an emergency. Occasionally, candidating ministers and search committees will take the position that the candidate should be the minister on call for emergencies in order to demonstrate their approach to ministry, but this view is not widely shared. The more common view is that the interim is still fully the congregation's minister; the candidate is not.

During candidating week, the interim's major obligation is to be completely absent from the premises. Some interims do offer to meet with the candidate in person away from the church if the candidate wishes. Others, having provided cell phone numbers and itineraries to the candidate and the church office, leave town and aren't to be found until after the congregational meeting to vote on calling the candidate. If they leave the area, it is of course up to them to arrange for some other colleague to be on call in case of emergency.

After Candidating Week

At the end of candidating week, if the vote is affirmative, the congregation has a new minister! They are ready and excited to begin a new era in the life of the renewed congregation they have first envisioned and now created. Even though the work is never done, they have good reason to feel anticipation, zest, and confidence in both their own ability and the ability of the minister they have called.

Now the interim's role is to affirm the congregation's enthusiasm about their decision, as in "I can see that you are excited about this decision," not "I think you have made an excellent choice." The interim needs to make space for the congregation to embrace their new minister at their own pace. At the same time, the interim extends congratulations to the newly called colleague. Beyond this congratulatory communication, the extent of any continuing relationship should now be determined by the newly called colleague. The interim asks, "In what way can I, in the time left in my ministry here, best assist you?" and "What information do you need?" The interim then takes cues from the newly called minister. If asked, the interim answers factual questions as fully as possible but is wary when answering questions of opinion or perception. This distinction encourages the new minister to form their own opinions.

But candidating week may not end with an accepted call, in which case the interim will probably need quite suddenly to become pastor to a disappointed congregation and a Search Committee in deep grief and uncertainty about what to do next. And, unless this turn of events occurs at the end of the interim's second year with the congregation, the interim may not be leaving after all. Of course, if candidating week does come at the end of the interim's second year, the congregation's Board will likely go into immediate search for a new interim minister for the congregation's third interim year. In that case, the current interim will still be leaving and will need to leave well.

Whether the next minister is to be another interim minister or a newly called one, immediately following candidating week is a good time for the interim minister to pointedly speak of "you" and "your congregation" rather than "we" and "our congregation." Ideally, the interim has been scrupulously making these word choices all along, although the congregation may not have noticed. Over time, individual interim ministers' personal practices evolve as they find various ways to draw attention to the impending conclusion of their time with a congregation. Some use visual cues. For example, an interim who ordinarily wears a clerical robe when leading Sunday worship might cease to robe after candidating week if there has been an accepted call.

Now is the time to engage with the leadership in discerning what to do about the remaining tasks on the to-do list. The congregation should not begin new initiatives. The interim and leaders should determine which of the pre-existing goals are reasonable to attempt to complete and which will remain unfinished business to attend to with the next minister, whether that minister is called or another interim. The interim can make a list of the many people to thank personally for their help during the transition time. Offering public thanks to congregational leaders and others who have been especially cooperative or encouraging can itself serve as a parting gift of leadership development. Also, the interim can give special attention to members who joined during the interim period. While for the majority of the congregation the interim has been understood all along to be temporary, new members are about to lose the only minister of this church they have ever known.

Supporting the New Minister

The interim also works with the newly arriving minister, whether called or interim, by clarifying what will happen during any impending gap in ministerial presence. Two commonly asked questions are:

- When does the incoming colleague want to begin preaching? The interim will need to take responsibility for finding area colleagues to cover any Sunday services during the gap if there are not worship associates or other members of the congregation who can take on this responsibility easily and well.

- If someone dies after the interim leaves and before the new minister arrives, will the new minister want to officiate at the memorial service? If not, the interim will need to arrange with an area colleague to be the minister on call for pastoral emergencies.

What the interim leaves behind for the new minister can be as extensive as the checklist presented in the *Janus Workbook* prepared by the Interim Ministry Guild (IMG) and the Transitions Office of the Unitarian Universalist Association (for more about the *Janus Workbook* and the IMG, see "The History, Philosophy, and Impact of Interim Ministry"), or as minimal as a clean desk and information only the interim minister can impart: pastoral concerns, the names of supportive local non-Unitarian Universalist colleagues, major congregational anniversaries, and staff birthdays and anniversaries of employment.

Some interims offer to meet with the new minister at General Assembly in June to pass along sensitive information, such as the names of sex offenders in the congregation. Others offer to meet with the newly called minister, if possible, on site. This can also be an opportunity to go to the bank with the incoming colleague to take care of transfer of discretionary fund signatures.

From the time of the accepted call of the new minister to the interim's departure, the interim must protect the new minister from unreasonable congregational demands. They have waited a long time for their new minister and are eager to see that minister in place. The interim must be prepared to say, more than once, "Rev. X doesn't start until ____." The interim reinforces this fact and helps maintain boundaries for the new minister by clearly remaining the minister until officially gone.

Leave-Taking

Now the reality that the interim is departing becomes obvious. The promise, from day one, that the interim would be leaving becomes real. It is time to move into a farewell mode, giving careful thought to leave-taking rituals with the Board, the Transition Team, the staff, and the congregation as a whole. If possible, the interim can allocate professional expense money for taking out to lunch the entire staff, including of course any ministerial colleagues on staff. All of this can take an emotional toll on the interim. Part of exiting gracefully is acknowledging this fact personally and with staff and colleagues. Appearing to be unaffected by all these good-byes would be inauthentic and would undermine the whole idea of leaving well. (For more about skillful departures, see "Working with Staff.")

If the interim ministry began with the interim minister and congregation speaking words of covenant to each other as part of the liturgy on a Sunday morning, then during the final Sunday worship, the interim and the congregation should release one another from that covenant. The final Sunday in the pulpit and a well-planned good-bye party spread out the emotional impact for both interim and congregation. The public finale to every interim ministry should be a celebration of what has been accomplished as well as acknowledgement of the mixed feelings that are natural at leaving time.

The interim can ask the Transition Team to plan and organize the celebration well in advance, and can suggest to the team the type of publicly given good-bye gift the interim would welcome most. Gifts need not be elaborate or expensive. One thoughtful option is a gift card to an interesting store or well-known restaurant in the interim's next location. The religious education director should be asked to have the children take part in the farewell celebration. It is part of the interim's work to teach the congregation via the Transition Team what their parts are in a good good-bye. The interim needs to leave having received many thanks, expressed in a variety of ways. (For more about the role of Transition Teams, see "A Different Country.")

Just as grief is seldom only about the presenting loss, so too saying good-bye is not only about the interim and congregation saying good-bye to one another. Done well, this ending can provide closure for previous leave-takings that, for whatever reason, did not go well. The interim may leave with some sadness but not with regrets unnamed, unspoken. So far as possible, disappointments need to be addressed, hurts soothed, relationships mended.

The interim needs to make sure that the interim's presence is removed from the church website and that information about the new minister is substituted. The interim should remove church contacts from Facebook accounts, and see that the office deletes his or her name from all email lists. The interim likely has another congregation to serve, which deserves all of the interim's energy now. At the same time, the interim should make space for this congregation to bond with their new minister. With mission accomplished, the interim can leave without looking back, smiling because of leaving well.

From start to finish, transitional ministry is about loss and leaving. From the time the settled minister's departure is announced until the interim clears out the office and drives on to the next church to be served, there are opportunities to practice the art of leaving well. Effectively leaving a congregation includes giving the clear impression that the minister is authentic and genuine throughout the process, remains engaged in the work until the very end, and tries to take into account the needs of the differing groups affected by the interim minister's departure.

Modeling leaving with grace is a gift interims provide every congregation they serve. It is an art that they are privileged to practice, and fortunately, each time they leave a congregation they learn a little more about themselves.

PART IV

Challenges
and
Special Cases

Predictable Roadblocks

JOHN NICHOLS

■ ■ ▨ ■

When a congregation loses its minister, many enter a time of grief. Since no one has died, they may not recognize it as grief. But the departure of a familiar minister—no matter how well or mildly liked, or even heartily disliked—creates uncertainty about what's going to happen next. Parishioners have lost a sense of security in their church.

The reality that things really will be different usually comes home to people in September when the interim minister steps into the pulpit. I will always remember the first Sunday in one congregation, about fifteen minutes before the service was to begin, when a little girl rushed into the minister's study. Upon seeing me, her excitement dissolved quickly into fright, and she rushed back out screaming, "Mommy, Daddy, they've done something to our minister!"

I had no doubt she had been to the former minister's retirement party in the spring and knew that he was leaving, but his departure just didn't become real to her until that first Sunday when she raced into his office and found me. I am quite sure that many adults have a similar reaction when the interim time begins. What happened to our minister? Oh, she's really gone.

When people are grieving, they often seek a shortcut through the confusion and the pain. They typically present one of several reasons for eliminating, cutting short, or refraining from engaging in the work of the interim period.

"Two years!? In my shop, we could bring a new VP on in three months."

It takes two years to do a proper job of settling a minister who follows a long-term predecessor. This news comes to parishioners as an unwelcome surprise. Many, drawing on their experiences in the secular world, will comment that the search process seems to work more efficiently everywhere else. Why does the Unitarian Universalist Association (UUA) insist on a more complicated system?

The bare bones of the process could take no longer than a year. Many congregations have members who served on previous search committees, and they will remember that. However, when the departed minister has had a long tenure, especially if much loved, or has left under a cloud, it takes longer for people to let go of their feelings about that minister. Search committees that decide in haste tend to choose someone who is either the mirror image or exact opposite of the person who just left. They are reacting rather than reflecting, and they may also be working with an image of ministry that no longer serves the congregation well. In some instances, they may be trying too hard to fix a situation that takes time to mend.

When parishioners suggest that the search for a new minister is something like that of a new vice president or a superintendent of schools, they don't realize that the new minister will be brought into a position of intimacy and trust not matched by any position in the secular world.

A new VP is not asked to confront the anguish of a newly widowed parishioner or the anger of a broken marriage. A new VP is not placed in front of the company once a week to preach to them about how to live. The congregation has a much closer relationship with its minister than any company has with its VP. Before and even while engaging the mechanics of the search process, the congregation needs time to sort out its relationship with its last minister and what it most needs from the next one.

"Why don't we offer the position to Mary?"

When a congregation has another minister on staff, some will be tempted to offer the vacant senior minister's position to the minister they already know to shorten the anticipated painful transition time. But they will first have to vote yes or no on the proposed staff member, to make her an "inside candidate." We'll call her Mary, the associate minister.

Mary and the congregation will have to follow the UUA rules for an inside candidate. These state that the congregation must vote on whether to call Mary as the settled senior minister before it receives a list of names of other ministers to consider. The congregation will get the list of names from the UUA only if Mary is not offered the position. This rule ensures that everyone is treated as fairly as possible: the congregation, Mary, and any other minister interested in the congregation. After all, in any search, the in-house candidate has an edge over others because she is well known and liked while others are not known.

Many parishioners will not understand why the inside-candidate rule is necessary when a different set of rules operates in every other business or profession. Some will wonder why Mary can't be considered along with those who apply through the UUA's settlement process. When they discover it cannot work that way, they may become confused or angry. But the rule exists not only for congregations. Ministers must be in good relationship with other ministers and agree to follow by these rules as professional standards.

The rule prevents a potential dilemma for the Search Committee. The committee would probably be under pressure from Mary's supporters to choose her and Mary's status as an in-house candidate would cause other applicants to withdraw. This would seriously hamper the committee's work and limit their options. A Search Committee that follows the rules not only has more options for a minister, but also will know their new minister is in good relationship with the wider UUA ministry.

When congregants begin addressing the interim about their wishes regarding Mary, the interim must be careful not to be seen as taking a position for or against her as the next minister. The minister may also need to serve as Mary's counselor, encouraging her to consider all her choices should this one fall through. If she does not receive a vote sufficient enough to call her to the senior minister position, then it would be awkward for her to remain at the church for much longer.

If Mary assents to the process, the congregation enters a time of discernment that may last several weeks or months. Mary's supporters will assume that the outcome of this vote is a foregone conclusion because, after all, who doesn't like Mary?

There probably will be, however, some serious problems down the line.

Over the years, even a very successful minister accumulates an opposition of at least 15 percent of the membership. These people are not violently antagonistic toward the minister, but given a choice they'd prefer someone else. Mary starts out with that 15 percent against. Add to that those members (at least another 15 percent) who are opposed to the rule on voting for the inside candidate first. They want to know who else is possible, but their vote to protest the process counts against Mary.

There is a good chance that Mary will receive a negative vote of 25 to 30 percent, and that's a lot of people with reservations about your candidacy. Few ministers will accept a call under those conditions. Such an outcome leaves everyone unhappy. The candidate's friends in the congregation will probably protest that she got a raw deal, some suggesting that she was the victim of prejudice. Those who opposed her will point out that they had every right to vote their conscience, and they don't appreciate being attacked for having done so.

The interim must explain the rules—and the reasons for them—over and over to different groups within the congregation, and even then, a great deal of healing must take place in the aftermath of inside-candidate votes. This pastoral work may be the hardest and most valuable thing the interim can do for the congregation.

Mary's situation could conclude somewhat differently. A few congregations have a system whereby the associate minister is selected with the understanding that she could take the helm when the senior minister leaves or retires. The nautical metaphor applies: The assumption is that the congregational ship will founder if the "captain" or someone appointed by the captain is not in charge. In this situation, Mary, having been chosen with the understanding that she was being groomed to be eventual senior minister, simply steps into that position when the senior minister retires.

There are some inherent difficulties with this system. First, it doesn't address the grieving that follows a long-term senior minister's departure. Mary is not in a good position to handle the grieving because she's been in that minister's shadow for several years and now would like to come into the light just when the congregation is feeling its loss. Second, the perceptions that individuals have had of Mary have changed over the years while she has been waiting in the wings. Some no longer see in her what they thought they saw when she was called, or they've come to believe that a different kind of minister would be better at this point. There may be some who have always believed that Mary was handpicked to maintain the church in patterns they now believe need to change.

Finally, there is an enormous risk of misunderstanding and resentment among those members who have joined the church since Mary was chosen and never had a word to say about her joining the staff, much less becoming senior minister. When people feel that something happened that deprived them of choices in selecting a senior minister, they become resentful, which could have painful consequences for minister and congregation. To be clear: It is "legal" for Mary to ascend to the senior minister's position under these circumstances. The more important question is whether it is wise to set this process in motion in the first place.

The inside-candidate rule also covers any other minister on staff, including community ministers. They would have an advantage over other candidates for the position because members of the congregation know them, and so they must be voted on first before a list of candidates can be released.

Interns are another tempting choice for congregational attentions at a time of ministerial loss. Interns are often beloved by the congregation that trains them, which is probably good for their development. Because they are clearly learning the role and tasks of ministry, they are usually corrected gently and forgiven much. This training is not realistic for taking over the role of leading the same congregation, particularly a congregation large enough to be able to afford an intern. It is far better for a new minister to take on a congregation where it is possible to start from scratch, bearing the full weight of congregational hopes and expectations. The UUA supports this notion by insisting that interns must wait three years before applying for a position in their internship congregation. Ministers who choose to apply must get a waiver from the Ministerial Fellowship Committee and the UUA Transitions Office. More often than not, the Ministerial Fellowship Committee does not allow the ministry to count toward final fellowship, and encourages the minister to pursue other options instead.

"It will never be like it was when Bob was here."

It is a tribute to our ministers that many parishioners become very attached to them and their ways. Parishioners get used to their minister's tone of voice, mannerisms, approach, style of presenting ideas, and personal priorities which have guided the congregation for many years.

The departure of the former minister is a big loss, and when it happens, many find ways to avoid accepting it. These ways could include phoning the former minister, whom we will call Bob, for advice on current church situations; inviting him to social events in the parish; asking him to visit parishioners in the hospital; requesting that he officiate at memorial services and weddings; making trips to hear him preach in his new parish; making constant public comparisons between Bob and the interim minister; and in some instances holding out hope that he will be convinced to return when the interim minister leaves.

Professional ministerial guidelines should direct Bob's responses to these offers. Common-sense guidelines can direct the congregation's leadership. They are as clear as day to many ministers, but unfortunately they seem counterintuitive to parishioners, who can't understand why they would not continue to enjoy a relationship they had nurtured with Bob over ten or more years. If the interim simply relies on the professional guidelines, which many laypeople regard as the ministers' "union rules," the interim will not win understanding and may create antagonism. This situation requires from the interim tact, empathy, and—particularly if Bob proves unable to extricate himself from former relationships—the help of the Good Offices Minister, a minister from the UU Ministers' Association (UUMA) designated to help ministers in some sort of conflict. The Transitions Office of the UUA can also be of assistance.

Perhaps Bob was voted minister emeritus. This usually means he had a distinguished ministry, and the congregation wishes to reward him by establishing that they would like to continue in some kind of relationship with him. If Bob continues to live in the community near the parish from which he retired, he might be invited to preach annually, make some hospital visits, and attend some major celebrations of the congregation.

Navigating the relationship between the interim and Bob is tricky. The two should enter into a written agreement, specifying how they will interact with each other. It should cover how often Bob will be invited to preach, and how Bob and the interim will negotiate weddings, memorial services, and pastoral calls. It should be discussed with the congregation's leadership and publicized to the entire congregation. When the new minister is called, a new agreement should be written by Bob and the new minister, reaffirmed by both, and again publicized. In this way, both ministers and the congregational leadership reaffirm the importance of ethical behavior. A lot of hurt, and possibly the career of the next minister, can be saved by attending to these matters.

Let's say that Bob is not a minister emeritus, and he retires and lives in the community where the congregation is located. And let's say that, although he understands how important it is to stay away from the congregation, he will likely meet congregants when shopping or walking the dog. Some will want to fill him in, sometimes adding their opinions, on recent events at the church. There is a very great temptation for the former minister to comment if the interim or settled minister involved

remains a stranger to him. The importance of the interim minister and the former minister forming a working relationship
cannot be overemphasized. Helping a congregation not latch on
to one minister as "their minister" is crucial for the future of the
congregation. A covenant between the two colleagues should
be undertaken early on and publicly, to honor the needs of the
congregation.

Interims differ greatly on how they handle these matters.
Some congregations are better served if Bob hews strictly to the
UUMA professional guidelines, at least until the new minister
is called. Others could be well served if Bob returns to give the
occasional eulogy for someone he has known well for a long
time. But the interim might decide to ask Bob to sit in the congregation rather than on the chancel and to come forward only
to deliver the eulogy. The interim might also ask Bob not to
wear a clerical robe, and Bob might not be invited to participate
further in leading the service. He might be expected to leave
when the service is over and not stay to greet old friends.

Sometimes these recommendations don't work. Sometimes
the former minister does not feel bound by any guidelines
or, for whatever reason, refuses to cooperate. If the situation
becomes serious enough, the interim may need to appeal to the
congregation's leadership to recognize that holding on to the
past can only prevent them from moving forward and may affect
the stability of their ministerial leadership.

In some cases, a minister has left because of a negotiated
termination, meaning that the minister and the congregational
leadership have agreed that this ministry should not continue.
Negotiated terminations can produce very complicated endings.
The minister might believe that even if the minister could obtain
a majority affirmative vote of the congregation, it would not be
a sustainable majority, and so settles for being rewarded financially for resigning. Such resignations are sometimes in the best
interest of minister and congregation, but result in unresolved
emotion and grief. There may be conflicting feelings among
congregants, and not all congregants may know that the ending was negotiated. Some congregants think that everyone must
believe as they do about the minister, and become entrenched

in their positions. People forget that the minister had different relationships with different people in the congregation, and the apparent contradictions can be difficult for many to understand. The interim's concern here is how to help the congregation put this situation into perspective and move on.

"It would not have happened if Alice were here."

Some interim ministries are delightful from beginning to end. It is more usual, however, to experience bumps in the road, as the congregation adjusts to major changes. Most commonly, segments of the congregation will grumble about the interim minister. In comparisons between the interim minister and the now beloved and idealized former minister (we might call her Alice), the interim is seen to fall short in leadership, pastoral presence, and sensitivity to others or in preaching. Because these criticisms arise out of grief for the former minister, they may seem harsh and unfair. Some regular attendees at worship show up far less regularly and, if asked, tell everyone that they don't find the new minister inspiring. Those who didn't like Alice may return to worship to make that point, and they tend to balance out those who are boycotting.

At worst, this grieving over the loss of a popular minister may translate into a diminished pledge drive as some express their discomfort with their checkbooks. It is vitally important for the interim to help the congregation understand that the pledge drive is not a referendum on the minister who happens to be in place, but an assessment of how much the congregation values itself, an assessment that will convey itself to the candidates for their ministry. This perspective will be new for some.

Sometimes, there is active opposition, in the form of organized resistance or open hostility to the minister or Board, or criticism of the search process. Understandably, these tactics can make the church leadership anxious or angry themselves. They probably have never had to deal with something this unpleasant, and don't know what to do.

Interims often talk about maintaining a non-anxious presence, and know that this is far easier to describe than to achieve.

In a situation fraught with tension, the interim will not add their own to the mix, at least not obviously. The interim may respond to criticisms by saying, "I'm sorry you don't like my sermons, my personal style, or some of my decisions, but this is what learning to live with a new minister is like. This is why I am here, so that you can experience a different style, and if it's not your style, then by all means tell the Search Committee."

The interim may respond to criticism by asking questions rather than appearing defensive and anxious. "What is it about my sermons you don't like? How different is my style of ministry from that of Alice? How would she have handled that situation? How are you feeling about Alice's decision to leave, now that it's a year later?" The interim should meet regularly and informally with church leaders so that if such moments arise, the leaders will know how to defuse them.

Interims will also make deliberate changes. The order of service may be changed so that it makes more sense to the minister. Certain things that were expected of the congregation's previous minister may be dropped. For example, one interim declined to spend every Sunday afternoon delivering the altar flowers to shut-ins and organized a pastoral care committee to do it instead. New committees may be organized and set to work performing with considerable creativity tasks that were undertaken by the previous overworked settled minister, and sometimes it becomes necessary to consolidate committees and help them to redefine their mission.

These changes are not brought about because the interim has an itch to do something different, but because the interim thinks they will in the long haul make things better and easier for the congregation and for the next minister. The interim is willing to risk some momentary loss of popularity to make a change that a settled minister might not attempt for several years. And of course, anything that gets changed can usually be reversed if the congregation feels strongly about it.

"You can't say that in this church!"

In some congregations, one of the changes may have to do with language. Every minister gets comfortable with a certain kind of theological language that may leave some people out. Unitarian Universalist congregations and ministers are deeply concerned about increasing the number of people from diverse races, classes, and nationalities in their midst. This emphasis implies that our experience will be enriched when we embrace diversity. Presumably, this includes theological diversity.

Reverential language—words such as *God, grace,* and *faith*—make some Unitarian Universalists very uncomfortable, particularly if their local congregation never uses them. Yet many Unitarian Universalists are looking for a liberal congregation where they can learn to use reverential language and become exposed to the ideas this language signifies.

Interim ministers represent the accumulated wisdom and breadth of a larger Unitarian Universalist movement in which considerable theological diversity prevails. The interim can introduce the possibility that a broader acceptance of religious ideas and language might attract people who would like to be more involved with the congregation. That acceptance might even include the person who would be the best choice to be their next minister.

The interim can offer a sermon or two presenting different ways of looking at religious language or more specifically at the word *God.* Prayers and meditations can use alternately humanist and theistic language. An occasional theist-oriented hymn will prompt resistance from some, but will also elicit positive responses from those who are delighted to have their theology publically acknowledged. Workshops or listening circles may reveal diversity which some will find surprising and, hopefully, welcome.

Generational and cultural differences around theology are real. Some people grew up in a culture in which going to church was expected. Others wonder what this "church thing" is about. Personal histories create different reactions among people in the congregation. The next generation of Unitarian Universalists will, if history repeats, be very different from the current one. Feelings of loss may cause some older people to react to these generational changes. Some may understand the need for greater theological tolerance but have their own sense of how far the tolerance should go.

Unitarian Universalists can be more rigid about theology than they are on many other issues. Strong reactions may be an example of lingering trauma from an earlier time in their lives. These reactions may also arise out of a sense of loss: Their congregation is now a different place, no longer the comfort or refuge it had been. Arguments over theology are opportunities for congregational education and pastoral care. They can expose unspoken and sometimes unconscious rules that may contradict what people say in a congregational search survey, cottage meetings, or other forms of feedback. Mostly, they are opportunities for a congregation to examine itself and decide how to balance who they are and who they want to become.

Congregations willing to attempt this examination publicly and respectfully, to become clear yet not rigid about their actual diversity, are more likely to be attractive to both new members and potential ministers.

"We've always done it this way."

Some congregations are happy the way they are and want an interim minister who will preach tolerable sermons and otherwise leave them alone. A few of these congregations have a way of life that works for them. Because they don't think anything is broken, they don't think anything needs fixing. In most instances, however, the path on which they are set actually works only for a segment of the congregation, excluding others who haven't been able to muscle into the leadership circle. Congregations firmly convinced of their own efficiency and goodness make for challenging interim periods.

The interim brings a complex message to this situation: "There are different ways to do what the congregation has been doing the same way for years, and some ways seem more effective than what is in place here. Why not try them?" Concurrent with this suggestion is the message that change is coming anyway. The glove that the former minister left will not fit a new minister. Why not start getting used to changing step by small step?

There are all kinds of ways to be rigid. Time-honored traditions may be rituals for some people and ruts for others. The interim period is a time to see what still fits, what needs altering, and what needs to be let go. Again, raising questions and trying new things allows tacit practices in a congregation to be discussed and examined. Is the intent still being practiced well, or even needed, or is there another option? Prospective ministers will be intrigued to see if a congregation has the agility and flexibility to accommodate a new ministry, new people, and new ideas.

"Isn't this the entire congregation's decision to make?"

Frequently, when a difficult decision must be made, some Board members will suggest that the congregation be polled in order to help them decide. They suspect that if they decide something without polling, those who disagree might accuse them of abusing their power. When the congregation was smaller, which may be in recent memory, they were easier to poll, and the resulting discussion could sometimes have been a charming part of congregational life. As a congregation grows, acquiring property and more staff, decisions become more complicated and sometimes more sensitive. They require intensive study by several members of the Board, a recommendation, and then a discussion in an atmosphere that allows members to speak more freely. Polling is no longer an option. The Board must decide.

And yet when I tell parishioners early on that I am going to ask the Board to make some decisions, their eyes search the ceiling and, with amused countenances, they wish me good luck in a way that suggests I'm not likely to have it. In all likelihood, no one had ever suggested to new Board members that they were elected to lead the congregation. More likely, they understood that they were expected to act in place of the congregation because it wasn't practical for the entire congregation to sit in a meeting once a month.

Interims seek to encourage, strengthen, and support leadership in the congregation. Needed changes do not happen in a congregation of more than a hundred members unless a group of people studies the issues, opts for the change, and then commits to helping the congregation understand it. The process of teaching leadership should begin at the first Board retreat and be led by the interim or a consultant brought in for this purpose. There is a world of materials on leadership in congregations that can be duplicated and mailed beforehand to Board members. Many of these are available from the Alban Institute, including *Governance and Ministry* by Dan Hotchkiss. Board members may be relieved to discover that they are supposed to be decisive, imaginative, and creative on behalf of the congregation. They do not need to spend their terms living in fear of tackling those issues that have stymied everyone else for years and are still left undecided. Their job, they are pleased to be told, is to lead the congregation out of the forest they find themselves in, rather than, as previous Boards may have done, wandering around in it looking for a place to hide.

If possible, the interim should have regular informal meetings with the Board chair or leadership team so they can determine which issues need more information and which need a decision immediately. At Board meetings, the interim may act as an informal process observer, making sure that the approach to an issue is as clear as possible, gently pointing out when the Board has avoided a decision. The interim can also begin to educate the congregation through newsletter columns and perhaps an occasional sermon on how congregational process depends on trust. *Friedman's Fables*, by Edwin Friedman, provides good material for this education.

Nothing frustrates parishioners more than finding that their congregational Board has stymied itself by allowing a few people to either terrorize or stall them on every issue. The Board and the interim can count it a victory every time they are able to decide and move ahead on a previously intractable problem.

A congregation may ask, "Shouldn't we wait and get the new minister's input?" The reality is that the new minister will probably not risk popularity on any new change for at least a year, maybe more. So the congregation can lose two years on the chance to make a change that could work better for everyone now. Most people would prefer to try a change that intrigues them rather than wait for the unknown new minister to decide it's a good thing to do.

Often, the immutable ways of many change-resistant congregations have been in place throughout the leadership of the previous minister. Right or wrong, these ways are experienced as that minister's. These ways are "bequeathed" to the congregation, and scrapping them too readily will be perceived as a disservice to that minister's memory (see "The Temptation to Rush the Search").

Congregations haunted by the memory of their previous minister require a great deal of patience. It may take a year for those feelings to be sifted and finally let go. That is why a two-year interim is usually recommended, since the first year may be spent getting used to the former minister's absence, and the second year may be spent testing new ways of doing things.

Change-resistant congregations can be frustrating. Yet sometimes, what draws people back to their houses of worship is what stays the same and provides stability in a transient world. Sometimes the interim would be well advised to balance the role of change agent with the more traditional role as pastor. Interim ministry is both. Change in congregations does not happen easily or without a sense of loss by some and relief by others. Congregations benefit from realizing that loss, relief, and hope can live side by side—and those aspects should co-exist, in order to look to the future without forgetting or being trapped in the past. The interim both honors the past and helps the congregation make room for possibility—the possibility that the congregation will continue to serve its members and the wider world as the world spins forward into a new time.

The Temptation to Rush the Search

ROBERT T. LATHAM

■ ▨ ▥ ■

Often, congregations just want to get through the interim period, and do it for only one year. And earlier in our denominational history, one year of interim ministry seemed right. But over the past few decades, we have recognized that for most congregations, a two-year interim ministry is needed. Over 90 percent of all Unitarian Universalist congregations now do two years of interim ministry. As with all crucial institutional learning, this approach has developed as a result of experience.

Most of a congregation's most urgent needs lie just beneath the surface of its story. And when we are a part of this story, we may not recognize these needs. The following dramas, based on real congregational stories, can help with sorting out the needs of any given congregation.

The Happy Valley Story

The Happy Valley UU congregation's minister had just resigned after an eighteen-year relationship. The church and minister had grown up together, but a larger congregation had lured the minister away. Happy Valley was a strong, effective community. It had a lot of pride and a positive public identity. The Board of Trustees decided that the congregation needed an interim min-

ister for only one year—just long enough to find the best new
minister available. They assumed that any minister would jump
at the chance to serve such a grand congregation. The rumor
was that Happy Valley was a plum for any new minister.

However, several denominational leaders suggested that, following such a long-term relationship, special issues would need to
be addressed. They recommended considering a two-year interim
period to explore this possibility. But the Board rejected this rea-
soning, seeing no apparent issues in the congregation's life.

A one-year interim was set up, and the search process immediately began. A new minister was called. Excitement was high,
and the future looked good. Then the new minister began to do
things differently. What had been sanctified in the past relationship was being changed. Many viewed this situation as a betrayal
of the congregation's values and a dishonoring of its past minister. Tensions grew. The new minister's style was also different,
prompting further disenchantment. Problems escalated.

After three years, dissatisfactions grew to almost insurmount-
able proportions. Bitterness developed, dividing the congregation.
The relationship with the minister ended in a negotiated settlement. The congregation's sense of self was severely damaged. Now
a two-year interim period was essential, but this time it was needed
in order to heal and restore the congregation's spiritual health.

Why did this happen? The congregation was not prepared
for change. The past minister and ways of doing things under
her leadership had become sacrosanct. The status quo and the
holy had become synonymous. Preserving the past rather than
embracing the new had become an unwitting devotion.

Congregations that consider themselves successful are the
most likely to think that a one-year interim period before settling a new minister will be sufficient. But the Happy Valley story
illustrates an often-overlooked truth of congregational life. A
successful relationship between congregation and minister that
ends well is as likely to create problems for the congregation's
future as that of a terminated problematic relationship.

Indeed, the issues created by success may be more difficult
to deal with than those created by failure because failure issues
tend to surface in congregational life, while success issues tend

to hide themselves. Leaders are apt to assume that when issues are not apparent, they do not exist. This understandable conclusion can easily end with a congregation deeply wounded by what it did not recognize.

Happy Valley was a successful congregation, yet beneath the surface, multiple land mines awaited the next relationship. These land mines, created by the relationship's very success, represented the dark side of this success—the confusion between how things had been done and the success the doing had produced. Further, this confusion attached itself to the congregation-minister relationship because the success had happened on that relationship's watch.

This story is one of the oldest in human history: the confusion of symptom with cause. It is the failure to recognize that the same symptom can be created by different causes. The land mines communicated a message: Don't tinker with this success story by changing what seemed to create it. The new congregation-minister relationship was eventually blown apart when the minister stepped on these land mines by doing things differently. For example, he decided to make changes to the worship experience. Rather than recognizing that this change would open a new door into spiritual exploration, the congregation viewed it as a violation of the holy.

The moral is: Do not assume that a past congregation-minister success story means that a congregation's relationship with its next minister is free of hidden land mines. The exact opposite is more likely to be true.

The Slumber Gap Story

The Slumber Gap UU congregation had had a mediocre, six-year relationship with its minister, characterized by neither love nor hate. The parting was dully amicable. The congregation's perspective—that they had no relationship issues to address—fostered an immediate move into the search process because they hungered for an exciting ministerial leadership.

But several denominational leaders expressed the need for caution. They knew the congregation was not in a state to choose a new minister wisely because it was in maintenance mode. It needed to awaken from its slumber, renew its sense of mission, and consider its leadership needs.

The Board decided that this advice was wise, so they established a two-year interim ministry and confronted numerous critical issues lurking beneath the surface of their slumbering lifestyle. During the interim period, they had time to evaluate their state of being, address their needs, and create a vision for a new future. They came fully awake. Then they engaged the search process and called a new minister.

It has been four years and, despite inevitable bumps and disagreements, things are going well. The congregation is vibrant and feels itself growing into a new future.

This relationship continues to mutually inspire both congregation and minister because the congregation spent two years of interim work unearthing hidden issues, resolving them, and elevating its spiritual health, which in turn maximized the possibilities of the new ministerial relationship.

Does the Congregation Need Special Care?

Lay leadership should discuss whether or not its congregation requires special care during the interim period. The term *special care* is not derogatory. It is a statement of assessment. It implies only that factors emerging from the congregation's past ministerial relationship hold the possibility of sabotaging the relationship with its next settled minister. These factors are as likely to rise from success as from failure. To preclude such sabotage, these factors must be handled with insight and skill. Fortunate is the congregation whose leadership recognizes both the potential for such sabotage and the need for trained interim ministerial leadership to deal with the issues so that their portent does not become reality.

Most congregations have more special needs than they realize, so leadership should assess the needs for the interim period before beginning the ministerial search process. This assessment means looking beyond the surface and includes both listening to those outside the congregation who know it well (regional staff, for example) and engaging in self-assessment.

Acknowledging these special needs has led over 90 percent of our congregations to engage in interim ministry for at least two years. There are many reasons why a congregation needs this interim time. Just one example is size transition. Many of our congregations have been in the process of transitioning their size for so long that it has become a lifestyle. Empowering a congregation to recognize the debilitating nature of this lifestyle and then to forthrightly address it will require more than a one-year interim period. (For more about size transition, see "Size Transitions.")

Congregations should be approached with an eye toward their unique needs and how the now standard two-year interim period can best address those needs. Experience shows that anything less than a two-year interim period will leave the impending professional relationship vulnerable to unresolved issues that could negatively affect the congregation's future well-being.

The most common types of congregations fall into four categories: the bereft, the benumbed, the betrayed, and the bequeathed. The following experience-based observations describing these categories will, if heeded, empower lay leadership to make wise decisions about its needs during the interim period. If a congregation fits any of these scenarios, it qualifies as a special care congregation. There is nothing absolute about these symptoms. They serve only as clues to a possible state of being.

The Bereft

One type of congregation is characterized by bereftness. Beneath this bereftness is a success story. The congregation's long-term relationship of loving, mutual admiration with a professional minister has ended. This loss could have been initiated by the minister's choice, by death, or by some other circumstance of life. Whatever the reason, the beloved has been snatched from the congregation's bosom, and the congregation is experiencing emotional trauma.

Together, the congregation and minister had experienced the glories of a metaphorical Promised Land. But when the minister left, the Promised Land vanished because it was not a place but a relationship.

It is the loss of the relationship and not the reason for the loss that matters, because the end result is the same: a sense of abandonment, denial, anger, guilt, depression, anxiety, loss, and defensiveness. Any minister stepping into this circumstance, even on a temporary basis, will be viewed as a rival of the lost minister and will become a target of projection for these negative feelings. Thus, the primary characteristics of such a minister must be the ego strength of self-differentiation and non-anxious presence, combined with a spirit of persistence.

The interim minister must deal with these feelings of loss in a straightforward fashion. The interim must help the congregation achieve a new state of spiritual health by encouraging them to accept the loss and anticipate a new ministerial relationship. Together they need to confront the experience of the lost Promised Land, and develop a new story identity that both incorporates the past minister and yet is separate from this minister as well. The congregation must be led to envision a new Promised Land. The capacity and desire for a mutually enhancing relationship must be restored.

This kind of acceptance and anticipation cannot occur in less than two years. The formula is a year for grieving and a year for turning. However, the two may become intertwined rather than sequential since they can easily enhance each other. Nevertheless, two years will be required.

The Benumbed

The benumbed congregation has had a lengthy relationship with a professional minister that was characterized by blandness. The numbing brought about by remaining static is the spiritual apathy produced by lack of inspired vision and the spiritual slumber that lies beneath layers of boredom. Temporary moments of restored feeling brought about by flirtation with conflict were usually smothered by fomenting civility. This congregation is experiencing real trauma that is likely to go unrecognized because of its surface life's placidity. Placidity is often confused with peace and satisfaction.

Rip Van Winkle represents an apt metaphor for the

benumbed congregation. In Washington Irving's story, he was a man who drank a special concoction and fell asleep for a long time, missing the American Revolution. The benumbed congregation, having drunk too deeply of that elixir of blandness and comfort, has fallen into a slumber that has permitted time and progress to pass it by. Whatever energy is expended during this slumber merely keeps the community's pulse beating. Its visible organizational expression is outmoded and in a state of minimal maintenance. This congregation cannot be awakened by a gentle nudging. Only the trumpet blare will stir its slumber.

The benumbed congregation's sense of mission is at a low ebb, and perceptions of possibility must come from without. Resurrecting motivation from numbness demands a high output of energy and a long period of time. A year of interim ministry may be required simply to arouse the sleeper. In this case, negative reactions to change might occur in the second year rather than the first, when they would normally happen. The reason is that negative reactions can be made only by an awakened membership. Moreover, suddenly aroused people are sometimes irritable.

But this delayed reaction may create a special problem. Normally, the necessary changes made during a two-year interim are initiated in the first year, and people have the second year to accommodate and see their benefit. However, if a year is required to awaken the Rip Van Winkle congregation, then a vital year for processing change is lost due to this arousing activity. In this case, even after two years of interim ministry, congregants may still be processing change issues during the first year of the newly settled minister—a year that could be fraught with danger to the new settlement. Congregants with unresolved issues around these changes may pressure the new minister to reverse the changes and, through this pressure, sabotage the relationship before it has a chance to become grounded.

Other consequential problems confront the interim period. For instance, due to the congregation's lack of spiritual growth over an extended period, the level of institutional wisdom is as low as the congregation's slumbering blood pressure. Upon awakening, they will tend to make decisions commensurate with pre-slumber-time wisdoms—wisdoms that were current when the congregation went to sleep but have long since been bypassed with newer perceptions.

In a benumbed congregation, the maintenance mode they have been operating with is like hibernation. A maintenance mode is characterized by low vision, low energy, low commitment, and low giving. Consequently, people willing to step into key positions of leadership over long periods are not only appreciated but applauded. The longer the congregation slumbers, the longer the possibility that the same member will inhabit the same position. And the longer the person holds a position, the greater the tendency to accrue unwarranted powers.

The deep emotional attachment of individual members to their power and a subsequent identification of this power with self-worth may create serious conflicts and dramas that drain vital energy away from transition needs. Moreover, the congregation may have elevated the status of such persons to a state of maintenance sainthood and be reluctant to address the issues inherent in this power aberration. This scenario can be explosive and damaging.

Given these issues, a minimum of two years is required to bring the benumbed congregation to a vital awakened state. The interim minister with a full leadership tool kit can combine the necessary awakening and envisioning processes over this period. The required leadership traits include motivational inspiration and institutional wisdom.

The Betrayed

Another congregation type is characterized by a sense of betrayal. Whatever the length of the professional relationship, something has happened between the congregation and the minister so that one or both feel betrayed by the other, and the congregation has been left in a state of intense emotional trauma.

This sense of betrayal could have been induced by unethical behavior on the part of the minister. It could have been initiated by issues arising from a dysfunctional congregational lifestyle that the previous minister tried to end, perhaps in a way that was perceived as heavy-handed. It could have been generated by a small conflict that was allowed to escalate beyond the capacity to manage. Whatever the source, an irresolvable sense of betrayal ensued that ended an unpleasant, and possibly recriminating, relationship. Like a battlefield, the issues found resolution through combat strategies. This mentality produced a no-win situation—both congregation and minister lost.

Lay leadership can seek a more ethical parting under such circumstances through a negotiated settlement. Sometimes the minister initiates leaving the congregation, compelled by the omen of a negative future. Whatever the style of ending, the drama has created in the congregation a variety of feelings toward both themselves and the minister: defeat, anger, distrust, victory, failure, disgust, glee, revenge, depression, and woundedness—feelings generated by warfare.

These feelings must get resolved. Forgiveness must happen, wounds must be healed, trust restored, well-being elevated, and unity instilled. In addition, an inspiring professional ministerial relationship with the congregation must be modeled, and the congregation's energies directed beyond self-preoccupation. This will require patience, gentleness, and wisdom. The quickest way to heal spiritual wounds is through the congregation looking up from its current morass to its larger vision and mission. This moves their energy from the past and present on to the future.

This process cannot be completed in less than two years. The formula is a year for healing and a year for turning. However, these processes are best interwoven in both focus and time.

The Bequeathed

The last type of congregation requiring special care can be called the bequeathed. Some ministers have suggested that a minister who has been in a congregation for six years owns it. This seemingly arrogant statement really means that people who join a congregation during a minister's tenure do so because of that minister's appeal or, at the least, because the minister does not turn them off. Over time, enough members who like the minister join and enough who do not leave, so that the congregation converts into a pro-minister community. Moreover, over time the minister engages the membership in every manner of life transition, further cementing the relationship. The majority of the congregation can now be persuaded by the minister's vision, which leads to the perception of ownership. This is not a problem; it is a characteristic of effective leadership.

This transformation normally takes place within six to eight years. Thus, when leaving, the minister bequeaths a legacy— a congregation that basically reflects the minister's theological and institutional perspectives. And sufficient time has passed for this legacy to have become institutionalized. This institutionalization is the key issue of transition.

Ghosts serve as the metaphor for this bequeathal. Ghosts are dangerous because they appear at unexpected times and often critical moments in life, inducing fear and diverting attention from the business of living. Moreover, ghosts claim to have ownership of what they appear to represent and threaten to harm anyone seeking to contest this ownership. Any new minister immediately following this bequeathal will spend a great deal of time during their first several years discovering and dealing with this ghostly legacy. This minister's relationship with the congregation will likely be victimized in some serious way by attempts to exorcise these ghosts. Ghosts resent being made homeless and will seek to rid their haunts of the intruder.

The negative possibilities in a bequeathed situation argue for a two-year interim period. Some mistakenly assume that two years are not needed because there are no visible symptoms of conflict. The conflict is not apparent because another ministerial relationship has not challenged the legacy's ghosts. Once challenged, the trauma will occur. Thus, potential harm waits beneath the calm surface of congregational life. It is the shadow side of success. If this situation is not confronted adequately, the next relationship may well become a ghost story.

When dealing with a bequeathed ministry, it is better to be safe than sorry. One never knows what will appear when a closet is opened in the life of this congregation. The normal formula is a year for exorcising and a year for turning, although they are often wisely meshed.

Healing and Turning

The goal of the interim process is to empower the congregation to come to a maximum state of spiritual health. If this happens, the ministerial relationship that follows will also have a maximum possibility of success.

It might be possible to deal with the visible symptoms of the special care congregation in a year's time. But equally important is the re-visioning of identity, mission, and ministry that moves the congregation's focus away from self-absorption and permits the healing process to conclude. Healing is greatly facilitated by looking up from the wound to that which is transcendently noble.

So another way of stating the formula is that the first year is spent dealing with the congregation's special care needs, and the second year is spent moving its focus outward toward mission and ministerial nobility. These two focuses, often intertwined, will usually unfold sequentially. Each needs its own caring time and attention. And each requires different professional skills to complete the process in just two years.

Postponing the Ministerial Search Process

The first year of the interim period requires significant energy in order to adequately address the congregation's peculiar issues from the past. Immediately beginning ministerial search process activities will drain off vital energy and bifurcate the congregation's focus during a time when the entire membership needs to zero in on exploring and elevating its spiritual well-being. Indeed, initiating the search process may actually derail the focused work the congregation needs to do. Other reasons to avoid starting the search immediately include:

- Some of the congregation's most perceptive and influential leaders will be elected to the Search

Committee. Their contribution will be invaluable in addressing the congregation's primary issues of healing and essential need for change. Thus, electing a Search Committee at the beginning of the first year will divert the attention and insight of these critical leaders when their leadership will be most needed for moving the congregation toward spiritual health.

- Search Committee members must be reconciled to the congregation's transition issues so they can honestly represent the congregation's real state of being. Engaging the search encourages them to take their finger off the congregation's pulse and miss subtle changes.

- The congregation will see both itself and its needs differently nine months into the interim period. To be good representatives of the congregation, the members of the Search Committee must reflect this difference.

- Waiting eight or nine months into the interim period will allow time to establish a more creative and thorough selection process, and a more deliberate consideration of members elected to the committee.

These reasons underscore the notion that the Search Committee will bear a heavy burden in selecting that ministerial candidate whose leadership will help determine the congregation's destiny. Wisdom dictates electing this committee when the congregation's spiritual health is at its most robust.

If congregations immediately move into the ministerial search process, they are likely to elect committee members who represent an old past rather than a new future. This is an invitation to failure. Congregations are prone to rush the process because they are anxious about the future and wish to feel in control. Being clear about when the committee will be elected will help ease this anxiety and release the congregation to focus on its spiritual health issues.

Ministers in search are likely to be suspicious of congregations who rush the process, asking questions about what the congregation might be in denial about and concerned about unresolved problems that may surface in the next ministry. The most attractive congregations are those that have taken the interim period seriously, worked diligently toward a new future for the congregation, undergone a self-assessment of their past, and hold a vision of their future. These congregations have wisely given special care to what they are and what they want to be. They have taken the time they needed to do interim work well as opposed to doing it quickly.

Often, the desire for a one-year interim indicates that a congregation is not self-reflective, that everyone is content, that there is nothing to address, and that "we just need to get through this so things can go back to the way things were" before the minister announced her departure. Only if none of the stories mentioned in this essay ring true on some level should a congregation enter into serious discussion with regional and national UUA staff about doing a one-year interim.

Large Congregations

MAUREEN KILLORAN

■ ■ ▦ ■

"When it comes to interim ministry, large churches are different!" Because of my own interest in serving large congregations in transition, I was intrigued when a colleague voiced this opinion over lunch one day. "You're wrong," a second minister responded with some heat. "Large churches are churches—whatever the size, transition work is the same." Both turned to me, as the only intentional interim minister at the table. "Which of us is right?" "It's like the blind men and the elephant," I replied. "Both of you are right, and neither has the whole picture." We settled in for what turned out to be a lengthy conversation.

In response to the colleague who insisted that transition work is the same regardless of congregational size, I drew on the work of Alban Institute senior consultant Susan Beaumont, who argues in "Core Competencies of Large Church Leadership" that certain core competencies—consistently effective preaching, willingness to engage conflict, organizational skills, and personal resilience—characterize successful ministerial leadership in large congregations. "Aha!" exclaimed my colleague. "Surely you'll agree that these qualities contribute to the success of any ministry." "You've got a point," I admitted, "but I contend that, in large churches, these qualities are not just useful but essential. In large congregations, expectations tend to be more intense and demands more direct." These differences can be illustrated in four primary areas:

- entering the congregational system

- preaching and worship

- governance and leadership

- the church as a relational entity.

Entering the Congregational System

Every interim minister in some sense steps onto a moving train. The congregation has ongoing programs, plans, and policies, and many lay leaders are invested in their smooth persistence. This energy is intensified in large congregations: five-, ten-, and even twenty-year plans may be on the books, and sometimes are even being followed. The large congregation likely has a strategic plan, and some leaders may offer robust resistance to derailing it, whether as a result of conflict or simply by the departure of the lead minister.

Daryl Conner, a specialist in organizational change, notes in his blog at www.changethinking.net that the larger the organization, the more change agents will encounter "significant political pressure to keep pet projects alive beyond their viable life span." The interim minister needs to work with the governing Board, lay leaders, ministerial colleagues, and staff to acknowledge current realities and, where necessary, to adopt a triage of focus. While every interim should be intentional about developing appropriate lines of relationship that facilitate this work, some characteristics of large churches make this vital.

Unlike settled clergy who, in the Unitarian Universalist tradition, are generally called by and accountable to the congregation, interim ministers work *for* and at the same time *with* the church's governing Board. In large congregations, this group, and the next circle or two of leadership, represents the lay constituents with whom the interim minister will have the greatest personal interaction. Thus, the interim must be alert to the risk of receiving—and potentially accepting—a limited description of the church's problems, self-definition, and needs.

Another significant characteristic of the large church is the probable presence of ministerial colleagues and perhaps other senior staff, such as a long-term administrator or music director. One or more ministerial colleagues may have served on the committee that identified and hired the interim. The interim must be sensitive to the blend of social capital and wisdom embodied in these colleagues and staff members. The perspectives of senior staff offer unique windows on the congregation; they are valuable resources for the interim minister's initial understandings.

A high-functioning Transition Team is essential in the large church, where the interim is likely to have relatively impersonal relationships with the majority of congregants. The team serves as extensions to the eyes and ears of the interim. They work in partnership to access the breadth and depth of the congregation's story, while acknowledging that the feasibility of getting everybody together is inversely proportional to congregation size. (For more about Transition Teams, see "A Different Country.")

Especially with younger or tech-savvy congregants, electronic communication can increase both the saturation and the effectiveness of the minister's interpersonal connection. As the number of congregants increases, diversity of communications becomes increasingly important. The interim will be wise to consider a range of possibilities for communication, including electronic media such as clergy blogs, Twitter feeds, video conferencing, and social networking.

Preaching and Worship

Large churches expect what Beaumont terms "consistently effective preaching [that] projects the identity and character of the congregation through worship leadership presence." Many are justifiably proud of their history of stellar pulpit performance. Although interims will, of course, bring their own preaching style, they must be prepared to respond to high expectations in terms of presentation and content, as well as repeated and explicit comparisons to the "saints" who have gone before.

Depending on its recent history, the large church may expect its interim senior minister consistently to bring a leadership perspective to current issues of injustice and politics. Congregants may expect their interim's preaching to be more prophetic than pastoral, more visionary than specifically grounded in the current life of the congregation. Every congregation attracts what Scott Thumma and Dave Travis, in *Beyond Megachurch Myths: What We Can Learn from America's Largest Congregations*, call "marginal participants"—those who attend church solely for the sermon. But in large congregations, these people may constitute as much as 30 percent of the attendees at worship. One of the interim's challenges is to use the pulpit to deepen congregational involvement in the transition process while recognizing that the gathered community regularly includes several hundred people who are intentionally uninvolved in congregational structures and processes. Reaching out to and inspiring these marginal participants may be a key aspect of a highly successful transition.

In addition, the large church may provide a range of technological, music, and other worship resources. The congregation may be accustomed to particularly formal or elaborate worship. The interim may lead a team of highly skilled paid and volunteer worship participants, including other clergy, a music director, vocal and instrumental musicians, dancers, worship associates, and administrative staff. In addition to practicing excellent personal time management, the interim must establish clear lines of accountability and expectations around regular meetings, communication, and deadlines to ensure consistent quality of the Sunday worship experience.

Governance

Although examples may be cited of large churches that entered their transition period with a well-functioning and size-appropriate governance paradigm, this is often not the case. Both congregations that have come from long-term, stable ministerial leadership and those that enter transition after a period of conflict may have experienced "governance drift." That is, without due diligence, governance itself tends to drift away from what may be more appropriate or effective for a congregation, toward what is convenient or what fits the preferred style of a current leader, or what leaders may recall from another organization or another era in the life of a congregation. Other congregations may be operating with a governance system that reflects either an earlier stage in their life and/or the leadership style of their departed senior minister. This condition may or may not be optimal going forward.

The interim must be governance savvy, well versed in size-appropriate governance options and possibilities. The interim begins as diagnostician, seeking to discover what is working and what is not. Next comes the role of change coach, as the interim opens doors of process and options, encouraging lay leaders to move toward appropriate governance paradigms. The congregation may benefit from the expertise of an outside consultant, which may be financially possible for the large church. The interim should be ready and able to suggest this option and to identify potential resources.

Staff Leadership

Interims in large congregations enter a complex and relatively large staffing system that includes other ordained clergy and possibly long-term staff, all of whom may have accumulated significant social capital. Some staff members are likely to be grieving the departure of the former minister. Others may feel anger, remorse, or relief. Almost all will have some degree of anxiety about their work environment and even their continued employment.

Central to the interim's understanding of the system is clarity about the hopes and expectations of staff, particularly but not exclusively those of ordained colleagues. These collegial understandings must not obscure the reality that over time even senior staff may have become embedded in the system in less than optimal ways, or that the time may be approaching or have arrived for other kinds of staff change.

One of the first priorities of the interim must be establishing collegial relationships with other ordained staff, including a written covenant of understanding. This relationship may need to extend to other senior staff, such as a long-term music director or director of administration. In addition, the congregation may have one or more ministers emeriti or affiliate ministers who may or may not be functioning under covenants or letters of agreement. Clarifying these relationships with the individuals involved, and with the governing Board and congregation, may be an essential and delicate task for the interim period.

Responsibilities for core tasks of ministry may be shared among ordained and other staff members. To some extent, these allocations will have derived from the skills and interests of the departed senior minister and may or may not be clearly articulated. The interim and colleagues will assess these allocations and, in dialogue with appropriate lay leadership, may need or choose to redesign the various portfolios of ministerial and other staff.

In large congregations, human resource management is central because of the significant budgetary expenditures represented by staff and the extent to which large congregations rely on staff to carry out the policies and daily operations of the church. While staff supervision may fall under the purview of a director of operations, interims in large congregations must have experience in developing and motivating staff teams, as well as knowledge about personnel policies and employment law. Regardless of who is formally responsible, interims must ensure that the policies and functioning of human resource management are well designed, current, and fair. (For more about staffing issues, see "Working with Staff.")

Public Ministry

Large churches may have a long tradition of social justice leadership in the wider community. Smaller congregations in the area may look to the large church to serve as a rallying point for other Unitarian Universalist voices. While expectations will vary depending on the degree to which the former senior minister filled these roles, the interim needs to be both competent in and prepared for the responsibilities of public ministry. The interim should take a lead in clarifying and negotiating role expectations with both the governing Board and other clergy on staff at the outset of the interim ministry.

Succession Plans

Some large congregations may have either a succession plan or a tacit understanding that a minister already on staff will be called as their next senior minister. In these situations, the interim can partner with the rising colleague and the Board, to address mutually determined issues, such as staffing changes, governance adjustments, and worship transformation, that could present problems for the rising minister in their new role. (For more about potential problems, see "Predictable Roadblocks.")

The Church as a Relational Entity

Some large churches are characterized by what political scientist Robert Putnam termed "bowling alone," in *Bowling Alone: The Collapse and Revival of American Community*. As a consequence of their considerable internal pools of expertise, comparatively large financial resources, and the fact that the preponderance of denominational resources is designed for smaller congregations, large congregations are vulnerable to patterns of self-sufficiency. It is not uncommon for large congregations to feel disconnected from their wider denomination, and thus to have stepped away from their responsibilities as "flagship churches," in denominational leadership and financial support.

The interim period offers a window for the large church to develop a greater sense of relatedness. Denominational resources may be both appropriate and essential companions as the congregation searches for new ministerial leadership. Lay leaders, some for the first time, may become aware of the richness of resources their denomination can offer. The congregation will be well served by the interim using this window to broaden staff's and lay leaders' knowledge of denominational and other external resources. At the same time, both the congregation and the larger religious movement will benefit from the church's deeper awareness of and commitment to its role as a programmatic and financial leader.

When it comes to interim ministry, there are many ways in which large churches are indeed different. Because large congregations tend to enter their transitions with high expectations of clergy performance, detailed plans, and complex staff configuration, they are qualitatively as well as quantitatively distinct from their smaller counterparts. From the outset, the large church requires particular sensitivity on the part of the interim minister seeking to enter its system. Congregational size and complexity tend toward particular challenges, for example, in the areas of preaching, governance, staff leadership, and congregational relatedness. At the same time, these very differences bear witness to the fact that large congregations, including those with existing succession plans, can be well served by a skilled and qualified interim minister.

Small Congregations

KAREN BRAMMER

■ ■ ▨ ■

The ministry to small congregations, including interim ministry, differs from that of congregations with over 150 members precisely because of the internal dynamics of being smaller. A minister's role in pastoral care, decision making, communication, and the welcoming and integration of newcomers will naturally vary by congregation size. Although the relative health of a congregation does not depend on its size, adjusting to meet the needs of a congregation based on its size can affect its health.

Interim work may be needed for the health and vitality of a smaller congregation, whether or not a minister trained for interim service does the work, and whether or not congregational leaders recognize the work to be done as interim work. If trained interim ministry is an option, the congregation has a much greater chance of success with that interim.

The smaller congregation is likely to revolve first and foremost around connections between people, resulting in a tendency toward informality about church matters. How information is communicated, for instance, may be inconsistent or rely on people seeing each other, which can be hard on newcomers trying to learn how things work. This state may continue even as the congregation grows unless leaders are convinced that more formal structures will help. Even if more structure is perceived as good, leaders will need to consistently commit to new behavior to avoid reverting to a pattern that is comfortable for those who have been around since the congregation was smaller.

Lay Leader Accountability and Partnership

In an interim period, a small congregation must quickly learn how decisions are made and carried out, and by whom. Generally, the governing Board makes decisions, and the designated committees or individuals follow through. In some congregations, however, a governing Board makes decisions that unofficially change "in the parking lot" after the meeting and follow-through is interrupted or taken over by someone other than the responsible committee or person. This happens when the Board in a small congregation consists of committee chairs who then act on the Board's decisions. Who is accountable for what is not always clear.

Many small congregations have survived over time because a small number of members have taken personal responsibility for every aspect of the life of the congregation. As the congregation starts a new chapter during interim ministry, that core leadership may have a hard time changing their behavior. They may need to be asked directly (privately or in a smaller meeting) to let go of the savior role. It can help to publicly thank those core leaders, recognizing the ways they have taken responsibility. A long-term leader may be able to mentor an upcoming leader, or be responsible for a different aspect of the congregation. For some leaders, this letting go is a relief, and for others it's a major identity crisis.

One minister coordinated a "retirement party" for a long-term member who was having difficulty relinquishing control. As a result of the public acknowledgement of change, fellow congregants were less likely to turn to that person for decisions and resources. Pastoral support was important to help the long-term leader find another way to see her own value. She was able to understand and value the need for the congregation to become responsible for its own health, even if they failed a few times.

The interim should encourage long-term core leaders to share leadership. This sharing goes hand in hand with more members of the congregation acting as if all members are responsible for its health. These two efforts get easier as the congregation learns to intentionally train new leaders and more consistently uses an exciting vision to drive the work. Together these changes will make it less likely that one individual overturns group decisions. (See "Changes in Leadership" for more guidance.)

Unintentional Interim Ministry

Small congregations are often unable to find interim ministers, particularly if the ministry is part-time. The number of interims interested in interim ministry positions decreases dramatically for less than three-quarter-time ministries. This means the transition work that interims are trained to address often falls to part-time ministers who are not trained for it. Nearly as often, if not more so, congregational leaders have not anticipated the need for interim work, which may eventually get expressed through intense pressure on the ministry. In other words, the next settled minister may end up needing to do interim work.

All too often, a new minister comes to serve a congregation where interim ministry has not taken place. This minister must undertake interim work without having been trained in it or fully comprehending what it is or why it is important. When the minister does not do this work intentionally or well, the minister has a short and unsatisfactory ministry. We sometimes call this an "unintentional interim ministry." When new ministers in such circumstances are astute and make it their business to learn about interim work, they can turn a potential case of unsuccessful *unintentional* interim ministry into a story of successful *intentional* interim ministry.

This happened to one fifty-member congregation whose previous minister had served six years part-time, although she worked many more hours than she was compensated for. She focused primarily on pastoral care, doing little work on lay leadership development or clarifying how lay and professional leaders would share the congregation's ministry. Once she decided to leave, the congregation chose against an interim ministry, wanting someone who would serve part-time for longer than the one or two years of interim ministry. In the year it took to find a minister, a few lay members stepped in and ran the congregation, swinging even further away from sharing authority with a professional minister.

When a new minister began, tensions rose early on. Members expressed unhappiness that he did not do enough pastoral care, while claiming they could not do without him if he left. Members who had stepped in for the past year were not comfortable handing power over to a minister who might not stay, yet those leaders complained of being tired.

Frustrated by the mixed messages and feeling routinely undermined, the minister spoke with a trained local interim and began thinking about the dynamics of the congregation as if he himself were an interim. Developing shared ministry was one of the congregation's stated goals on which he had based his first year of ministry. Because the congregational leaders seemed unaware of what would be needed to "share ministry," the minister realized that a different goal was more appropriate —pointing out behaviors that consistently contradicted their stated goals, and teaching skills that would bring them closer to being partners in ministry.

He had to decide whether he could sufficiently challenge lay leadership to change without risking his ability to pastor to them and serve over the long term. Interim ministers ordinarily do this work, knowing that the disequilibrium can make congregants unhappy with them. But their stay is temporary, so they leave behind congregational leaders who are more ready for ministry that can help them move where they said they wanted to go.

With close help from denominational staff, this unintended interim minister adopted a strategy designed to challenge the leadership and congregation, and at the same time support his ability to remain in this ministry over time. A team of lay leaders was invited to district and regional trainings, engaging in a learning partnership for three consecutive years. The team worked slowly and consistently to educate the congregation, with minimal buy-in. But when a crisis of leadership happened, the team was ready to reframe it to the congregation in terms of congregational patterns rather than blaming an individual lay leader or the minister. This response required intentionality and calm in the face of discomfort, but the leadership remained consistent and saw long-stuck congregational dynamics suddenly begin to shift.

Partnering with district staff and a trained lay leader team increased the minister's capacity to support congregants and encourage change without the minister wearing a target on his back. Lay leaders listened and reframed the anxiety of those who thought the minister's encouragement to decrease their dependence on him was callous or a signal that he was leaving.

Ministers who take on what becomes unintentional interim work in small congregations will fare much better if they resist isolation, especially if they are part-time, which makes it hard to participate in ministers' gatherings because of lack of professional expenses or time. Ministers engaged in unintentional interim work need to seek regular support and outside perspective. This is particularly important as small congregations turn more frequently to seminarians, talented lay leaders raised into ministry without adequate support, and local non-Unitarian Universalist ministers.

Congregational Self-Stories

Through the years, I have observed leaders of small congregations who will not let go of their power. It has to do with being stuck in a victim mentality rather than moving through survival and into "thrival" mode. I know some leaders of vibrant small congregations who think of themselves as competent, even inspired, partners with their professional minister and the denomination. But some other leaders in smaller congregations become demoralized by reacting to what they perceive as a common preference in this country for whatever is larger rather than smaller. Some congregational leaders construe this preference as a rejection of the value of their small congregations. For some, this leads to resentment of the prevailing culture. For others, it leads to buying into the rejection themselves with resulting lowered self-esteem. Either way, the ultimate result is congregational leaders who, without help and encouragement, are not likely to work to increase vitality in their congregations.

So much more is understood now about what it takes to support people or organizations as they move from victimization to strength and vitality. Being smaller within an overall culture that devalues smallness does not, of course, carry the same impact as, for example, the abuse and betrayal of ministerial misconduct. The persistent sense that bigger is better has negatively impacted the morale of some congregations, but is now becoming less an issue in our faith movement. More often, small congregations hear that they matter to the denomination, and fewer hang onto feeling devalued by the larger system.

However, in the past some ministers who lost their positions due to misconduct were sometimes informally guided to take positions in small congregations, where it was hoped they would cause less damage and could perhaps redeem their ministry. The small congregations were often rural ones. Often the outcome actually redeemed neither the ministers nor the congregations. As a result, some small congregations still distrust denominational structures and ministers. (See further discussion in "Congregations with a History of Misconduct.")

Congregation Infrastructure and Negatively Powerful People

Unfortunately, small congregations may follow practices that intensify this distrust. Leaders may hold onto their positions simply to outlast a minister they do not trust or like. The informal infrastructure common in small congregations provides little leverage to alter the situation, even if other leaders want change. If the congregation has infrastructure that clearly states term limits and articulates the nominating process, there may be more opportunity to help the congregation evolve. Without that infrastructure, too many skilled ministers and lay leaders give up trying to help and decide to leave congregations when leaders do not allow change.

Another practice that continues without appropriate infrastructure has to do with ministerial searches. Leaders of small congregations who do not use denominational best practices for their search process may invite someone who preaches occasional Sundays to be their part-time minister without checking references. Clergy who are not in good standing with their denomination—or who do not want to follow denominational procedures but want to be in ministry—are more likely to find small congregations open to working with them. The lack of infrastructure and formal policies may invite a problematic minister with no stated expectations, contract, or accountability.

Even if some congregants realize that this minister is causing damage, others may feel allegiance to the minister. What are their options? There is no established set of expectations and no process of review. Congregations split over such difficulties, or develop cultures of secrecy and distrust that can last for many decades. These congregational leaders should reach out to their denominational staff for help.

Where ministerial misconduct, addictive behavior, or a history of mediocre ministry is part of the congregation's story, interim work may require support for people to tell the stories in ways that help them build a culture of truth telling, compassion, and forgiveness. The work must include helping the congregation to extract themselves from a cycle of victimization and to learn to deal with negatively powerful people.

Negatively powerful lay people (and damaging ministers) affect a congregation's ability to thrive and grow, and create a damaging partnership between minister and lay leaders. When this happens, the congregation tends not to feel strong and may be more likely to feel victimized. As a result, congregants may want to have a minister or lay leader "fix" or "save" them rather than to rely on their own agency and resilience. But the next time something goes wrong, the congregation can blame the "savior," and the sad story continues. If negatively powerful people do everything in a congregation that sees itself as unsteady, the congregation is not likely to risk losing them. Members of that congregation may feel obliged to forgive them or inclined to deny that bad behavior exists.

More often than this scenario, however, is the tendency for people in small congregations to try to be kind, rather than honest, with someone exhibiting bad behavior. Not holding people accountable can actually drive them to worse behavior as they seek the structure they need, or the power they desire. Redefining kindness and accountability can be so contrary to the way people in small communities operate that significant work must be done to help leaders combat their own resistance to setting limits.

Interim work can help members learn that not being truthful is not the same as being kind, and that denying the truth can in fact damage both the person whose behavior is disruptive and the congregation. Congregational leaders can learn new, clear ways of responding to bad behavior. They can adopt anti-disruptive behavior policies, covenants, and contracts. But writing those documents is only one step. They must use them consistently.

For instance, if a person with a known record for sex offense wants to be part of the community, congregational leaders and the person should sign a contract stating when that person can be in the building(s) and with whom. Leaders should be clear about how they will communicate this information to the congregation, how they will monitor compliance, and what will happen if the contract is broken. Further, this information has to transfer to the next leadership.

Boundaries help a community to be safe, and help people who have damaging behavior stay out of trouble while they remain in community. Sometimes a well-bounded congregation is the only place a person with difficult behavior can remain safe. When boundaries effectively maintain safety for both the individual and the community, the congregation expresses the beloved community we dream about.

Negative people sometimes retain power because small congregations value informal relationships and the creativity or rights of one person over the vision or decisions of the group. Leaders of small congregations are more able to share power appropriately with the minister as they learn how to balance the polar opposites of individual and community rights and needs. Interims are well situated to introduce this way of framing conflict and to encourage different behavior.

If a small group can embrace a compelling vision for their future, this can override the power held by a few individuals and uphold the desires stated by the whole group. But this vision is hard to state and claim when the congregation holds a sad story about themselves. As an interim affirms the strengths and dreams of the congregation, and the congregation chooses a more positive story about itself, a shift is more likely to happen. Congregants may be more able to identify goals that are important enough to risk disempowering damaging folks. Unhealthy or stuck small congregations must build a positive congregational story to stop bad behavior.

As interim ministry works on the congregation's self-story and builds its capacity to hold individuals accountable, the congregation is more able to become a covenantal community. A strong statement of covenant backed by a clear and consistently used anti-disruptive behavior policy will help a small congregation live guided by love.

Right-Sized Infrastructure

The small congregation working with an interim minister should take into account its current direction. Is it growing or able to sustain growth if supported well? Do demographics indicate that the congregation is trying to act larger than it can reasonably become, or that it needs to reduce its real estate, governance, staffing, or programs? Is the congregation profoundly stuck and not likely to change until certain internal or external factors change? Is it time to enter a hospice phase and end with dignity? An interim ministry helps congregational leaders assess whether they can grow, downsize, stop trying to change for now, or dissolve.

Working with congregational leaders on their idea of church, how they build relationships, and their governance can help them make choices about becoming the right size for their current reality. As interim ministry helps them shift, they become more adaptable to ongoing changes.

For some generations the image of "church" has revolved around the building and worship. To the extent that leaders and congregation can imagine church as less defined by a certain type of building, or a building at all, the more an image of their true purpose will inspire them. Leaders often feel driven and exhausted by the belief that they must support a specific model of worship and religious education every Sunday. What might evolve if they were freed of assumed responsibility and encouraged to put their resources into responding to deep needs, meaningful connection, and engaging the world they live in? For example, they might alternate worship with group gatherings or justice work every other Sunday.

Interim ministers ask compassionate questions about buildings and traditions, support alternatives to the exclusive patterns of friendship, and encourage connection in other meaningful ways. Newcomers and people outside existing friendship groups can more easily participate in small group ministry, or in short-term groups that work together on a justice or congregational project and do theological and group reflection about it. These are great ways to build groups across generational lines as well. Congregations can break out of their fossilized idea of what they are supposed to be, and claim a living, evolving image.

Adhering to past styles of governance can lock congregations into decline rather than steer them toward potential growth. Boards of small congregations may spend most if not all of their meetings managing details of the congregation, such as how to pay bills, or how to fill committee vacancies. If their time is consumed by these details, at what point do leaders observe the congregation as a whole?

When do they organize the congregation to identify a rising sense of purpose and move toward it? And who decides by what standard of community they live together? The Board will serve better when leaders know that helping the congregation determine where it is going and who it intends to be is at least as important, if not more, than the endless day-to-day tasks of keeping the doors open and running the programs. Interim ministry can help a Board balance this work.

The sheer size of the Board and committees can stifle congregational health and growth. Sustaining infrastructure that is too big is exhausting and can feel like digging holes to fill them up again. Cumbersome governance is unresponsive to new ideas or current realities of lay leaders, such as changing expectations of volunteer time, or needing to feel a sense of meaning from volunteer work. Governance that is too small may lack clear procedures to help newcomers and others know how to participate, and may encourage well-meaning individuals or mavericks to accomplish what they want rather than moving forward with what the congregation prioritizes. Interim ministry can help frame congregational conversation that equips leaders to make better governance decisions and lead in ways that help the congregation discern and meet its next ministry.

Sometimes, the next ministry for a congregation is to right-size itself, to continue to be a congregation but let go of something that is not working even though it has been historically important. Clear, compassionate leadership helps a congregation stop doing what is not effective, such as by ending a traditional fundraiser, selling a building, or cutting back professional ministry. Once they do, new energy may surface for the next right thing in their ministry together.

One congregation of ninety members figured this out. This congregation is located at the literal crossroads of their town. The leaders remember when the congregation was the most influential institution in town, initiating justice work and education in the community. But since then the town has experienced terrible economic decline. To adjust to the new economic reality, the Board in agreement with the then full-time minister, decreased professional ministry to three-quarter time. The Board asked the minister to figure out and communicate the details of the changes to the congregation. As people felt the loss of the minister's diminished presence, they expressed anger at the minister. For a year, the congregation, Board, and minister struggled with frustration and hurt feelings. The minister was close to resignation and asked for help from denominational staff.

Staff began to work with the Board and the minister on covenant and refocused on the purpose of the congregation. Then they worked together to articulate the core of their ministry, clarifying what the congregation needed the minister to do, and what specifically the minister would let go of. The third aspect of their work was to educate the congregation on the core functions of ministry, and to communicate the decisions for part-time ministry (now down to half-time) to the congregation.

The Board also realized it was their job, rather than the minister's, to field dissatisfaction, since they were the ones who decided to cut back the minister's time. Taking this responsibility was new for the Board because for many decades, everything happened by the authority and instigation of the minister. Following the decision by the Board and minister to reduce the minister's time, the Board understood their moral authority and responsibility—in partnership with the minister—for ministry of the whole. Almost two years later, the minister reported more energy in the congregation than ever, because the congregation claimed its deepest reasons for being a congregation. Letting go in this case was the right interim work that ignited imagination and conviction.

However, for some congregations letting go is not enough. They need instead to face the fact that it is time to dissolve as an entity. One congregation suffered for decades from terribly difficult core issues. Ministers, consultants, and denominational staff were invited over time and attempted to help. The financial situation was dire. Sadly, core and long-term members did not allow new lay leadership to take hold, and difficult behaviors of the long-term leaders drove other newcomers away.

Denominational staff and a minister emeritus started working together. They supported the leaders to bring members together to discuss, and then vote to dissolve as an entity. They did this before running out of money so that the building could be passed on more or less intact, and the historic artifacts lovingly distributed. The minister emeritus officiated a celebration of the life of the congregation as it closed with dignity rather than struggling against the inevitable in denial and shame. With broad training in congregational health, denominational staff often helps the congregation determine what might be helpful— even if that is dissolution—and may then arrange for appropriate consulting, ministerial, or staff support.

Rural Possibilities

Not all smaller congregations are located in rural areas, but many are. Anyone contemplating interim ministry in a rural area must consider certain aspects of rural congregational life, whether the rural area is failing or thriving. Perhaps most helpful would be to evaluate whether and how the members and programs of the congregation are interconnected with the area. If the congregation is not well connected, the interim minister needs to be prepared to help the leadership to overcome a sense of "us versus them" that may play out around religion as well as politics, economic class, "locals" versus those who have arrived within the last two generations, and levels of education.

While a sense of isolation is not unique to congregations of any size, the interim minister who goes to serve a smaller rural Unitarian Universalist congregation is likely to find that it is the only religiously liberal institution in an otherwise conservative region. If congregants conflate liberal religion with liberal politics and conservative religion with conservative politics, they may have difficulty connecting outside the congregation. If they only focus inwardly or succumb to arrogance, they will aggravate the polarization.

The interim minister who serves in a rural area for the first time will also likely discover that government is less able to reach into rural areas the further people are from urban centers. This can impact the relative sense of safety of those who identify as being in the minority, either politically or regarding their personal identity. They may feel they will get second-rate treatment under the law or when receiving help in disasters. Thus in rural areas there is often a level of self-reliance that can be quite surprising to a minister who moves there from an urban area.

Rural areas sometimes have specific terms to describe people whose families have lived there for generations and people who have arrived in the last couple years (or couple generations)— terms such as *locals* and *from away*. Bringing up such terms for honest, caring conversation might be unpopular since racial and class tensions are likely to surface. But if interim work is about helping a congregation see itself honestly and claim its intentions for the future, such conversations could provide perfect fodder for that work. They could lead to profound personal, spiritual, and congregational growth.

Conflicting values are not exclusive to smaller or rural congregations. But these congregations often have a special ability to grapple with the conflicts they face because the members are neighbors and have principles that may bind them in compassionate dialogue. Interims are in an ideal position to ask innocent questions, not only about unhealthy dynamics in a congregation but also about congregational patterns of relating to the local community. These may have gone unacknowledged in order to keep the peace, yet have served also to maintain imbalances and foster secret hurts. If addressed honestly and with compassion, unearthed issues can grow people of faith spiritually, across boundaries, and numerically.

The "Start-Up" Workshop

The "start-up" is a workshop designed to help a minister and congregation with relationship, expectations, and goals. Not all start-ups are the same, and not all regions have the denominational staff capacity to offer start-up workshops for all congregations in transition. However, the components of a start-up workshop can be very useful to jump-start a successful interim ministry in a small congregation. The smart interim minister will get in touch with local or regional denominational staff early on to schedule a start-up workshop if possible.

Start-up workshops often use storytelling to share history that helps integrate newcomers, including a new minister, and can give leadership a window into their congregation's strengths and self-image. Start-ups can identify congregational norms that are important for the new minister to know about. Sometimes articulating those norms at a start-up workshop can lead to a congregation intentionally deciding to change norms that are unhealthy. The workshop helps the congregants state expectations they hold for the minister, and helps the minister express expectations of the congregation, but can also clarify when expectations are unrealistic. Start-ups can create covenants between leaders and agreements about process and goals.

Because start-ups are typically attended by denominational staff or by someone who will report back to staff, they can forge a working relationship between staff, minister, and Board president. This can be particularly helpful when the incoming minister is not trained to do interim work. The minister and president will reach out for perspective and assistance from denominational staff as things develop. The workshop is an opportunity to articulate a clear process for evaluating ministry and undertaking the next ministerial transition. It may help the congregation to reflect on itself and evolve, making more space for interim work to be done well.

The many hundreds of small congregations are for the most part well situated to significantly impact the communities in which they live. My hope is that the leaders of small congregations will claim their inspired hopes, and with support become equipped to adapt to a changing world. May small congregations be the engines of faithful connection, growth, and depth they are so well placed to be.

Size Transitions

SUZANNE REDFERN-CAMPBELL

■ ■ ▦ ■

Since the 1980s, much conversation about church growth has focused on congregational size. Alban Institute consultants and others have helped us see that churches of different sizes are, in effect, different animals. Lyle Schaller, in *Looking in the Mirror: Self-Appraisal in the Local Church*, used a church typology based on animal names, such as cats and collies, with widely different ways of being and doing church. Thus a small rural parish with 50 active members has a very different structure and culture from that of a large metropolitan church of 2,000 members, and both differ from a suburban congregation of 350.

The most influential size typology, at least in Unitarian Universalist circles, was set forth by Arlin Rothauge in *Sizing Up a Congregation for New Member Ministry*, in 1983, when he was working at the Episcopal Church Center. His framework, based on worship attendance, includes congregations of family size (0 to 50 worshippers), pastoral size (50 to 150), program size (150 to 350), and corporate size (350 to 500+). More recently, the Alban Institute has kept the basic scheme while revising the numbers, setting the boundary between Pastoral Size and Program Size at 400 worshippers rather than 350, and establishing the Corporate Size range as 400 to 1,000, according to Alice Mann in *Raising the Roof: The Pastoral-to-Program Size Transition*.

If these numerical categories are at least in general correct and meaningful, then several likely consequences follow. One is that congregations need to "act their size" in developing structures, carrying out ministries, and setting expectations of clergy, staff, and lay leadership. For example, a congregation of 600 that expects its clergy to know every member on a personal basis is setting itself up for disappointment, and its ministers for burnout. Conversely, a church that once numbered 600, but now struggles to survive with 80, is likely to have structures and expectations out of keeping with its current size. This church could well have the potential for vibrant ministry, but only if it shuns the temptation to lament its glory days and organizes itself according to present reality.

Another consequence of size analysis is that congregational growth is incremental only up to a point. At the upper range of each size category, a church will likely reach a steady state, or plateau, in which one member leaves for each one who joins. When this happens, the church serious about membership growth must transform itself. For example, a church of 120 active members might increase its rolls to 150 members through a concerted effort to strengthen its ministries of invitation and hospitality. But if it wishes to grow beyond that point, it must make a size transition—a fundamental shift in its way of being and operating.

This essay explores questions about congregational size transitions during the interim period. When a congregation is between called ministers, is it appropriate for its leaders to work on size transitions? Is it an appropriate issue for an interim minister to raise with them and work on? If the interim and lay leadership do decide to work on a size transition, what can they realistically expect to accomplish, and what steps can they take to achieve it? Finally, might size analysis have other uses during the interim period, so that doing the work is helpful even when making a size transition is undesired or unrealistic?

These questions were sparked by my work as interim minister with the Unitarian Universalist Congregation of Danbury, a pastoral-sized church in southwestern Connecticut. Since I use their story as a lens through which to view broader questions, I'll focus especially on the specific size transition they were exploring—the shift from pastoral to program.

I start from the hypothesis that if a pastoral-sized congregation is fundamentally healthy, the interim period is an ideal time for its leaders to explore a possible shift to program size. I base this supposition on the assumption that the interim period is the time that congregations are most poised to re-examine their ways, addressing systemic and cultural issues.

Every congregation I've served (four as a settled minister and two as an interim) has said that it wants to grow. But all too often this desire is accompanied by a fantasy that to do so, "All this church needs is a dynamic, charismatic new minister." There is little recognition that sustainable growth comes from within, with shifts in system, culture, and identity, and that therefore the congregation itself has significant work to do beyond choosing its next called minister.

The role of clergy in a pastoral-sized church must also be considered. In his article "How to Minister Effectively in Family, Pastoral, Program, and Corporate Sized Churches," Roy M. Oswald, former Alban Institute consultant, points out that "the cost of moving from a Pastoral to Program Church usually comes out of the pastor's hide." This stems from the changed behavior required of any minister trying to make the shift. When clergy do what is required—withdrawing their energy from individual pastoral care and redirecting it toward worship preparation, organizational development, and outreach—congregational anxiety tends to rise. If this anxiety is not managed well, ministers may become scapegoats.

Intentional interim ministers are uniquely positioned to absorb the cost of the pastoral-to-program transition. They are trained to be carriers of congregational anxiety; indeed, they expect to take on this role. They can help change members' expectations about who should attend to pastoral needs, and as a non-anxious presence, can weather the slings and arrows accompanying the shift. As a result, the new called minister will come to a congregation that has let go of its size-limiting expectations, at least to some extent.

With these general considerations in mind, let us look at the case of the Unitarian Universalist Congregation of Danbury, Connecticut (UUCD).

Like many Unitarian Universalist congregations in Connecticut, UUCD has its roots in Universalism. Its presence in the small manufacturing city of Danbury began in 1822, with twelve dissenters holding clandestine Sunday meetings. The First Universalist Society eventually joined the row of respectable churches along Main Street, but closed its doors in 1967. Soon thereafter, the remnant of this congregation combined forces with a new Unitarian fellowship to form the UU Society of Northern Fairfield County (UUSNFC). In 1970, this group bought farm property in the affluent rural town of West Redding, and began to worship in a building known as the Barn.

After growing its membership to some 150 members, UUSNFC reached the classic pastoral-size plateau and stayed there. In many ways, this suited them well, as they enjoyed good fellowship at the Barn. But at some point, they became restless, sensing that their location and buildings limited their potential. In 1997, the leadership formed a Vision Task Force, which came up with the idea of pulling up stakes and moving back into Danbury. This task force imagined "a vital, relevant, caring religious community" with lots of space for new people. It called on the congregation to grow, both in numbers and in quality of ministry. Their dream included enhanced programs for children and youth, increased diversity and building accessibility, and a more significant "presence as a force for good and activism in the wider community."

After a three-year process of conversation and planning, the congregation made the vision its own. They sold the Barn, purchased a two-acre plot just north of downtown Danbury, and called a new minister, who was excited about the congregation's plans. In the fall of 2003, they began holding services at the local university, and by the fall of 2005, they had completed phase one of their building program.

By early 2008, some of the congregation's hopes had been realized, while others had not. Their justice ministries, focused on Danbury's immigrant communities, had expanded. But their hope for numerical growth had proven elusive, with membership hovering around 145. In addition, they encountered difficulties in getting code approval for phase two of their building, and their minister resigned for personal reasons. They were left feeling discouraged.

In their interim ministry application, the leadership named a continued desire for growth, and disappointment that it hadn't happened, as among their pressing issues. When I interviewed with the Interim Search Team, they asked me if anything had "jumped out at me" in reading their materials. I said I thought their lack of numerical growth sounded like a textbook case of the pastoral-size plateau, and they agreed. Within the week, they chose me as their interim for a one-year term, later extended to two years.

Taking to heart what I had been taught in my first interim ministry training, I started by "joining the system" before trying to analyze or change it, and resisted the temptation to make substantive changes until I had built relationships. A key element of this approach was the many one-to-one meetings held with lay leaders during the first few months. In these conversations, a desire for membership growth was a consistent theme, with several people telling me, in various ways, "It's time for UUCD to stop thinking of itself as a private social club." This stance reinforced my impression that the congregation—or at least part of it—was ready to explore the possibility of a size transition.

Wanting to gain more knowledge of the pastoral-to-program transition, I seized the opportunity to enroll in one of Alice Mann's Raising the Roof seminars. I returned with a useful, research-based tool, Alban's "System Change Index" (SCI), found in Mann's book, *Raising the Roof: The Pastoral-to-Program Size Transition*. This instrument is designed "to foster conversation about the congregation's progress through the transition zone between pastoral and program size." Using nine factors, such as the minister's role and the size of the paid staff, it invites church members to assess their congregation's readiness to navigate the pastoral-to-program shift.

Introducing the SCI to various leadership groups, I found it to be a useful conversation tool. It helped me get a sense of what congregational leaders had already learned about growth and their readiness to work on it. I also gained further insight into the congregational system and how it worked.

At the Board level, the SCI helped surface resistance to growth on the part of those members who hadn't been privy to earlier conversations. One of them, a relative newcomer to the congregation, said, "I'm very skeptical about this whole growth thing. There are some of us out there who really don't want to grow; we like being part of a small, intimate community." That gave other Board members the opportunity to talk about why growing the church was important to them. A new Board member said, "Well, the numbers really aren't important. If the quality of what we offer is high, then we'll grow without really trying." I acknowledged the partial truth of this. Indeed, numbers aren't everything and quality is important. But I also pressed them on the need to expand the congregational container, so it could hold the new people coming in.

With regard to congregational self-understanding, I worked to lay a theological foundation for growth. From the pulpit and in meetings, I regularly lifted up the dream that had led the congregation to leave the Barn and move back into the city. In doing so, I lifted up the words of Peter Morales, spoken in his successful campaign for Unitarian Universalist Association president: "Growing our movement is not an institutional need. Growing Unitarian Universalism is a moral imperative. It is the moral equivalent of feeding the hungry and housing the homeless." I also consistently pointed out that numerical growth work can never be undertaken for its own sake, or to help the congregation meet its financial obligations. Rather, it stems from a deep practice of hospitality, of welcoming those who hunger for the Unitarian Universalist way in religion, but who don't yet know we exist.

I was also very deliberate in my approach to clergy role definition. Congregational understanding of the minister's role can be either a bottleneck or an enhancement to growth. Churches who expect ordained clergy to meet all of their pastoral needs directly are in effect asking their minister to serve only current members—those who are already there. In letting go of such expectations, they free clergy to focus on outreach and evangelism—ministry to those who are not yet there, but could be.

The former minister had been passionate about pastoral ministry, with a substantial focus on one-to-one care, and the congregation had deeply valued her work. But when I met with the Caring Committee, its members expressed a desire to carry more of the pastoral load; they had loved the former minister but wished she had given them more to do. Picking up on this, I took a stance opposite that of my colleague, employing a minimalist, although not hands-off, approach to pastoral care. I encouraged the Caring Committee to see itself as the primary care ministry of the church, while I responded mainly to hospitalizations and crisis situations. This approach was comfortable for me, because it was in keeping with my community organization training, where I learned to see the minister's role as that of leader/organizer rather than chaplain.

When I arrived, I sensed that UUCD was moving away from single-cell operation. Although members appreciated the congregation's sense of intimacy, most of them understood that it had become impossible for every person to know everyone else. They realized that when a congregation grows, the need for closeness must be fulfilled in different ways. In response, they had established Chalice Circles, a successful small-group ministry program providing multiple points of entry and connection. But despite this movement in one area of UUCD's life, such progress was lagging in other areas. The Board, for example, was still attempting to function on a single-cell model, feeling directly responsible for everything that happened in the congregation, and the culprit was the bylaws. Needlessly detailed and prescriptive throughout, they saddled the Board with an eighteen-point list of responsibilities guaranteed to bog them down in micro-management. As a result, I spent many hours on bylaw revision, working with a committee to redefine the Board's role and to streamline the entire document.

UUCD had a history of creating specialized task forces and planning teams. When I arrived, the most recent example was the 2020 Vision Team, which a few years earlier had conducted a congregation-wide planning process. Building on this history, I proposed the formation of a Growth Team that would study the congregation through the SCI lens and make recommendations to the Board. This team, once appointed, went right to work, and was in the midst of its deliberations when my ministry ended.

This congregation was full of talented people, but its aspirations toward excellence were sometimes compromised by its culture. Three years before my arrival, a significant church fight had erupted when the minister and Board attempted to eliminate the Milestones (or Joys and Concerns) section of the Sunday service. In the face of a congregation-wide petition drive, the leadership had backed down, and Milestones had remained, with a negative impact on the quality of worship. Soon after my arrival, the Sunday Services Committee chair approached me, saying, "I've been reflecting on congregational growth and thinking that every committee in the congregation ought to contribute to it. Do you have any suggestions for making the worship services more visitor-friendly?" Recognizing the gift that had just been presented me, I suggested that Milestones were interfering with worship quality. Acknowledging the political difficulties of trying to drop them, I suggested that it might be helpful to place them toward the end of the service, rather than at the beginning. The chair picked up on this immediately, saying, "Yes! Visitors come for the sermon, not for Milestones— but Milestones go on so long that the minister doesn't get to start preaching until 11:45!" Almost immediately after making the change, we noticed that Milestones had become more prayerful—and much shorter. No one, to my knowledge, ever complained.

Soon after my arrival as interim, lay leaders began to complain about the membership infrastructure. The Membership Committee, they said, seemed disorganized and unfocused. In interviews with members of this committee, the reasons became clear. The group making up the committee had joined it in a bloc, staging something of a coup. Dismissing the existing membership procedures as cookie-cutter approaches, this group dismantled them without offering anything to take their place. Furthermore, they had completely redefined the committee's mission, seeing their role as being "to examine every aspect of congregational life." Slowly, painstakingly, and with as much diplomacy as I could muster, I worked with this group to bring it back to its focus of welcoming and incorporating new members. Until this was accomplished, I knew that I would have to take a very hands-on approach to new member ministry, consistent with the pastoral-church model in which newcomers are welcomed and incorporated primarily through the work of the minister. Systems appropriate to a program-sized church would have to wait. Eventually the committee acquired new leaders who understood the value of a methodical approach to membership. They reinstated some of the dismantled systems and began to create new ones.

In the two-year interim period, UUCD increased in size from 145 members to 165. Although this is not a spectacular level of growth, and hardly amounts to a definitive pastoral-to-program size transition, it did help the congregation get past a certain psychological barrier. No longer could they lament, "We've never been able to get past the 150 mark," for they had done it! In the spring of 2010, when they called an experienced minister with a gift for preaching and a track record of growing pastoral-sized churches, the future looked bright.

Recently, I called the new minister to find out how things are going. She reported that membership figures have declined slightly but that religious education attendance is increasing and financial pledging is very strong among new members. The new minister predicts that the size transition work will pay off in five years.

Case studies, based as they are on a specific set of facts, can never be prescriptive for other situations. Nevertheless, my experience with the Danbury congregation suggests that size analysis is a useful part of the interim's repertoire, and that under some circumstances, size transition work is appropriate during the interim period. The SCI can be helpful in discerning congregational readiness, and can assist ministers and congregations in determining areas of focus.

As with any interim work, size transition work needs to be done in partnership with lay leadership. With UUCD, it helped immensely that most lay leaders were not only familiar with the concept of size transitions but had been asking appropriate questions long before the interim period began.

My Danbury experience further suggests that size transition work must be undertaken with the long term in mind, without any expectation of immediate results. The shift from pastoral to program size involves major shifts in congregational culture and will therefore take longer than a one- or two-year interim period allows. Living into the transition requires ongoing effort in partnership with the new called minister.

Finally, I believe that as long as a congregation is healthy, this work is worth the effort, even if it never results in a size transition. It can help a congregation become more welcoming and mission-focused, even when it doesn't lead to growth in numbers. Through size transition work, interim ministers can help a congregation grow into more effective ministry, knowing that most of the transformation will happen long after the interim time is over.

Congregations with a
History of Misconduct

DEBORAH J. POPE-LANCE

■ ■ ▓ ■

Misconduct by a religious leader can have a significant adverse impact on a congregation, often considerably more persistent and pervasive than initially thought. An interim period provides opportunities to address this adverse impact.

A religious leader's misconduct is experienced initially by congregation members as deeply disappointing, regrettable, and embarrassing. The immediate aftermath disrupts programs, angers and hurts people, and often divides the membership. Attempts to limit the upset and manage the conflict often discourage open discussion and the expression of feelings, fostering a culture of secret keeping and non-transparency in decision making. This can negatively affect relationships among members and with subsequent ministers. Too often, "moving forward" means that those with minority views must leave the congregation. The loss of membership leads to crippling losses in resources. Day-to-day functioning of a congregation becomes chronically impaired, and this jeopardizes future viability. These cultural changes and unhealthy practices further incapacitate a congregation in ways that are not remedied by the usual approaches—such as healthy congregation workshops, regional staff interventions, and able clergy.

In general, interims and leaders serving congregations with a history of misconduct will want to understand that history, consider what specific impact it has had or continues to have, learn what previous efforts, if any, have been made, and assess what might be done or begun in this interim period to redress any further negative impact. Strategic work, in addition to that needed to maintain regular services and programs and address customary interim tasks, can be undertaken to reduce harm, lessen the long-term effect on a congregation, and prepare a more auspicious welcome of a new minister.

But in some congregations, strategic work will be slow going and bring modest results. A congregation can be so disrupted by the disclosure of a former minister's misconduct that its continued survival through the immediate crisis will be an interim's primary work. In another congregation, new concerns about long-ago misconducts may be addressed in concert with other interim work. Still another congregation may be so rattled and raw after a series of conflicted ministries and unhappy departures, or after multiple ministers' misconducts and removals, that ministering to their pain and grief will be all that should be attempted in the interim period. Other work must wait for some healing to occur lest its result be short-lived or make matters worse.

Common Symptoms

The persistent adverse impact on a congregation from misconduct by a religious leader was discovered by a group of ministers quite by accident. A group of clergy began meeting together regularly for mutual support. Each reported that ministering in their current congregation was unusually stressful and difficult. Each expressed concern about the effect of this stress on their health and families. Nearly all worried about how long they could last. Some reported having questioned their call or considered leaving ministry for other lines of work.

Meeting and talking, they discovered their congregations all had some striking similarities. Each congregation was thought to have had promise, but over several decades, that promise had not been realized. Many were marginally viable. Most were chronically dysfunctional, conducting their business in disturbingly ineffective ways. These congregations appeared to lack the capacity to run a successful canvass, welcome new people, secure their building, follow procedures, or carry out decisions. They suffered from what might best be described as a failure to thrive.

Members of the congregations did not get along and treated one another rudely. Decision making was hindered by repeated conflict. Differences among members or with ministers quickly escalated and polarized. Often these conflicts were resolved only by the departure of one side or the other. Many of these congregations had been served by a series of ministers whose short tenures ended unhappily or explosively.

Each congregation had a reputation for being hard on ministers. Some were overly dependent on them, refusing to do anything without their approval or involvement. Others hardly noticed the ministers, routinely excluding them from decision making or failing to notify them of meetings.

Membership and leadership displayed a reactivity to the person of the minister. Ministers reported feeling pushed and pulled. They described members or leaders who expected too much or too little, who exacted their compliance with threats, or who solicitously curried their favor. Navigating these reactive relationships every day was extremely stressful, if not impossible.

Nothing adequately explained why these congregations were so similar or why these congregations of otherwise nice, smart, capable people failed to thrive. Then the ministers discovered that all of the congregations, every one, had in the past been served by ministers who had engaged in some sort of sexual or other misconduct.

Each congregation's specific experience was different. Some had endured misconduct by a religious leader recently, others long ago. In some, the misconduct was a secret; in others, it was widely known. In some, the misconducting leader had been dismissed or moved on; in a few, the minister remained despite proven misconduct. But regardless of these variations, every one of these congregations exhibiting this failure to thrive had experienced misconduct by at least one minister or other leader.

These ministers came to realize that the current condition of their congregations was rooted in the common experience of misconduct. Something in the experience of a minister's misconduct damaged a congregation's health and viability. Something in the experience or its aftermath remained in the culture of these congregations long after, hampering subsequent efforts. Something before, during, or after a previous minister's misconduct continued to be expressed in subsequent relationships with ministers.

Ramifications and Coping Strategies

What is it about sexual misconduct and its aftermath that can cause congregations to be significantly damaged and derailed? A minister's sexual misconduct betrays the trustworthiness and integrity expected of ministers. This betrayal undermines people's faith and their confidence in religious institutions and leaders. It undermines the authenticity of what ministers and congregations purport to stand for and those meanings and purposes people hold dear.

Sexual behavior by ministers with those they are called to serve violates the intended purpose of the ministerial role and relationship. Ministerial relationships are intended to be professional and pastoral and to serve the needs of those in whose service a minister is called. When sexual behavior occurs, the relationships become personal and unable to fulfill their intended purpose.

A minister is accorded power and authority along with a duty to use these resources responsibly and in the service of those they are called to serve. Ministers' sexual behavior is misconduct because it misuses this power and authority to meet a minister's own needs. Sexual behavior engaged in by a minister with those who seek counsel, care, and support at times of spiritual crisis or other need is also misconduct because it misuses trust to take advantage of vulnerable others. Health concerns, family matters, and other inevitable life challenges make members vulnerable. Sufficiently needy, they are unable to give informed consent and willing to tolerate behavior that, if engaged in elsewhere, they would know was wrong.

Ministerial misconduct is not only sexual. A seemingly end-less list of nonsexual behaviors often co-occur: theft of money or property, failure to follow proper procedures for congrega-tion vote, confidentiality violations, or harassment of staff and members, to name only a few examples. These types of behav-iors are also misconduct because they are harmful, negligent, and incompetent.

Misconducting ministers are described as generally "behav-ing badly." They are experienced as intrusive, presumptuous, solicitous, and inconsistent. They can be controlling, demand-ing, self-absorbed, and manipulative. These behaviors, taken together, form a pattern of relating to others that varies in inten-sity from not listening to yelling obscenities, from not being pleasant to being boldly inconsiderate, and from being hurtful to violent, according to another's vulnerability, tolerance, or lack of power. This varying pattern of behavior constantly pushes, disregards, or violates the personal boundaries of others.

Systemic family therapy sees families and other human orga-nizations, such as congregations, as emotional systems whose complex, interdependent dynamics maintain the system and secure its survival into the future. In response to life's messi-ness and challenge, families adapt and evolve. Congregations respond similarly to changing conditions and new challenges. Like families, they endure terrible setbacks and losses; a few experience devastating trauma. A congregation's well-being and future depend on its capacity to respond to grief and trauma in ways resilient enough to recover, to bring healing and to restore meaning in their aftermath. A religious leader's misconduct may be for a congregation a loss so great or a trauma so devastating that their capacity to recover is insufficient to the challenge. Like those who have lost loved ones and never fully grieved or who have endured trauma and remain deeply shaken and injured, they are never quite the same or fully healed, and can remain only marginally functional or viable.

Like families, congregations evolve strategies that over time may cease to serve their best interests. One common strategy is keeping secret and not discussing unpleasant and threaten-ing events because the resulting conflict and discontent might destroy the congregation. Over time, keeping secrets becomes a chronic, intractable dynamic, stifling conversation, discouraging consensus, and despite its original intent, generating repeated conflict. In this way, the chronic, intractable dynamics common in misconducted congregations are the result of past strategies developed to respond to and survive a minister's misconduct and its aftermath. Likely thought to be useful at the time, these strategies now undermine the health and vitality of the congregation.

In all emotional systems, the attitudes and behaviors of leaders —whether fathers or mothers, clergy or laity—powerfully structure and restructure the system. Leaders' interactions are patterned and repeated, and thereafter come to regulate all of a system's interactions. For example, a child who sees parents yell angrily when they disagree may yell at playmates when disagreeing. This happens in congregations as well. In congregations where a minister commonly makes unilateral decisions or dismisses or ignores others' input, congregants may come to tolerate or exhibit this same behavior. Long after a minister departs, the pattern of interactions persists, pervading the culture of the congregation and regulating the dynamics of all relationships.

In this way, the minister-congregation relationship is formative. A minister's conduct significantly influences and, over time, alters the way a congregation conducts itself. A minister's pattern of relating imprints a congregation and becomes the dominant pattern of relating throughout the congregation. This imprinting generates the cultural similarities found in misconducted congregations. For example, in congregations where the boundaries of ministerial relationships have been violated by misconduct, a pattern of violating other relationships or ignoring other boundaries will be evident. In congregational cultures where a misconducting minister's relational manner distorted congregants into the divisive pattern of "those who like me and those who don't," conflict becomes a relational norm.

In congregations where multiple ministers and leaders have engaged in misconduct, strategies and patterns have evolved that have significantly compromised a congregation's functioning and health. They do not have sufficient capacity or adequate immunity to fend off misconduct and withstand its ill effects.

This lack of immunity may have existed before a first miscon-duct occurred and persisted, making them vulnerable to subse-quent misconduct. Or they may have lost what immunity they had through changes in the congregation's culture. They may have been overwhelmed by loss, trauma, or other crises. What-ever the explanation, their ongoing lack of capacity places them at risk for future misconduct by religious leaders. Unless the congregation's immunity is bolstered and significant changes in their cultural dynamics are made, they will be defenseless to prevent a recurrence of misconduct.

Beginning an interim ministry with a congregation with a history of misconduct, interim ministers and leaders can feel like first responders at a terrible traffic accident. Chaos and con-fusion dominate the scene. People are hurt, in pain, and angry. Many have left, and with them, pledge income and programs. Buildings are messy and untended. Day-to-day operations are disrupted and inconsistent.

Significant upset will have ensued prior to the start of the interim ministry. Rumors will have circulated long before alle-gations were made or disclosure occurred. Congregation lead-ers initially may have closed ranks, hoping to avoid scandal. Lack of knowledge, clarity, or agreement about what is and is not misconduct will have fueled debate that is still unresolved. A misconducting minster or leader persuaded to leave "for the sake of the church" may continue nevertheless to solicit sup-porters and foment upset.

Legal proceedings may have been threatened. An investigation by the Unitarian Universalist Association's Ministerial Fellow-ship Committee (MFC), the official body that grants or revokes ministerial credentials, may have involved members. The MFC's decision can take months or years, and when complete, prove inadequate to resolve divergence in congregants' opinions.

Triage

The immediate challenge for interim minsters and leaders is triage—determining what is most urgent and must be done first. But unlike after a traffic accident, the hurt and upset are not readily identified and set right. Congregations impacted by a recent minister's misconduct may remain volatile for months or years, certainly well into any interim period and likely past. Their fragility, unlike that of accident victims, may be inconsistent, either invisible or disguised as something else. Healing and recovery will take time and continue into the next settled minister's tenure and likely the next.

Interim ministers and leaders can first and foremost seek to set a congregation on a path toward recovery and healing. They need to make a beginning, however modest, that subsequent ministers and leaders can sustain and build on. And they need to do this in a way that does not make recovery any harder or cause any further hurt or upset. Most important, they need the interim period itself to go well, or at least not badly. The upset, conflicts, and, to be sure, misconduct of the previous era must not be repeated, or occur in some new way, fueled by or focused on the interim leaders.

The primary goal is to restore some semblance of order and basic service. A key intervention will be to operate the congregation as intended and expected. For some time, the congregation has attended to the crisis and been distracted from forwarding itself as a religious community. Supporting the work of the congregation with integrity will create the means needed to foster healing and viability, and to restore people's trust and commitment.

Similarly, an interim minister who does the work of ministry competently, consistently, with integrity and grace is a significant intervention. An interim whose interactions with others are marked by authenticity and humility, whose relational manner is appropriate and in keeping with good etiquette and good ethics, and whose conduct is trustworthy and not cause for further anxiety, conflict, or embarrassment will cultivate goodwill and cultural change. More by their actions than their words, interims can begin to clarify expectations of ministers and their role or relationships, and rebuild trust in ministers one relationship at a time. On the basis of this often painstaking process of rebuilding trust, other work may be attempted and will succeed, in time.

Grief

Equally important is the pastoral task of ministering to members. No matter what their opinion of the previous minister's conduct, everyone has experienced a great loss. Those who loved, respected, and relied on the minister and would have been willing to overlook even misconduct in order for the minister to remain will be grieved by the loss of their beloved minister and angry at those they perceive forced the minister's departure. Those who were outraged by this minister's conduct will grieve the loss of their congregation's reputation and feel betrayed by the minister whose conduct led to the loss. Those who have belonged for years or who joined only recently will grieve that the congregation is no longer the place they loved or had longed for. Reeling from these losses, everyone will grieve for some time.

Victim-survivors can be seriously injured and require intense support to heal and reclaim their lives. Their needs may be more intense than most ministers or leaders have skill or time to provide, and be best served by care providers from outside the congregation. Partners, families, and friends may have been betrayed and angered by both the victim and the misconducting minister; they will need time to sort out these complicated feelings, as will leaders. Often, leaders have been battered and bruised by the very membership they hope to serve, another by-product of misconduct and trauma. The interim will need to support leaders so they may continue their work or find graceful exits and remain members. There will be ongoing work to identify ways the congregation, shamed and threatened by the loss of their public reputation, may feel again some pride in their work and their community.

Ministering simultaneously to members or groups whose perspectives may be at odds can be challenging and may threaten an interim's or leader's pastoral access or capacity to minister. Members who think the misconducting minister was wrongly treated may feel betrayed by interims and leaders who too often discuss or too aggressively point out a predecessor's misconduct. Members angry that the minister was fired—only because those "fools or liars complained"—may be put off by interims and leaders who appear to spend considerable time with victim-survivors. Ministers and leaders must maintain a sufficient appearance of neutrality about conflicted issues that they can be in conversation with everyone and not be seen as on one side or the other. An interim must be every member's minister and no one's opposition.

Finding ways to acknowledge individual members' sense of loss will help interim ministers and leaders navigate the challenges of ministering to the variety of those who grieve. An interim or leader can say to one member, "I am sorry for your loss. I know the former minister was important to you and your family." And to another member can say, "I'm sorry for your loss. I know this congregation means a lot to you, and seeing it go through these difficulties is hard." These statements are both accurate and focus on members' common experience of loss rather than on arbitrating their differences. This focus in turn nurtures their common commitment to the congregation's future.

The work of Elizabeth Kübler-Ross in *On Death and Dying* provides useful tools for ministering to those grieving in the aftermath of a recent misconduct. Kübler-Ross explored the feelings and experiences of people facing terminal illness and impending death, and identified a five-stage process of grieving: denial, anger, bargaining, depression, and acceptance. She soon realized, as have others, that these stages describe how people feel and act when they experience any kind of loss, whether death of a family member, end of a relationship, or departure of a minister.

Interim ministers and leaders will readily recognize in these stages the feelings and thinking of those they encounter in congregations with recent experiences of misconduct. Denial: *Our minister could not have done this.* Anger: *Our leaders made a mess of this.* Bargaining: *If the minister just quietly leaves, no one will know and we'll be better off.* Depression: *I am too sad to come on Sunday.* Acceptance: *Even good people can make bad choices.*

The upset, anger, and conflict commonly seen in the immediate aftermath of misconduct is evidence of members' efforts to grieve. Their attempts to manage complicated feelings, minimize pain and discomfort, regain control, and recover some sense of normalcy are predictable responses to grief and loss.

Kübler-Ross observed that when people work through the five stages of grief, they move on after loss more ably and with renewed meaning and purpose. But when these stages are not worked through, when people are not encouraged to talk, grief remains unresolved. Then people can experience emotional or physical problems and greater difficulty finding meaning and purpose in their lives.

Chronic, intractable dynamics in congregations where a previous religious leader has engaged in misconduct suggest that the community has yet to fully grieve the loss. Ungrieved, these losses grow larger, infecting and impairing a congregation. Coping strategies that arose to respond to the crises but are no longer necessary or effective may persist tenaciously. For example, extreme reactivity to ministers, easy anger and disagreement, inability to make or follow through on decisions, or to care and secure the community's best interests, may be evidence that the congregation has not begun or completed working through the five stages of grief.

Helping the congregation as a whole articulate the meaning of the misconduct experience and integrate it into the congregation's story will facilitate individual and communal grieving. Information sessions should be held for members, if they have not been already. Conducted by congregational leaders for the membership, these sessions should convey what information on the recent minister's misconduct and later developments is known and can be stated publicly. An interim minister should not provide or deliver information during these sessions but participate as a neutral pastoral presence and support people's speaking and hearing well. Follow-up sessions may be necessary when additional information is available or new concerns and questions arise.

Educational and Healing Programs

Some congregations will be served, often later, by additional educational programs, such as workshops that build leadership skills and increase members' capacity to respond to the occurrence and aftermath of the misconduct. Programs on the ethics of ministerial practice and congregational life or workshops on congregation-minister relations can support the congregation's efforts to make cultural changes and to integrate the experience into the longer, varied story of the congregation. A way will need to be found to share the story of the misconduct and how the congregation weathered the crisis, learned from the experience, and changed, individually and communally.

Information sessions and related educational programs should include opportunities for members to process what they have heard. Some portion of a larger meeting should be set aside for members to reflect together on what they have just heard to help members, individually and as a whole, make sense of what they have experienced. Separate smaller break-out groups will provide opportunities for members to talk in greater depth about their thoughts and emotions, and to listen to others talk about theirs. Different factions in a congregation may never agree on the facts, but when they understand each other's feelings and appreciate others' grief, they will be better able to find common ground and go forward together in their common commitment to the congregation.

Listening groups—gatherings of six to twelve people—are one way to create this opportunity. Scheduled over the course of several weeks or months, these groups should be facilitated, ideally, by grief counselors, psychotherapists, or others with skills to help members discuss still fresh and difficult experiences and to keep conversation focused on appreciating each other's experiences, not on debating who is right or wrong.

Given that people process grief at different rates and intensity, some will need more opportunities to listen and talk than others. Some groups, such as staff, Board members, or victim-survivors, may be best served by separate, dedicated opportunities. Among these groups might be those whose relationship with a recent misconducting minister was intense or complicated, those who were involved in concealing or discovering the minister's misconduct, or those who worked closely with the minister and may feel particularly betrayed or responsible. Some members will prefer or be better served by individual listening opportunities; counselors should be made available for individuals by appointment.

Lasting Effects of Misconduct

Why some congregations who experience a minister's or other leader's misconduct suffer lasting effects and others do not remains unclear. Congregations in which recent misconduct has been disclosed early and who faced the challenge seem to do better. When acknowledged, misconduct can be openly discussed. Members can grieve and, making sense of the experience, move on in healthier ways. A few congregations are galvanized by the experience. Like grieving parents who start foundations to aid others whose children die, these congregations muster a resolve that makes them stronger, healthier, and more resilient.

Congregations whose misconduct histories have never previously been made known—and thus have had no opportunity to grieve the losses or make sense of the experience—fare more poorly than those whose misconduct was disclosed early on and fully. In those where misconduct has been kept secret, communication can become cut off, perceptions distorted, anxiety heightened, and decisions derailed. Congregations where misconduct behaviors were widely known but not acted upon can be extremely dysfunctional.

Sometimes congregations with no apparent history of misconduct demonstrate the chronic challenges commonly seen in congregations that do have this history. Not knowing the history but observing extreme dysfunction, interims and leaders may attempt to impose order, clean house, or upgrade practices. But then they find themselves inexplicably the focus of anger and conflict or in a situation gone from bad to worse. Interims and leaders who observe such chronic challenges would do well to wonder out loud, neutrally and dispassionately, if any past religious leader engaged in misconduct before attempting quick fixes.

Old misconduct histories come up during an interim time for a variety of reasons. Perhaps decades later, members feel distance or freedom enough to tell what happened. Or they feel safe enough, given the interim time or minister, to speak.

Inspiring the disclosure of a previously undisclosed history of misconduct is a significant intervention, creating the possibility that a congregation's story can be told. Even when delayed by many years, these disclosures create the possibility of healing, recovery, and change. Interims and leaders may then collaboratively engage in deliberate strategies as outlined above.

In some congregations where old misconduct is disclosed, telling the full story or addressing chronic dysfunction may prove difficult or impossible. Misconducting predecessors who are still congregation members or ministers emeriti may curtail these efforts or continue to engage in misconduct.

Some victim-survivors will leave a congregation in the wake of recent misconduct. But other members with whom the predecessor engaged in unethical behaviors and whose involvement is a secret will likely stay. In these congregations, whether to protect secrets long held or members much loved, leaders may dismiss interim tasks with inexplicable passion. For example, they may disparage the customary interim task of making sense of history, insisting that the past is not relevant. In congregations where duplicity has been used to conceal or occasion misconduct, congregations develop a culture-wide pattern of lying or dissembling about the facts. The interim will need to take steps to normalize this task "as just routine interim stuff" or work more slowly or cautiously than would be otherwise necessary, lest the resistance extends to all possible interim work and to the interim minister and leaders themselves.

Congregations with histories of multiple misconducts may pose additional challenges. They often believe wrongly that all will be well if they just find "a good one this time." Some become hypercritical and struggle to find, settle, or retain subsequent ministers. In others, a pattern of ignoring or confusing other boundaries—likely imprinted by leaders whose misconduct and manner violated boundaries—may help explain why they have an increased risk for misconduct by subsequent ministers, interims among them. Because relational patterns imposed by misconducting ministers and leaders persist, systemic pressures may covertly encourage subsequent ministers to violate boundaries. Interims and leaders should take special care to conduct themselves exactly in accordance with the highest standards of conduct.

The adverse impact of misconduct, if unrecognized and unaddressed, will persist and continue to reduce a congregation's viability. Recovery is not an easy or quick fix. But strategic efforts of interims and leaders will address issues head on, change patterns, and determine healthy courses of action. Often, fear and shame keep patterns in place. Those congregations that can move beyond these patterns will heal and transform past wrongs, and in doing so give fullest expression to that hope for reality that people seek in religious communites. Moving beyond misconduct and trauma means moving from acknowledgment to hard work, to hope and healing, and to new life.

The Interim Assistant Minister

CARLTON ELLIOTT SMITH

■ ■ ▨ ■

The roles and functions of interim assistant ministers have some distinct differences from those of interim senior ministers. Likewise, interim assistant ministers are distinct from other assistant ministers. Although members of a ministry team may share responsibility for worship, pastoral care, and administration, an assistant minister typically serves to support the vision of the senior minister, whom the congregation has entrusted with overall leadership. The senior minister holds more power than the assistant minister, but both will benefit from clearly defined expectations about how they will work together for the organization. Like any covenantal relationship, that between a senior minister and assistant minister requires trust, openness, and vulnerability in order to thrive.

When establishing their agreement, a senior minister and an interim assistant minister will need to determine if the interim assistant will be a placeholder or a change agent. If operating as a placeholder, the interim assistant performs the functions of the previous assistant minister while the senior minister identifies a new long-term assistant, often with the help of a Search Committee. An interim assistant in the role of change agent is more aligned with the traditional role of all interim ministers— that is, someone charged to help the congregation get unstuck as it anticipates the person who will follow the interim assistant or institutional restructuring.

Regardless of whether the interim assistant is a placeholder or a change agent, the senior and assistant must have a shared understanding of how they will function together. They could start by reviewing the guidelines of the Unitarian Universalist Ministers Association (UUMA), particularly those related to collegial responsibility. Or they could start with policy governance, according to which the senior minister is given veto power. Some ministers hold that under policy governance, the senior should be the only called minister in a congregation served by more than one minister, with any others serving at the senior's will. If the senior and interim assistant disagree, they will ideally each acknowledge the other's perspective and present a cohesive plan of action. In the end, both should be able to see their higher accountabilities to the congregation, to the spirit of life and love, and for some, to God. Toward this end, some ministry teams meet regularly with a coach or a therapist—sometimes funded by the congregation—to help surface and resolve issues between colleagues.

One interim assistant said that her senior colleague asked her to develop a list of outcomes that she would deliver over the course of her year. "Those agreed-upon outcomes gave me lots of room," she said. "I knew that if I just looked at them and created programs to achieve the desired outcomes, it would be okay." She also mentioned the importance of the two ministers having skills and work habits that complement each other. A detail-oriented interim assistant might be just the kind of support a senior whose strength is looking at the big picture might need. The themes cooperation and collaboration kept surfacing as she thought about why their working relationship went so well. It also helped that they avoided triangulation. "We had an agreement that both of us would be open to what congregants had to say, but we had a responsibility to tell each other what we knew others were saying behind our backs." Interim assistants should advise those with complaints about the senior minister to go directly to the senior rather than be the messenger of unwelcome news themselves. (For more guidance about avoiding triangulation, see "Mining, Minding, and Making Stories.")

Benefits for the Congregation

The interim assistant minister has a unique opportunity to affirm the good work that the congregation and the senior minister have done together. In one congregation where I served as interim assistant, the senior minister's tenth anniversary had gone unobserved due to certain events in the life of the community. I helped organize a twelfth anniversary weekend with a festive Saturday dinner program and a celebratory Sunday worship service. The occasion lifted up the congregation's history and underscored what was working in the minister-congregation relationship.

Sometimes the changes an interim assistant brings emerge from new experiences and new connections. As change agent, the interim assistant can take risks and build relationships with partners in the wider community. Shortly before I arrived in my current position as an interim assistant, the minister and staff selected "Immigration as a Moral Issue" as the congregation's social justice theme, in tandem with the Unitarian Universalist Association's (UUA) 2010 congregational study/action issue. With that focus, I nurtured our connections to secular organizations supporting immigration justice that led to our twice hosting a statewide annual Immigrant Advocacy Summit. Through a worship service I organized, we came into relationship with a group called the Dream Project that provides college scholarships and educational opportunities for youth from underserved immigrant families. These and many longer-term international endeavors are growing the congregation's identity as a hub for immigrant advocacy.

The interim assistant minister can support the congregation making connections with the larger denomination. Senior ministers deeply entrenched in the day-to-day operation of their congregation will have to make sacrifices somewhere as they handle the demands before them. Often neglected are connections to our wider Unitarian Universalist movement—participation on the district, regional, and national levels. Having led an Association Sunday service, served a variety of congregations in different districts, and worked with UUA staff, I can attest to the ways interim assistant ministers can be valuable resources for senior ministers to draw upon.

In his book *Generation to Generation: Family Process in Church and Synagogue*, Edwin Friedman describes three ways that leadership manifests in congregations. Leadership can be based on the *charisma* of the minister on one end of a continuum, or on the *consensus* of the whole community on the other. In between these extremes is leadership based on *self-differentiation*, in which the minister self-defines as the "head" but stays in touch with the rest of the organization, which in most cases will follow the minister's lead. Self-differentiated leaders are less vulnerable to sabotage, burnout, or over-functioning, because they are able to be a non-anxious presence in the face of the worry and fear of others.

Interim assistant ministers can help assistants who will follow by modeling self-differentiation. By setting their own course and staying in touch with the rest of the organization, the interim assistant, like an interim senior minister, can lead effectively and participate in transformation. In congregations where the previous assistant minister was deep in the shadow of a charismatic senior minister or disempowered by the leadership structure of the congregation, the self-differentiated interim assistant can lift up a new possibility for how to be in relationship.

Challenges

Some interim assistant ministers discover they will be the last to hold the assistant position in that congregation. Congregations add ministers when good times are rolling, the coffers are full, and dreams of expansion abound. If the minister or ministers have gotten caught up in strife, cash flow is drying up, and the financial future looks bleak, lay leaders are likely to ask, "Do we really need two (or more) ministers?" and "How can we reorganize so that we operate more efficiently?" An interim assistant minister who provides a non-anxious presence while these questions are raised can be of enormous value.

An interim assistant minister can help a congregation discern what kind of professional staff it wants and can afford. The interim can hold up a mirror to help the congregation see and appreciate the demands it has made of its senior minister. For example, the interim can help it understand if its need for pastoral care is more than the senior minister can reasonably be expected to do. Or the interim assistant might help the congregation determine whether its staffing for religious education is out of balance by having both a full-time religious education administrator and an associate or assistant minister focused on religious education.

In many congregations, the assistant minister's role is a wild card, particularly when filled by an interim. In some cases, at the end of the first interim year, a congregation may conclude that it can no longer afford as much ministerial staffing and reduce the assistant from full- to part-time, or even eliminate the position. In one congregation I served, the Interim Assistant Search Committee discovered that they had no funds allocated in the annual budget to fly a candidate in for an interview, and on that basis, opted to go for a second year of search.

Interim assistant ministers are often junior to their senior ministers in age, ministerial experience, or both. Although many congregations want diversity on their staffs, lesbian, gay, bisexual, transgender, and/or people of color might serve only in secondary ministry positions, as assistant or associate ministers, or as ministers of religious education. Each of these factors —age, gender identity, sexual orientation, ethnicity—can heighten the power imbalance between the senior minister and an interim assistant. The ministers and the congregation should be mindful of this possibility and establish lines of communication to head off strife among colleagues, and put them on the path to right relations (or at least, to resolution).

The Temptation to Candidate for the Permanent Position

Interim Ministers agree not to become candidates at the congregations they've served until at least three years following their interim tenure. Interim ministers agree, in standard contracts mandated by the UUA, that at the end of their contract, they will leave the congregation. They are indeed "pre-fired," which frees them to push congregations out of their comfort zones and make bold choices. An interim minister can help ineffective lay people or staff members find other opportunities to share their gifts with greater speed (and perhaps fewer repercussions) than a permanent minister can. As change agents, they help smooth the way for the permanent minister who will follow.

If an interim minister applies for the permanent position it presents a potential conflict of interest. As a change agent, the interim minister would have a hard time helping the congregation correct its course and make bold choices if the interim was also avoiding conflict in hopes of being called. The prodding and risk-taking effective interim ministry requires would be difficult to pull off while the interim was trying to convince lay leaders of the interim's superiority over other ministers being considered. It would not only thwart the process established among colleagues but would also deprive the congregation of the benefit of being served by someone with no self-interest. (For more about the search process, see "The Interim Minister's Role in Ministerial Search" and "Predictable Roadblocks.")

While most senior interim ministers mind the prohibition against applying for the permanent positions they occupy until at least three years after their interim tenure, the boundaries are not as clearly maintained for interim assistant ministers. In 2003, the UUA temporarily suspended the three-year rule for interim assistants, interim associates, and interim ministers of religious education who were either people of color or of other marginalized groups. The rationale was that because so few UU congregations would consider hiring marginalized ministers at all, ministers who had found employment as interims should be able to keep their jobs. I was one of the ministers invited into this experiment. With some philosophical reservations, I accepted, and eventually became the "permanent" assistant minister. In addition to two years of interim ministry, I also served four years of called ministry at that congregation before that position was discontinued.

I would encourage interim assistant ministers who have been invited to or are considering applying for the permanent position they hold to carefully weigh the pros and cons. Have you had a thorough conversation with your senior colleague about your concerns? How confident are you that your respective visions and intentions complement each other? How will you maintain communication, trust, and boundaries as colleagues? Even if it works well for you individually, what are the implications for the integrity of the interim ministry program itself if you break your original agreement to leave after one or two years?

With the best of intentions, congregations sometimes hold back information that would help the minister sooner rather than later. One minister recalls serving a congregation early in her career, where she was specifically *not* given the title interim assistant while they discerned whether the assistant position she held would continue or not. Her senior colleague and the lay leadership forgot to explain that if they did continue with an assistant minister, they could hire her in that role. Not calling her an interim gave them that option. When reconfiguring the staff, they discontinued the assistant position. The assistant minister says that knowing that at the point she initially accepted the position would have been helpful.

If there is any possibility that the assistant minister and the congregation might wish to work together beyond two years, I suggest negotiating a position description that is not called interim assistant ministry. *Temporary*, *acting*, and *consulting*, are among the alternative qualifiers to *ministry* used to keep the option of long-term employment open. The assistant, the senior minister, and perhaps UUA regional staff can work together to determine which fits best.

Benefits for the Interim Assistant Minister

Their position can give interim assistants new to ministry and contemplating senior or solo ministries a clear view of the challenges and demands of being the person the congregation looks to for guidance. "Being an interim assistant made me question whether I ever wanted to be in that role," one interim assistant says. "The senior minister—especially a senior interim—does a lot of heavy lifting. They dive into the middle of the hornet's nest. I was supportive in the interim assistant role, but I didn't have to dive in."

Congregants often ask interim ministers if they ever want a permanent position, and assistant ministers if they ever want to be senior ministers. In fact, interim ministry and assistant ministry are honorable callings themselves—the former, to help congregations through transitions, and the latter, to support the congregation's primary leader. Most interim assistant ministers are not committed to serving in temporary supportive roles for their careers, and some come to their positions with years of solo ministry experience. Some arrive after finishing seminary and see their tenure as another kind of internship—a chance to learn from watching a colleague before setting off on their own. In any case, the congregations served by interim assistant ministers value and affirm their contributions. With clearly defined functions and commitments between the interim assistant and the senior minister, and with clear agreements about how long the interim period will last, ministers and congregations are positioned for a favorable time together.

PART V

A Broader View of Ministerial Transition

Options for Ministerial Transition Other Than Interim Ministry

NANCY BOWEN

■ ■ ▦ ■

"Do we have to have an interim minister?" This is one of the most common questions congregational leaders ask of both the Unitarian Universalist Association regional staff and the Transitions Office. Often the question arises because congregants remember a difficult interim ministry in their past and they don't want to repeat that experience. Sometimes they have heard a story about a complicated interim period at a neighboring congregation. Sometimes congregants do not want to engage in any kind of transitional work because they believe they don't need it, believe they don't need to change, believe that stewardship and membership will suffer (possibly even die), believe that interim ministers only stir up anxiety when there is no reason for it, and ultimately believe they only need to get on to the next settled minister and they will be fine.

It is true that there are options other than interim ministry for a congregation after a settled ministry ends. They may choose contract ministry or developmental ministry. They may proceed directly to another settlement, become part of a multisite congregation, or have no ministry at all. Congregations do operate under congregational polity and definitely have the right to choose their own course.

What follows is a description of each option, a little history of each, some stories of how each has worked or not worked in the past, discussion of potential pluses and pitfalls, and some other information that may help a congregation decide which option is best if interim ministry is not going to be the next step. For most congregations, however, interim ministry is indeed the next, and the right, step.

Contract Ministry

If a congregation takes up this option, its Board enters into a contract with a minister for a specified period of time, usually one year with an option to renew annually. The contract minister agrees to fulfill some basic ministerial tasks, such as preaching on a specified number of Sundays and pastoral care. Sometimes other duties are included in the contract, such as attending Board meetings, helping with a particular committee or task, or supervising paid staff if there are any. If the minister will be coming from a distance, the contract specifies both time and mode of travel. It also specifies the amount of compensation, what benefits will be included, when the minister will be paid, and any expenses that will be reimbursed. The lines are clear, and the minister's time is carefully managed.

Most contract ministries are part-time, usually less than three-quarter-time. Contract ministry has been used with less success in full-time ministries, though it remains an option. Most notably, a contract ministry is helpful for a congregation that needs to build trust in ministry or rebuild lost trust.

In one congregation, where a full-time minister's resignation had been negotiated with difficulty—and it was the congregation's third such termination of a settlement—pursuing another call did not seem to be a smart option. Interim ministry had seemed unsatisfactory after the previous settlements ended. The congregational leaders thought the congregation simply needed time to hold steady. Many congregants would benefit from being able to slowly build trust with a minister. So the Board decided to look for a contract minister who would preach, do pastoral care, and supervise the three very part-time staff members. The Board felt that after a year with a contract minister, the congregation would be better able to take stock and renew its faith in ministry. Board members advertised the position through the UUA and found a minister willing to come for one year. They made sure they were very clear with both the contract minister and the congregation about exactly what would be expected of the minister.

The congregation had been split regarding the previous minister. Now, because everyone knew this new minister's contract would end after one year and because the contract was clear about the minister's role, both sides were able to breathe and be more present in the moment. With everyone knowing the limits of the ministry, the congregation settled into the year, and they saw that the minister was performing basic ministerial tasks more than adequately. The sides became less divided. Knowing the ministry could end after a year lessened the anxiety of some members; as a result, they became less critical of ministry in general. The following spring, the Board renewed the contract ministry for another year. After three years of contract ministry, with a fourth pending, the Board decided that now they could more readily and less reactively look at other options. At this point they were able to see how they had contributed to their problems with settled ministry. Consequently, the congregation and its leaders were now ready to tackle the challenges facing them. They brought in the regional staff of the UUA to explore what might be possible. After much conversation and discernment, the congregation decided that it should move toward developmental ministry, which the regional staff supported. The contract ministry had been a bridge for the congregation on a long road of needed, if unfinished, healing.

Another congregation, one with aging membership, liked having a minister and benefited from ministry, but their changing circumstances meant that they could no longer afford full-time ministry. Like their wider community, the congregation was dwindling. The leaders did an honest assessment and realized what the congregation could truly and fully support was half-time ministry. So they advertised for a half-time position. While the pool of ministers interested was small, one minister who lived three hours away was interested and seemed to be a good fit. The Board reached an agreement with the minister

to preach two Sundays a month, back to back, and to be with
the congregation for nine consecutive days each month, bridg-
ing these two Sundays. At other times, the minister could be
available at home via phone, video, and email for projects. The
minister would lead the two services, teach one class, provide
in-person pastoral care when on-site, do other pastoral care
from home, attend Board meetings, and work with the very
part-time staff—the director of religious education, the music
director, and the office administrator. The congregation's budget, which had been stretched beyond its capacity, became manageable again. The leaders had found a way for the congregation
to retain the services of professional ministry at a fair price with
clear expectations.

A third congregation decided, when their minister retired,
that they did not need or want an interim minister. The leaders decided to post a position for a full-time contract ministry,
hoping at some point to turn the contract into a called ministry.
The position was advertised, and to the congregation's surprise,
there were few responses. The two ministers they did interview
both asked the same question: Why have you chosen not to
have interim ministry, the path most congregations take? The
congregational leaders countered with two somewhat conflicting statements: They had not had a good experience with their
last interim minister and they just needed another minister who
would "be with" them.

The two interviewees came to the same conclusions. They
didn't trust that the congregation saw the proposed contract
ministry as anything more than a tryout, during which they
would continually be "singing for their supper." They were not
confident that the congregation would truly work to make the
next ministry a success. And they both concluded that the congregation not only didn't want to change but in fact wanted a
new minister like the previous settled minister, who had retired.
So both of them withdrew. The congregation was unable to find
a contract minister.

A fourth congregation, looking for part-time ministry, told
their prospective contract minister (or "consulting minister,"
the term used at that time) that they really wanted someone

to help them grow. What the congregation didn't say was that this goal came with a caveat: We want to grow as long as we don't have to change. We just want more people to come in who look and act like us and are willing to make substantial pledges. When the contract minister began the work of helping the congregational culture shift so that more people would attend and join, the congregation balked and ended the ministry. This episode exemplifies a common dilemma, congregations that want to grow without having to change.

These four congregations are like many of the congregations looking for a contract minister. A contract minister with specific, clear goals can be a real boon to a congregation. Lack of clarity, however, or even—in rare instances—deception on the part of a congregation, makes a poor context for contract ministry. Another thing to keep in mind is that the number of ministers seeking contract ministry is likely to be smaller than the number seeking settled ministry. In part-time ministries, a flexible ministerial schedule is crucial, at least in part because the minister is likely to have additional part-time employment that may offer little or no flexibility. Finally, congregations served by a part-time contract minister should not expect full-time ministry at a part-time price. Yet for a congregation that needs to "sit still" for a while, or one that can't afford full-time ministry and can set clear and reasonable expectations, contract ministry might well be the best option.

Congregations considering contract ministry are encouraged to have their leaders consult their regional staff about how a contract ministry might best serve them, talk with other congregations that have chosen this option and found it valuable, and be realistic about what needs they have, what they can expect of a contract minister, and how they will ensure that their expectations are reasonable.

Developmental Ministry

Developmental ministry is a five- to seven-year, performance-based commitment to sustained congregational culture change. The congregation, regional staff, and Transitions Office work together to identify a developmental minister suited to help the congregation identify and change unhealthy patterns and habits so that Unitarian Universalism may become a strong and healthy voice for love and justice in that location.

The term "developmental ministry" seeks to capture the deep commitment of congregations and ministers as they do the hard work of moving a congregational culture toward greater health and vitality. Often they are developing a new congregational identity, a new congregational ethos, and practices that will sustain these healthier patterns. A wide range of congregational challenges might prompt a congregation to consider seeking developmental ministry—challenges that are painful to the congregational community and require deep, intentional, and sustained work to overcome. Some of the most typical challenges are:

- a traumatic history of unresolved conflict

- a history of unresolved clergy sexual misconduct

- other patterns of sexual misconduct in the congregation

- deteriorating socioeconomic circumstances in their location requiring re-invention

- serious challenges or conflict over a historic or beloved building

- a history of repeated and rapid ministerial turnover

- a history of abusive leadership

- patterns that combine a lack of civility, an inability to analyze and resolve problems, and poor boundaries—patterns which together result in a lack of respectful relationships.

Congregants often come to recognize their challenging history and difficult patterns at the ending of a conflicted ministry or during an interim ministry. Occasionally congregational leaders recognize that the congregation needs to slow down and take a look at itself. However, most often it is an outside religious professional who is able to see the historical patterns dispassionately and ask the provocative questions that empower a congregation to consider alternative forms of ministry and ministerial search. This is work the regional UUA staff is prepared to help a congregation pursue.

The most important sign that a congregation is likely to have a successful developmental ministry is lay leaders' awareness that they are stuck in self-destructive patterns of organization and interaction and need radically different ones. They must believe that such changes are necessary for a healthy and sustainable future, and be willing to do the work required to make those changes.

Developmental ministry search and settlement differ from the usual search and call process in three significant ways:

1. **Congregational leaders recognize a pattern of "stuckness" and ask for help making changes.** The existing unhealthy habits, patterns, and culture have likely prevailed for many years, and have come to be accepted as "the way things are." With the assistance of UUA regional staff or an interim minister, congregational leaders ask the UUA to help them find a minister who can stay five years on contract and help them make changes.

2. **The congregation's leaders develop strategic priorities addressing the root causes of the difficulties they have experienced.** These strategic priorities are specific to the individual congregation. Typically, when root causes have been accurately identified, the congregation and developmental minister need to work together to find new paths to health. The congregational leaders acknowledge that these changes are necessary and champion the priorities in congregational life, in the budget, and in policies and procedures. They partner with the developmental minister in willingness to take on elevated risks in order to support these changes.

3. **Throughout the term of the developmental ministry, the developmental minister, congregational leaders, and regional staff collaborate as a team.** Their shared intention is reflected in both contracts and practices that clarify clergy authority, plans for regional staff involvement, and regular assessment to support both the ministry and the leadership.

I refined the concept of developmental ministry in my work with the congregation in Boulder, Colorado, which became the pilot and prototype for developmental ministry. This congregation could tell it was in need of significant, possibly long-term, help. I was serving as a regional staff member at the time, and in conversation with me the congregation agreed that the issues it faced were more complex and massive than a regular interim ministry could address. So the congregational leaders agreed on a plan with the regional staff. The congregation would work on specific goals for the next five to seven years, and the regional staff would provide help directly and also work with the transitions director to find a minister who could help them.

Several key factors contributed to the success of this project. The congregation agreed that the issues were theirs to address with the help of the developmental minister, rather than expecting the minister to solve their problems for them. The congregational leaders understood that the minister might have to say some very difficult things and ask the leadership to change. Since the congregation had historically tended to let ministers go when conflict arose, the congregational leaders agreed to a five-year contract. The contract specified that the Board could terminate the minister if they did not like what the minister did or said, but if they did this, then they would have to pay out the full contract regardless of how much time was left on it. The congregation knew it needed its collective feet held to a proverbial fire. This commitment was a key factor in their success, and perhaps *the* key factor.

After the completion of the developmental ministry contract, the congregation went into search and called a minister who still serves them with love and pride. A congregation that had dwindled at times to thirty people attending a Sunday service became again a congregation of three hundred, vibrant, engaged, and proud of the work they had done with the help of the developmental minister, the regional staff, and the Transitions Office.

Since then, variations on the Boulder model have been tried. The congregations that have been most successful have combined an awareness of the need for long-term work, a willingness to accept help from outside, and a realization that they must be willing to ride through rough patches.

I created a checklist to help congregational leaders discern whether they are in a position to consider developmental ministry. If they are leading a congregation that displays more than three of the unhealthy characteristics on the list, they might well consider inviting regional staff to come and help them undertake a congregational assessment. The checklist asks whether the congregation:

- is not actively engaging Unitarian Universalism

- is isolated from other congregations and regions, and from the UUA

- is not focused on a rewarding mission

- has not been successful in building an energized volunteer base

- has repeated short-term ministries or has never been able to consider professional ministry

- replays old conflicts again and again

- does not trust and authorize elected leaders to lead

- fails to build trusting relationships with ordained leaders

- resists ministerial and leadership authority

- is unable to forgive, learn, and move forward

- accepts or expects a self-centered, "me first," consumer approach to congregational life.

Developmental ministry should not be regarded as a ministerial tryout or as an opportunity for the congregation to merely watch and critique while the minister works. Trial-and-error efforts have shown both congregations and ministers that an option to call the developmental minister actually hampers the success of developmental ministry. Congregations reported that members focused too much on the option of call and not enough on the work needing to be done. Therefore, the option of calling the developmental minister no longer exists. However, congregations and ministers engaged together in developmental ministry may consider a one-year extension of the ministry if the work is not finished and the regional staff, developmental minister, and congregational leaders all agree that an additional year would help the congregation complete its developmental goals.

As of this writing, the most effective developmental ministries have been those that followed an interim ministry. A congregation in an interim ministry would discover, with the help of the interim minister, that more and deeper changes were needed, and greater work was to be done, than could be accomplished during the interim ministry period. With the help of the interim minister, who would involve the regional staff, the congregation would define its goals and move into developmental ministry.

The benefits of successful developmental ministry are clear. It is most likely to succeed when congregational leaders are unified in thinking that there is hard work to do and that they can't do it alone. And they must be committed to educating the congregation throughout the process. This unity and commitment lead to greater trust of ministry and connect the congregation better to the wider religious movement. Additionally, identified goals give the congregation some tangible work to do.

Congregations that take up developmental ministry also receive assistance in their search processes for both developmental and subsequent settled ministry. The regional staff and the transitions director select a limited pool of ministers whom they deem most likely to be good matches for these congregations.

Developmental ministry is not so likely to work successfully when a congregation has not brought to it clear goals and a clear commitment, does not trust the developmental minister, or lets old patterns overtake a desire to be truly changed. Such congregations often look to the developmental minister for answers and do not see the potential in themselves to take on these tasks.

Proceeding to the Next Settlement Without a Transitional Minister

Congregants often suggest that their congregation go directly from one settlement to the next, but few congregations actually try it. Most realize the need to take a break, regroup, and turn toward a new future. Only two congregations in recent history have attempted to proceed to the next settlement without interim ministry, and there were definite bumps in their process. Many ministers refused even to express interest in these congregations, fearing they would have to be too much like the settled minister who had just left. In one of the two, the newly settled minister later said, "I have no doubts my ministry here would have been easier had an interim minister preceded me," and later added that it felt as though it was necessary to be both interim minister and settled minister at the same time, and that the developmental work happened at a much slower pace than in a typical interim ministry. Most congregations who try going forward without interim ministry end up hiring an interim minister after all.

Regional staff have suggested that proceeding without interim ministry might be a viable option in one particular set of circumstances, when a small congregation is geographically isolated but in good health. As of this writing, a pilot program is under way to test this theory. In this program, these congregations, which interim ministers are often uninterested in serving, instead agree that they will get a new minister for a period of five years, usually someone who has just graduated from seminary, and that the minister will go into search in the last year of the five-year program. Several regional staff members and the Transitions Office know of stable, healthy congregations that have had frequent ministerial turnover, probably due primarily to their geographic isolation. The ministers who left these congregations reported they had had very satisfactory ministries and felt it was time for them to put this good experience to use by moving toward a new, larger congregation.

These healthy small congregations are currently known as teaching congregations, in large part because they are instrumental in helping new ministers to greater success. It is likely that more congregations will be considered for this form of ministry, and congregations who see themselves as being a good fit for it will work with their regional staff for an assessment of their fitness to be a teaching congregation. Ideally, the ministers will receive interim training at some point during their five-year tenure, to better understand the importance of transitional work and the minister's share of this work.

The great advantage of this program is that a smaller congregation in a hard-to-reach location might begin to see itself as a launching pad for good ministry in the wider world of Unitarian Universalist congregational life, reduce the amount of transitional time needed, and maintain its good health by avoiding upheavals in congregational life. The disadvantage is that the congregation may have a hard time letting go of a popular minister when the time comes for that minister to leave.

Two Other Options for Managing Ministerial Transition

A congregation may consider teaming up with a larger nearby congregation to be part of a multisite team. While multisite ministry is still in its infancy, it is likely to become more common in coming years. If a congregation has limited resources, joining its efforts with those of a larger nearby church can bring in additional staffing, resources, and support.

A second option is to go with no ministry at all, at least for a year. Sometimes a congregation needs to pay off bills or pay for the negotiated severance of a minister, and the costs of additional ministry are understood to be too high. A year off allows the congregation to regroup, feel less pressure, and become more prepared for interim ministry. Congregations that have taken a year off and then gone into search have more often than not been unsuccessful, but those that entered interim ministry after their year off have been very popular among ministers in search when they did begin seeking a settlement. And they were less anxious about finances while they did the interim work with an interim minister. In a few cases, they have taken advantage of a pre-interim program, such as the "jump-start transition" program described in the next chapter, or they have worked with regional staff to keep them focused.

Yet, while all of these options can be good ones, 90 percent of congregations in search have taken advantage of traditional interim ministry. Interim ministry is not always easy on a congregation, but it usually leads to a ministerial settlement. Interim ministry helps congregations manage the transition from one settlement to the next. If one of the alternative options described here does not stand out as a good fit for a congregation's circumstances, then it will be best served by interim ministry. Interim ministry continues to serve congregations well, even as congregations, ministers, and interim ministry itself change along the way.

Jump-Starting
Ministerial Transition

BARBARA CHILD

■ ■ ▨ ■

"Jump-starting the transition" is what I have dubbed the work I have done in two very different sets of congregational circumstances in which traditional interim ministry was not a realistic option. The results of this work were so beneficial that interim colleagues began asking me to describe it so they too might consider doing it. One interim minister jokingly told me that she wanted to serve only those congregations where I had jump-started the transition in advance of her arrival.

The congregations where I have done this work had found themselves, somewhat abruptly, without a minister. In one, there had been a hard-fought negotiated retirement. In the other, there had been a termination with virtually no negotiation. In the first case, the financial arrangements left the congregation without sufficient funds to pay for full-time ministry for a year. Even though this congregation knew they needed and wanted an interim minister, they were making do with a series of guest preachers and otherwise managing with only lay leadership. In the second, congregants were so angry that they wanted no interim minister and quite possibly no minister of any sort ever again. Here I focused on my role as a consultant, not on my status as a minister, though that was by no means a secret.

When I have described to colleagues the work I did in these settings, some have suggested other circumstances in which comparable jump starts might be just the thing. For instance, in a church with a succession plan whereby a called associate minister is expected to become the senior minister when the current senior minister leaves, there is still transition work to be done if the transition is to be healthy and the new senior minister is to thrive, but it is not work that the new senior minister can do. Jump-start work has also proved valuable in a congregation served by an inexperienced interim minister who brought in a recently retired accredited interim minister to do the heavy-duty transition work as a consultant, as described in "A Jump Start with a Twist." And it has always been common for an interim minister—or a called minister, for that matter—to bring in a colleague who is an expert in some area to facilitate a workshop. This jump-start transition work may be viewed as that practice writ large. Still another variation would be for serving interim ministers to adapt this program to jump-start their own interim work. Other possibilities await discovery.

I designed and have carried out this jump-start program as a recently retired accredited interim minister. I believe it is fine work for an experienced interim minister who wants to take a year off from full-time ministry without entirely leaving the work behind, or for one who is recently retired and wants to maintain skills, does not want to relocate, and prefers to work part-time in a challenging situation rather than serving as a supply preacher, sabbatical minister, or other placeholder. As I have put it, if I can get there with one suitcase in a car or an airplane, I am ready to be there for multiple weekends over a span of months. How many months the work will take depends on several things, and may or may not be possible to determine before it is under way. As of this writing, I am contemplating yet another variation—concentrating the jump-start transition into only about one month.

I want to stress that jump-start transition work is work for experienced interim ministers to do; it is not work for congregational leaders to undertake on their own. However, just as there are various circumstances under which an experienced interim minister might want to take it on, church leaders can learn here about various circumstances in which it might have value for their congregation. For instance, a well-led jump-start program might help them discern whether they should immediately search for a minister to call or would be better off applying for an interim minister or other contract minister, with whose guidance they could assess their congregation's history, present identity, and envisioned future, and prepare for a call and settlement. Or a congregation might have lost its called minister at an inconvenient time in the ordinary cycle of search for an interim minister. That congregation's leaders might discover here how they could make excellent use of the period before regular interim search by engaging an experienced interim minister to lead a short-term jump-start program. Lay leaders who are interested in pursuing jump-start possibilities for their church are invited to consult the Unitarian Universalist Association's Transitions Office or regional staff to learn about experienced interim ministers who might be available to do this work with them.

So what is this work? How does it come to happen? What does it look like? And why do I call it a "jump start"?

What Is This Work

Both times I have done this work, a professional staff member of the Unitarian Universalist Association saw the difficult ministerial transition under way and asked me if I would be interested in talking with the congregation's president to see if I could offer help. I think the lesson here is clear. Congregational leaders are not likely to seek this kind of help on their own; unless they have happened to read this book or heard about the program by word of mouth, they probably don't know that it is available. Experienced interim ministers who are interested in doing this work need to let regional staff, the UUA transitions director, and/or the director of congregational life know they are available for it. The more regional and national professional staff, as well as experienced interim ministers, know about this work,

the more likely they are to think of it when a potential need
arises. This work may be viewed as one element of the Targeted
Ministry Program (TMP) being jointly developed by the UUA
and the UU Retired Ministers and Partners (UURMaPA).

Preliminary Conversation

When congregational presidents are told by a UUA professional
staff member that they might want to get in touch with me, they
either email or phone me, but they generally don't know very
much about what they are asking. If the initial contact is by
email, I invite a phone conversation right away, because the first
step in getting this work to happen is getting the president (and,
through the president, the Board) to trust that I have something
to offer that they might want and that I know what I'm talking
about. I believe that mutual trust between the president and me
has been the *sine qua non* of success each time. It starts with that
first phone conversation.

In that conversation, I make clear that if I am to work with
the congregation, I need to learn all I can about them first, that
I do not arrive with a plan of action already formed. It helps if I
can say that I don't know anyone in the congregation. (If I do,
I make clear that what I know is minimal and that I depend on
what I learn from the president in our conversation.) I do let the
president know that I make a practice of speaking with someone on the regional staff about the circumstances there. I do not
speak with the former minister, as I would if I were undertaking an interim ministry. If I were to have such a conversation, I
think it would be essential for me to reveal that to the president,
and that might not help us establish mutual trust. I do read exit
interviews with the former minister and former Board members, if they are made available to me.

I tell the president in general terms that I would want to do
the following, in this order:

- Spend a week at the church, interviewing Board
  members individually, paid staff members, committee chairs, and anyone else the president identi-

fies as a key leader; interviewing other congregants in groups of up to ten; and meeting with the Board as a group early in the week and possibly at the end of the week as well.

- Write a report on that week describing what I have done, what I have observed, what I have learned, how I interpret it, and what I recommend for the remainder of our work together.

- Distribute the written report to every congregant as well as to UUA regional staff, the UUA Transitions Office, and the coach for the congregation's ministerial search if one has already been appointed.

- Return for whatever number of weekends we agree upon, perhaps with an understanding that when that time is up we will decide whether I should continue and, if so, for how many more weekends. One president made a good case for agreeing at the outset not only on how many weekends I would spend with them but also on the exact dates of those weekends. The larger and busier the congregation, the more likely this is to be essential, so that meeting space can be secured and the jump-start program can be advertised early enough and well enough for people to reserve time for it. Another president wanted to see how things went before committing to more than a few weekends.

- Plan the weekends to include a meeting with the Board on Friday evening; a workshop for the congregation at large on Saturday, probably in the morning; either consultation with individual lay leaders as needed or an adult religious education class on Unitarian Universalist history, thought, or practice, probably in the afternoon; and preaching on Sunday morning.

The Memorandum of Agreement

Once we have agreed in general on the work to be done, I write it up in the form of a memorandum of agreement, taking care to avoid assumptions and ambiguities. I send it to the president, who of course needs to get the rest of the Board to agree. That task is easier if I have been clear and have gotten the president excited about the program. Still, revisions may be proposed, and there may be some back-and-forth before the agreement is signed. The hardest part is likely to be getting everyone to agree on how many weekends and on specific dates. I find that the more specific I can be in the draft agreement, the more likely we are to be able to address and resolve logistical questions about scheduling, room choice, and the like at the outset, helping to avoid surprises and difficulties later on.

There are a lot of variables. For instance, the preaching schedule for the months in question may already have been arranged, and guest preachers lined up. There may be major congregational events—such as an art fair, rummage sale, building and grounds cleanup, you name it—on the calendar for Saturdays, and it is very important to me that no such events be scheduled against my Saturday workshops. The Board members may have different opinions about the best times for Friday evening meetings with me and whether they should be brown-bag affairs or early enough that everyone can eat afterward.

I do not wait for all these details to be settled before sending the president the first draft of a memorandum of agreement. Having something in writing often clarifies for everyone exactly what details we still need to resolve. It is easy to work through successive revisions online. Once everyone agrees on all the terms, I ask that the president print and sign two copies of the memorandum of agreement and send them both to me by mail; I sign both, keep one, and return the other, also by mail. Of course it would be possible to exchange final agreements by email, possibly with scanned signatures. However, I want to impress on the congregation's leadership that a final agreement is indeed final. I am not interested in haggling about it later. My system has so far not failed me, and I recommend it.

(Supplementary material for this essay, including sample memoranda of agreement, is contained in appendices available online. Access to them is managed by the UUA Transitions Office; for information, contact transitions@uua.org.

I have not been willing to negotiate about my fee or reimbursement for expenses. I don't see any point in that. This is hard and worthy work. I would not be doing it if I were less skilled. Congregations need to understand that it is worth it to them to pay for it. A sliding scale, in my view, drags everyone down and helps ensure that ministry is an underpaid profession. I have no interest in contributing to that phenomenon. In addition to paying my consultation fee, the congregation reimburses me for all travel expenses, including mileage and any airfare, lodging, and meals. I recommend they find me a motel close to the church that offers complimentary breakfast. I never, under any circumstances, accept home hospitality from a congregant. If the leadership wants to cut costs by chauffeuring me into town when I fly in, that's fine.

Preparing for Interviews

Someone on the ground needs to be in charge of scheduling my time during the interview week. The most likely person is the office administrator (however titled) or another staff person designated by the administrator, though the president must monitor the process—without micromanaging—to ensure that it happens appropriately. The interviews should be forty-five or fifty minutes long, with at least ten minutes in between. They may take place Monday through Saturday, in any two of the three parts—morning, afternoon, and evening—of a day. The schedule need not be the same on all days.

A meeting with the president needs to be scheduled very early in the week, and one with the full Board must also be held fairly early in the week. Each of these meetings may last upward of two hours. Appointments with each Board member, staff member, committee chair, and other key leader need to be scheduled as well. There may need to be some conversation with the president about what "key leader" means. In my view, it does not mean a matriarch or patriarch with no current official leadership position but lots of influence; it also does not mean a former president who has not managed to give up control. On the other hand, it may mean the editor of the newsletter, an unpaid choir director, or any other lay leader with a named, official position who isn't called a committee chair.

It is somewhat more complicated to schedule group interviews with the other congregants. To begin with, my coming, and the reason for it, needs to be publicized well enough for people to be interested in meeting with me. This publicity job is the president's and mine, not the scheduler's. I have typically written a letter to the congregation to be published in the newsletter, put on the website, and distributed in whatever other ways the president thinks are most likely to be effective. I have also provided a picture of myself and a short biographical statement. In one instance, the president wrote a letter to the congregation designed to entice people and encourage them to sign up for group interviews. It must be clearly communicated to the president that the success of the program depends on building congregational interest before my arrival, and the president must take this task seriously.

The scheduler presumably is the one who knows best how to manage the signing up, whether online, on the phone, with sign-up sheets on a bulletin board, or through some combination of these methods. It is essential that the scheduler—and everyone else—understand that no interview group may include more than ten people. No exceptions can be made. However, there is no restriction on spouses, partners, or friends signing up together.

It should be made clear that people may attend as many group interviews as they like as observers, but that they may speak and participate only in the one they signed up for. This is an important way for me to convey that these are public meetings, not secret ones, and that I will not be keeping confidential anything anyone says.

The group interviews need to be scheduled at various times of day and evening to accommodate congregants' schedules. They need to be held in rooms where up to ten participants and I can sit around a table, with a reasonable number of observers elsewhere in the room. (I have had almost no observers, but I still believe that offering that possibility is an important feature of the program. It highlights the values of both transparency and trust.)

Possibly the most critical part of the entire interview week is the questionnaire that I require every interviewee to complete in writing and bring to the interview. I call it a "ticket" to the interview, and word gets around quickly that I mean it. Everyone—Board members, staff members, committee chairs, other key leaders, and participants in group interviews—must fill out the questionnaire to participate. I keep a stack of blank questionnaires at hand. If someone arrives at an interview without a completed questionnaire, I insist that it be filled out on the spot if the person is going to stay in the room.

The questionnaires give me essential information, including demographic information that I include in my written report on the week: how many people I have interviewed, how long they have been in the congregation (which is not the same thing as how long they have officially been members, if they even are), how many Sunday services a month they typically attend, and how many hours a month they typically spend in church activities. But the questionnaire does more than gather demographic information. It invites people to reflect, before meeting with me, on what they regard as the important strengths and challenges of the church, what they hope I will prioritize in my work there, and what they especially want me to know about the church. I like having these papers in front of me during interviews. I sometimes make notes on them while people are speaking. The questionnaires are also a way for me to convey to congregants how seriously I am taking my work with them and thus how seriously I expect them to take it as well.

Initial Meeting with the Board

At my first meeting with the Board, I model for them, at least in a general way, how I want our subsequent meetings to go. I have no idea what their Board meetings typically look like, but I begin with what I call an ingathering. It includes opening words and a chalice lighting. I have a whole collection of chalice lighting texts, gathered from *Singing the Living Tradition*, the UUA's WorshipWeb (and its predecessor, the Unitarian Universalist Ministers Association's *Collected Worship Resources*), and a variety of other sources, such as the UUA's new collection of worship readings *Lifting Our Voices: Readings in the Living Tradition*. I have each one printed in fairly large type on a 5 X 8 index card. I use these not only at meetings with church Boards but also at workshops. I may simply hand someone a card and ask them to read it while I light the chalice, or I may give someone two or three cards and invite them to pick one. In any case, what I give them is consistent with the mood and thematic focus I want to achieve in that meeting. After the chalice is lit, I say some words of meditation and invite them into some moments of silence.

Then comes my version of check-in. It is anything but an invitation to go around the table and have everyone say how they are feeling or how their week has gone. At this initial meeting with the Board, I ask them to pair up, choosing someone they don't know well—and of course I am paying attention from the start to who does the choosing, who waits to be chosen, and what pairs end up together. I don't put too much stock in this initial information, but I put some, just as I put stock in every single thing I observe about interactions among congregants and about the look of the place, everything from upkeep to what is or isn't on the bulletin boards. If there is an uneven number of Board members present, I pair up with the one not chosen. Once the Board members are in pairs, I invite them to interview each other, asking these questions:

- Who are you at your best?

- Who are the people who made you who you are?

- What is an important learning experience you have had?

And then I invite each participant to introduce their interview partner to the rest of us. Inevitably they discover that they have learned some important things about their fellow leaders that they never knew, even if they have been working together for some time.

After this exercise, I describe in some detail what I believe I am (and am not) doing there, establish my credentials, and invite their questions.

I have them line up in order of when they started coming to the church and then invite them to consider these questions: Who is and who is not well represented on the Board? How much congregational history is carried in their collective memory? What gaps may be significant? If the group has generally spent past Board meetings ticking off tasks on a to-do list and if they are not used to having a minister take any interest in them as individuals, much less as carriers of congregational history and culture, they are likely to appreciate the attention this exercise pays to them.

At this point my agenda shifts and essentially mirrors the agenda I will use in my small-group interviews with congregants. I emphasize the difference between a group interview and a discussion. This is not a discussion. I will go around the table and invite separate answers from every person to the questions I pose; I will stop anyone who attempts to respond to another's comments. I think it is enormously important for them to hear each other's responses. It is also worth reminding them now that, in addition to this meeting with the whole Board, I will be interviewing Board members separately.

When I debrief with church presidents after concluding my jump-start consultations with their congregations, I ask what they think contributed to the success of our work together. They often specifically note both my directness and my honesty. Leaders and other congregants alike are sometimes surprised by what they may experience as bluntness, but they come to count on it and it contributes greatly to the trust that must develop for this work be to successful. One president noted that my references were candid about me, and the fact that I would choose such people to serve as references set the stage for my own candor.

In my initial meeting with the Board, I ask each person to tell me what I call a "signature story" about the church. I make the analogy between an individual's written signature—which may be quite illegible but is nonetheless immediately recognizable by anyone who knows the person well—and the signature of a church, which is conveyed just as recognizably by the stories congregants tell over and over. I want the Board members and others in my small-group interviews to hear the stories others tell. I also want to find out what stories are told in multiple groups by people who aren't aware that others are telling me the same stories.

The other question I am particularly interested in is this: What do you want more of here? This is an Appreciative Inquiry question, as discussed in Diana Whitney and Amanda Trosten-Bloom's *The Power of Appreciative Inquiry* and Diana Whitney et al.'s *Appreciative Team Building*. The answer may identify something the respondent is missing and wishes were present; it may equally well identify something the respondent believes is present and would like to see in even greater measure. In either case, the question does not focus on problems to be solved. It does not ask what is wrong here but what is right and could get even better. It signals the approach I try to use throughout my work.

At the end of my initial meeting with the Board, when I have described my plans for the rest of the week, I ask whether the Board members would like to get together with me as a group again at the end of the week, to hear my initial reflections on what I have learned, before I go home to write my report. Such meetings can prove enormously important to the whole consultation. One Board that chose to have this meeting initially believed I could concentrate the work of a whole first year of interim ministry into a few months, enabling them to choose a Ministerial Search Committee that spring, have that committee go to work with their coach (then called a ministerial settlement representative), and bring in an interim minister the following fall to do just one year of interim work, which they were thinking of as the second interim year, while the ministerial search would be in progress. What I learned during my week of interviews in that church was that this plan was completely unworkable. The congregation was so fractured that no seven of them could have been sufficiently trusted by the rest that they could have successfully served as a ministerial search committee. These people needed the better part of a year of interim ministry with a full-time interim minister on-site before they would be ready even to think about selecting a ministerial search committee. I knew I needed to demonstrate this in my written report, but I also knew the Board needed to comprehend this conclusion and support it before I put it to the congregation at large. Of course, I could have sent the written report to the Board in advance of sending it to others, but that would have been a pale substitute for talking it over with them and making sure they understood its ramifications. It was a complete stroke of luck that they had agreed at the beginning of my interview week to get back together with me at its end. That second meeting was a learning experience for them and for me. They learned they needed two years of interim ministry in addition to the preliminary work I was doing with them. I learned how I needed to present this necessity to the congregation. This experience also taught me to always urge the Board to reconvene with me at the end of the interview week. That second meeting might turn out to be a godsend.

Small-Group Interviews

Before I do anything else at small-group interviews, I make sure I have a completed questionnaire from each person at the table. If anyone has not brought the completed questionnaire, I set them to work on it immediately and make clear I need to have it in hand before they leave the room.

In the course of these interviews, I use two forms that help me work with all the groups the same way. It is essential to use the same process and ask the same questions, in order to complete the interviews in the allotted time and keep the resulting data manageable. These are absolutely essential, if for no other reason than to preserve the interviewer's sanity.

The first form is an agenda for myself, which includes the opening words and chalice lighting, a few quiet moments for centering, introductions, a description of my role, an invitation to tell signature stories, interview questions (which will be answered by each person in turn, not offered for group discussion), and closing words. My typical introduction technique, which I learned long ago from Rachel Naomi Remen, is to invite each person to describe some object at home that they could have brought along to put in the center of the table that would tell us something important about them that they would like the rest of us to know. After the introductions, I describe my own role in the work we are doing, and then I turn to my standard interview questions. These are listed on my second form. I use one copy of the form for each group, noting on it people's answers to each question.

Individual Interviews

My individual interviews with lay leaders and paid staff members are more informal, though they are still bound by the same time restrictions as the small-group interviews. I am not likely to light a chalice or ask for a moment of silent meditation. I am more likely to engage in back-and-forth exchanges, so that the sessions feel more like conversations and less like interviews. However, I still have standard interview questions on the standard form, which I use in every interview.

My Report

My general plan—a week of interviews followed by a written report that includes recommendations for follow-up work—is adapted from what I learned from Speed Leas in an Alban Institute workshop on intervention in severely conflicted churches. The churches where I have done my jump-start work were considerably conflicted, but this program is adaptable for use with churches in a variety of circumstances, not only conflicted ones.

I have found it important to write my report as soon as possible after the interview week, partly so that as much as possible is still fresh in my mind and partly because I want the congregation to receive my report while their curiosity is still high. I think the report itself is probably the best publicity device for getting high turnout for the workshops that follow.

Each report I have written has been upward of forty pages long and has gone into great detail about the church; while I don't regard the reports as secret, I don't believe they should be available outside the congregation, except to those with a professional need to know the details. Here is my standard outline for the report:

Agreement with the Board

I quote from the actual memorandum of agreement, giving the purposes of the consultation and the dates of the interview week and anticipated weekend visits.

What I Did

I summarize my activities during the interview week, including the total number of people interviewed, the number of individual interviews of lay leaders and staff members, the number of small-group interviews, and the number of people interviewed in small groups. I attach a copy of my interview questionnaire. If I have read exit interviews with former Board members or a former minister, I mention that fact, and I also give the names and positions of any UUA staff I have spoken with about the church. I also mention having read the church bylaws, and the policy book if there is one.

What I Learned

- I give the number of each gender I interviewed, including how many of each I know to be transgender, if any. I indicate how many of those interviewed are official members, how long they have been at the church (in ranges of years: zero to two, two to five, and so on), how many times a month, on average, they attend Sunday services, and how many hours a month (in ranges of hours) they spend in activities related to the church.

- I enumerate frequently told signature stories, frequently mentioned strengths of the church, and frequently mentioned challenges, concerns, and unresolved conflicts, and give an unabridged list of everything people report they want more of.

* I indicate which issues interviewees hope I will prioritize, and I assess what we can and cannot realistically expect to accomplish during the remainder of my consultation with the church.

What's Next

I describe my plans for my weekend visits to follow, including Friday evening meetings with the Board, Saturday workshops, and possibilities for a monthly adult religious education course. If it is generally understood that a year or two of full-time interim ministry will follow my months of consultation, I give a very brief introduction to what interim ministry actually is, who provides it, and what the congregation's tasks are during the interim period. If the congregation, particularly the leadership, have not so far committed themselves to interim ministry following my work with them, I describe what I see as their options and the ramifications of their choosing each.

Distribution of the Report

I make clear who will receive the report, including all congregants, either electronically or in hard copy. I list other recipients, who may include, as appropriate, the UUA transitions director; regional professional staff; the coach, however titled, who will serve the church and its Search Committee during subsequent ministerial search; and the interim minister when that person is selected. (If specifically requested, I have also sent the report to the former minister.)

Concluding Note

I conclude the report with a personal note of thanks to all who have assisted me in my consultation so far, everyone I have interviewed, and all who have welcomed me graciously into their midst. I express my happy anticipation of our continuing work together, and I sign the note with my full name but no title.

I send the report to the president before it is shared with anyone else, but on the understanding that it will be distributed exactly as it is—even if there turn out to be errors in it that I will need to correct later. In other words, nothing in the report is subject to negotiation or redaction.

Weekend Visits

Friday Evenings with the Board

I always prepare a detailed written agenda for myself and send a less detailed version to the president about a week in advance for distribution to the rest of the Board. Doing this helps elicit issues for discussion that they know about but I don't. I establish from the start that all of my communications with the congregation will be through the president. I am not to be copied on anybody else's email, and no one else is to write to me directly. This mode of operation has served me extremely well, and I cannot imagine ever changing it. If there is dissatisfaction among congregants with the president in particular or the Board in general, or if other Board members are dissatisfied with the president, it becomes evident soon enough without anybody writing to me about it. And I have no wish to be triangulated.

My agenda for meetings with the Board has generally followed this plan:

- We begin with opening words from me and a chalice lighting, with words on an index card handed to a Board member to read.

- Then I offer a reading from *This Day in UU History* if we are meeting on the anniversary of something I can put to good use.

- I ask everyone to check in, using a question I have derived from either the chalice lighting words or the entry in *This Day in UU History*. For instance, after I read to a Board about the Unitarian Universalist ministers who showed up on Bloody Sunday in Selma, Alabama, my check-in question was: What is something important that you have shown up for since we last met? More commonly, check-in questions arise from chalice lighting words. Some examples: What is something that lifted your heart or brought you joy during the past week? What is something you discovered of worth in some other person during the past week, and something of worth you discovered in yourself? What is something significant that happened in your church life since we last met?

- Check-in is followed by a reading from *Bless the Imperfect: Meditations for Congregational Leaders*, edited by Kathleen Montgomery. This book is a gold mine, and I am determined to make every church leader I work with aware of it. After my first meeting with a Board, I get a commitment that at least one Board member will buy the book and choose a reading for our next session, and other members take turns choosing ones after that.

- In my first Friday meeting with the Board after the interview week, I make time for their questions and comments on my written report, which they have had time to digest by then.

- Also in that first Friday meeting, I share with them Michael Durall's nine criteria for his willingness to consult with a church, which he lists in *The Almost Church: Redefining Unitarian Universalism for a New*

Era. They include "a willingness among church leaders to keep open minds in reviewing current patterns of congregational life, and a willingness to consider different methods if they hold promise; a willingness of church leaders not to have the keenest minds focused only on institutional maintenance . . . but on outreach efforts, as well; . . . a willingness to clarify and, most likely, raise the expectations of membership, including the expectation of charitable giving in good measure; . . . a willingness to challenge the attitude of scarcity . . . ; . . . and a willingness of church leaders to lead—to make decisions without taking surveys 'to see what people think' before instituting new policies." I put the complete list in the agenda. I do not invite discussion about it at the first session, but get each Board member to choose one of the nine criteria to ruminate about and report on at our next meeting. My overarching question is: If I operated according to Durall's criteria, would I have come to work with you? And the follow-up, assuming the answer is no: What will you do to meet these criteria?

- The next item on the agenda is standard for each visit: What issues, if any, have surfaced since my last visit that it would be good for us to discuss? If issues have arisen, we then determine whether discussion on the spot would be useful or whether it would be better instead for me to meet separately at some point on Saturday with one Board member and perhaps one or more other interested and affected lay leaders as well. This point in the meeting is also an opportunity for Board members to share with me how they think the congregation is reacting to our work so far and whether adjustments to my plans might be in order.

- During the Friday evening meeting, I always brief the Board about my plans for the Saturday morning workshop—what I plan to do and what I hope to accomplish. I get commitments from as many Board members as possible to attend the workshop, and we determine who will do what to bring the learnings from it to congregants who do not attend. Since there is so much value in Board members attending all the events of the weekend, and since Board members are likely to be especially busy people, it is important to give them as much notice as possible about what is planned so they can set aside the needed time.

- At all these meetings, I have a check-out question. At the first session, I ask: How was this meeting different from your usual Board meetings—not how do you feel about it, just what differences did you notice? At subsequent sessions, I ask some variation on this question: What is something from this meeting that you know you will continue to think about, or that you will remember for a long time?

- At our final meeting, we spend considerable time assessing where they are with respect to interim ministry. If they have committed to hiring an interim minister for the following year, we talk over the interim selection process, where they are in the process, how it is going for them, and any feedback they have for the UUA Transitions Office about it. We also talk about how they can best prepare for the coming interim minister, what documents to gather (including those generated in workshops, which should have been saved for this purpose), what issues they want to ask the interim minister to prioritize, even what attention might need to be given to the minister's study to make it inviting for its new occupant.

    One cautionary note: I have learned from one interim minister who followed my jump-start work how important it is for me not to leave the

Board with too definite an assessment of what the interim minister's priorities, methods, or approaches to the work should be. Interim ministers need to be unfettered in making their own assessments and choosing their own methods and approaches. Both of the congregations I have worked with in the jump-start program did commit to having an interim minister the following year. However, if a congregation did not make that commitment before I finished my work with them, I would have a heart-to-heart conversation with the Board about their options for religious leadership and the likely ramifications of choosing each of those options.

■ At my final Friday evening meeting with the Board, we take some time to assess our work together, addressing the following questions:

- Was my work here what you expected it to be, or did it differ? If it differed, how so?

- What did we accomplish together?

- What didn't we accomplish that you wish we had?

- What suggestions do you have for me when I do this kind of work again with other congregations in the future?

I think it's fair to say that my overarching intention, in every meeting with the Board, is to establish and then maintain trust among us so that we all are willing to be honest with each other and take on hard issues, even if they make us uncomfortable. No congregants other than Board members have ever sought to attend my sessions with the Board; if any had, I believe I would have declined the request. The presence of others in the room would almost certainly have changed the group dynamics significantly—and there is no need for these meetings to be open. They are not official Board meetings, where policy decisions are made. They are meetings of parties to an agreement, who are discussing and implementing that agreement. We need to be honest. We need to be able to be vulnerable. We need to be able to acknowledge mistakes. We are partners in a delicate and important effort. In my meetings with the two boards I have worked with as jump-start consultant, we were sometimes uncomfortable, and the gnashing of teeth could sometimes be heard, but I believe that we enjoyed each other's company and profited in important ways from our time together, all for the greater good of the church.

Saturday Morning Workshops

If the jump start is going to make its way into the congregational consciousness and culture, it needs to be offered to congregants directly, not transmitted from the top via the Board. The two opportunities for doing this are the Saturday workshops and the Sunday sermon. I will say more about the sermon in a minute, but I do believe the best opportunity is the Saturday workshop, even if there are fewer people there than at Sunday service. It is important, however, to get as many people as possible to attend the workshops, and this requires a big marketing operation, especially for the first one. If it is engaging and thought-provoking, word will get around, and it will be easier to draw a crowd for later workshops.

The tricky part is coming up with appropriate advertising copy for a whole workshop series long before anyone knows what will be needed or appropriate. My solution has been to initially advertise, well in advance, a series of only four workshops, on the principle that further ones, however many there turn out to be, can be advertised later. In describing these workshops, I use the same principle I have often used in composing sermon blurbs for newsletters, that is, I mainly raise provocative questions. The good news is that not once has anyone ever accosted me afterwards to complain that the workshop did not answer the questions raised in the advertising. My flyer full of questions is posted all over the place, including on the church's website and in the newsletter as well as on bulletin boards. Congregants also have as advance publicity my letter to them and my biographical statement, which includes a picture of me. And the Board serves as an advance marketing team, with the president as cheerleader in chief.

A great deal is riding on my first workshop. I make myself a very detailed agenda for it, although I do sometimes deviate from it according to the dictates of the moment. The first such workshop I gave focused on what it means to be a Unitarian Universalist community. I gave this workshop in many churches I served as interim minister, and I believe it is a fine way for a group to gain a realistic view of, and begin to come to terms with, its present identity. I ground it on descriptions of Unitarian fellowship, the Unitarian Universalist Church, and beloved community gleaned from Michael Durall's *The Almost Church* and Tom Owen-Towle's *Growing a Beloved Community.* Participants find it an eye-opener, and I would almost certainly offer it first in future jump-start work.

In the interest of preventing needless difficulties during workshops, it is helpful to say a little at the beginning of each one not only about its focus but also about the process by which it will operate. This has at least some chance of heading off at the pass anyone who might otherwise try to turn it into a venting or complaining session. Especially if people in the congregation have been used to sharing "Joys and Concerns" during Sunday services without monitoring, they are likely to require some instruction in workshop protocol.

In both churches where I have done this work, the focus of later workshops differed, and changed from weekend to weekend because I constantly rethought what to do next depending on what needs I discovered and also on my deep discernment shared in conversation with the Board. I cannot stress enough the importance of working in partnership with the Board. More than once I was inclined to do one thing, but conversation with the Board convinced me to do another. In this work, it simply does not do to operate over and against the Board. It is their church. I come with the clear eye of the outsider, but they carry the culture. And since they are there when I am not, they know far better than I how the congregation is reacting to our work so far and whether it has given rise to additional issues.

Saturday Afternoons

Saturday mornings work best for workshops. This leaves Saturday afternoons open. I haven't worked with a church yet that couldn't benefit from deeper understanding of what it means to be a Unitarian Universalist. In both churches where I did jump-start work, therefore, I offered to teach an adult religious education class on Saturday afternoon. One church took me up on it; the other preferred I leave Saturday afternoon open to consult with individual leaders as needed on whatever issues might arise. In truth, they came up with something every single Saturday afternoon I was there. However, I am fairly sure those consultations could have happened around the edges of other scheduled programming. Nonetheless, I respected the president's assessment that adult religious education is not part of the substance of transition work and could be offered by others at any time, while our work needed to remain sharply focused on issues related to transition. If a jump-start program is offered in a congregation where there has been a lot of tension and the leaders have learned to expect emergencies to happen frequently, it is understandable that they would want the jump-start consultant to be available as much as possible for consultation.

The class I taught in the other church was a joy to teach, and I recommend that such a class be part of the jump-start program if the leadership is open to it. It may be a hard sell, because the congregation and its leadership may not realize that they need to understand better what it means to be a Unitarian Universalist. It is of course also going to be difficult to get people to spend most of their Saturday in church, attending a workshop in the morning and a class in the afternoon. And to tell the truth, if they are going to choose only one of those two opportunities, I would rather they attend the workshop and forego the class. A book that has worked very well for me as the basis for such classes in churches I served as interim minister is John Buehrens and Forrest Church's *A Chosen Faith*. Any minister will have favorites. All of them can serve well.

The Sunday Service

In one of the churches where I have done jump-start work, the lay leaders of Sunday services were inexperienced and unsophisticated enough that I took on much of the responsibility for the services when I was there, in part to show the congregation some different ways of doing things. In the other church, expert lay worship leadership had developed, and I felt that making significant changes in the Sunday service would be beyond my purview. Besides, I knew that an interim minister would be arriving fairly soon. Whatever changes in the service might be appropriate would be far better managed by that minister, who would be on the ground full-time, than by me, an occasional presence.

In both churches, the Sunday sermon gave me the opportunity to reflect on the theme of the Saturday workshop and on what had happened there. Now I was speaking to people who had not been there as well as those who had. I always had to remember I was speaking to visitors as well, and they needed not to have the uncomfortable sense that they had wandered by mistake into some other people's family reunion. Thus it was important that I be clear and straightforward, without relying on allusions or hints. Inside jokes were not in order. I liked the way my sermon completed the weekend. It was the denouement, so to speak. And all but the last one could help draw more people to succeeding Saturday workshops. But I never felt that the Sunday sermons carried nearly as much weight as the workshops. I continue to see the workshops as the real heart and soul of the jump-start work.

The work is a joy to do. I cannot recommend it enough to experienced interim ministers and other ministers in a position to offer some variation of the program described here, and to congregations in circumstances that could make it valuable, whether those circumstances are among those I described at the beginning of this essay, or are ones I have not yet even dreamed of.

Congregational leaders have offered positive assessments of our work together. Their comments have included:

- Through our jump-start transition work, both leaders in particular and congregants in general were able to get an objective picture of current congregational life.

- We came to understand interim ministry well enough to not be afraid of it but instead welcome it and even look forward to it, with an appreciation of how important self-examination is and how long it takes to do it well.

- Our work was "smart, spirited, honest, and targeted." This was at least partly because our jump-start consultant came to us as an independent contractor and worked according to an agreement that we forged together.

If asked to advise leaders of another congregation who were trying to decide whether to hire a jump-start transition consultant, one congregation president I worked with would ask them, "Why *wouldn't* you want to set yourself up for a successful decade ahead?"

A Jump Start with a Twist

OLIVIA HOLMES

Shortly after I retired from my work as an accredited interim minister, I signed an agreement with a Unitarian Universalist church for a five-month transitions consulting ministry. Simultaneously, a ministerial colleague of mine signed an agreement to be that church's interim parish minister for six months. She had over fifteen years' experience as a minister, but none as an interim minister and none in Unitarian Universalist parish ministry; she had only recently achieved dual standing with the UUA. Our two agreements grew out of my bringing her into the conversation that the church originally began with me.

Our ministries were both to begin in January. Nothing untoward had happened in the church; their beloved minister had decided to step down at the end of December and enjoy a well-earned retirement. To his enduring credit, he and the leadership gave the congregation ample warning of his departure. The congregation rallied together to give him an appropriate and thoroughly affectionate send-off.

Because the congregation was in search for an interim minister for an eighteen-month interim transition to begin in January, they were out of sync with the regular search calendar for Unitarian Universalist ministers, which expects ministers to begin in mid- to late summer. In addition, the congregation was offering less than full fair share compensation and no moving expenses whatsoever. Under these circumstances, the Interim

Search Committee did not think they would be able to attract an interim minister with the level of experience they had hoped for.

I was seventy years old and knew it was time for me to slow down and turn my energies toward the enormous "bucket list" of retirement projects I had accumulated over a quarter century of Unitarian Universalist ministry. I felt I no longer had the energy and vitality for the full-time interim ministry I had loved so well. However, the UUA transitions director thought I should at least speak with the Interim Search Committee of this church, which happened to be very near my home, to see whether something helpful to the congregation could be worked out.

My plan was to offer to serve for six months, to enable the congregation both to search for a well-matched interim minister for the full year to follow and to increase their commitment to and understanding of stewardship so they could become fair compensation employers in every way, or at least get closer to that goal.

Barbara Child had shared with me her work in developing the concept of a jump-start transition. As I began conversations with the congregation's Interim Search Committee, I realized that I did not honestly feel I had the energy to work even half-time, let alone the three-quarter-time they hoped for, and that their budget would allow. So I contacted my colleague, who I thought might be interested in considering Unitarian Universalist interim ministry after her years of successful parish ministry in another denomination. I suggested we consider offering ourselves to the congregation as a clearly defined shared ministry team, with her as the interim parish minister and me as the transitions consulting minister. She was as fascinated by the possibilities as I was.

The church was planning on eighteen months of transition. We all eventually agreed that, for the first six months of that period, my colleague would serve half-time as their interim parish minister, responsible for rites of passage, pastoral counseling, preaching, staff supervision, and the other usual responsibilities of parish ministry. I would serve the congregation quarter-time as their transitions consulting minister, focusing exclusively on helping them prepare for someone else (neither myself nor my colleague) to become their interim minister for the following year. This arrangement allowed the congregation to become fair compensation employers of the equivalent of a three-quarter-time position, shared between the two of us, something they and we could be proud of having worked out.

The agreement I signed with the church made clear that I would not be functioning in any way as a parish minister. I would, however, preach once a month on an issue relevant to the congregation's understanding of their strengths, challenges, and norms, and write a monthly newsletter column regarding the ongoing work of transition.

In creating the agreement, I followed fairly closely the model Barbara Child had created for her jump-start work. The plan included a monthly meeting with the Standing Committee that was separate from their regular monthly business meetings. Our monthly meeting was intended to enable me both to share what I was learning about the congregation's strengths, challenges, and norms, and to offer them tools to more deliberately define the congregation as it was and as it envisioned becoming. It also enabled us to develop new goals for our work together.

Since my colleague was brand new to both Unitarian Universalist ministry and interim ministry, I took formal responsibility for mentoring her in her role as the interim parish minister.

My agreement also called for:

- presenting a workshop to the entire congregation approximately once a month (or having one presented by an expert I would recommend), on a subject agreed upon by me and the Standing Committee,

- working with the Stewardship Committee to review the strengths and challenges of the congregation's current attitudes and practices of stewardship,

- and assisting in designing an approach to the upcoming stewardship campaign.

The agreement further called on me to work with one or two additional church committees, whichever seemed most relevant to the Standing Committee and me. Finally, it specified that the

Standing Committee would set aside $2,000 to provide for possible transitional program expenses, such as but not limited to:

- consultations by other experts in areas of leadership development

- attendance by lay leaders at relevant Unitarian Universalist district or regional workshops

- books and other supplies for workshops

- other expenses deemed appropriate in advance by the president or her designees and me.

The leaders had no experience with a minister having authority over such a line item in the budget, and as a result, the Standing Committee thought the authority for allocation of these funds was theirs. As the one who included it in the contract, I thought the authority was mine. Anyone drawing up an agreement for jump-start work should take care to be very clear about who has the authority to allocate such funds.

The work I actually completed varied somewhat from what was envisioned in the agreement. The truth is that you really don't know, until your feet are on the ground, what work will turn out to be most important, and whether it will be what you had anticipated. It is a good idea for the agreement to use language like "such as" and "for example," to assure the congregational leaders that they and the consulting minister will determine their most important objectives together.

The very first work for me to do after my colleague and I had introduced ourselves to the congregation, which we did by letter, was to hold one-on-one interviews with each of the congregation's leaders and staff members, followed by group interviews with between eight and ten members of the congregation at a time. We committed ourselves to providing feedback to the leadership and congregation the following month regarding the information we had gleaned from the interviews. I used the model questionnaires Barbara Child had created for her jump-start program, and they worked very well. In total, over half the congregation participated in the interview process.

It would have been impossible for me to work so exclusively on connecting with so many members of the congregation had I been the sole interim minister. As it was, I had no preaching, pastoral, or staff responsibilities to distract me. The result was significant. Congregants knew that I had listened to them intently at the very beginning of the interim time, and that I would share with them what I had heard and learned. That knowledge went a long, long way to alleviate their fears and anxieties around the transition time and process. The congregation's president said afterward, "The interviews were incredibly valuable, and I recommend them as a way to look deeply into the true life and issues of the congregation. They required a tremendous amount of the consulting minister's time and energy, and I doubt that they could be done by a single interim minister; the team was essential for allowing this work to take place."

During the interviews a number of people asked the question all experienced interim ministers come to expect: Why does the transition have to take so long? I addressed this question in my newsletter column. I stressed the importance of the congregation addressing its grief after the departure of a beloved minister. I stressed the need for the congregation as a whole to look toward understanding its strengths, challenges, and mission before any minister, interim or settled, could determine whether their skill set would be a good match for this church. And I also stressed the importance of the Search Committee's knowing that finding a good match in a minister is far more important than finding a minister within a certain time frame. This was a critical message, which I had to repeat many times before the congregation and the Search Committee really understood it. In the end, the Search Committee did not find a match in the first round, and its members were comfortable going into a second round and considering another year of interim ministry. This was a major step forward in their understanding of the importance of both the interim work and a good match with an eventual settled minister.

One great advantage to having two ministers serve during this time was that my colleague's presence, both in person and in her newsletter columns, was far more pastoral, more spiritual, and more inspirational than mine. We both saw this as a

great advantage in a jump-start interim time. She could assure
the congregation that their interim parish minister loved them
and cared for them with the same commitment they had found
in their previous minister. I was free to speak the truth—gently,
perhaps, but to speak it nonetheless. The president commented
that however gently I spoke the truth, it was hard at times for the
congregation to receive it. She felt this was partly because some
of their perceptions were naturally different, and partly because
"the congregation was sometimes resistant to that 'truth.'"

My colleague, the congregation, and I all had to learn something about boundaries in the beginning. People would come
to me with pastoral issues, and I would have to redirect them
to my colleague. People would go to her with transition questions, and she would have to redirect them to me. The good
news is that it did not take very long for all of us, including the
two ministers who were used to working solo, to create clear
boundaries. The clear difference between our roles offered
an opportunity to practice clarifying boundaries and responsibilities, something about which the congregation had a lot
to learn.

I soon realized that, while the congregation had a mission
statement, no one really knew what it was or why it might be
important. Further, they had no statement of affirmation or
shared covenant. So the Standing Committee and I designed a
"dot process" to be implemented during community hour (coffee hour) on two Sundays the following month. We printed the
mission statement on two large sheets of newsprint and posted
them at opposite ends of the parish hall. Each person arriving
for coffee was given a certain number of dot-shaped stickers to
place over the word or words they thought most important in
the mission statement. The children were included in the process, with dots of their own in a different color from the adults'.

The results showed that the words most people found most
important in the mission statement were the action words: the
verbs *nurture*, *witness*, *support*, and *inspire*. I was able to adapt
a chalice lighting reading to include these four verbs so that
people could begin to remember them over time just by speaking them together every Sunday. Further, my colleague and I

introduced a unison affirmation also to be spoken nearly every Sunday morning, a variation for this particular congregation of the affirmation said in many Unitarian Universalist congregations that begins, "Love is the spirit of this church." While a unison affirmation is not a covenant or a grievance policy or a disruptive behavior policy, it is a place of grounding in which to begin conversations should conflict arise.

Two diagnostic tools I shared with the Standing Committee in those early months were Michael Durall's nine criteria for a church to be able to move forward, from *The Almost Church* (page 272 in this book) and Dan Hotchkiss's "Snapshot of Church Finance" (danhotchkiss.com/snapshot-of-church-finance). Each member of the Standing Committee independently evaluated the congregation on each of Durall's criteria. I compiled the results and presented them to the Committee. A majority of them found that their congregation met only one of the nine criteria. They could see for themselves how much work was needed. The president reflected, "This was an excellent tool, as it allowed the leadership to see for ourselves how we measured up against the criteria."

Dan Hotchkiss's "Snapshot of Church Finance" was equally helpful in giving the leaders specific diagnostic information to use in setting goals. For example, they discovered that only 51 percent of the operating budget of the church came from pledges. Hotchkiss suggests that "anything less than 80 percent runs the risk of weakening the congregation's sense of ownership and responsibility." Knowing their level of stewardship was low helped inspire the Standing Committee to work toward being more direct and proactive in moving the congregation away from an attitude of scarcity and toward one of abundance over a period of years.

Over the next couple of months, I guided the Standing Committee through two critical transition activities. The first was understanding and following best practice in the selection of a Search Committee. The second was moving the understanding of stewardship from a narrow focus on money to the importance of nurturing the ministries—all the ministries—of the congregation.

Our area's ministerial settlement representative (the coach of the Search Committee) and I were used to working very closely together in guiding a congregation toward best practice in selecting a committee. In this church's case, I led a training for the Standing Committee in how to talk to the congregation about the work of a search committee, the extensive time commitment required of search committee members, the kinds of interpersonal and functional skills they would need to be successful in working together, and how then to ask the person they were speaking with to suggest names to be considered. Congregation members might also volunteer for consideration themselves.

The Standing Committee then shared the task of phoning every member of the congregation to discuss the matter. Once they had a list of names, they called the top four potential committee members recommended by the congregation. They wanted to be absolutely sure these people understood the depth of commitment that would be required of them and were willing and able to serve. When these four had agreed, the Standing Committee worked to round out the Search Committee's shared skill sets, including by recruiting other members whose names had been suggested by the congregation, again calling those they felt would be the best first to be sure they understood the commitment and would be willing and able to serve.

A special meeting of the congregation was called, immediately following a worship service, for the purpose of naming, electing, supporting, and blessing the Ministerial Search Committee. I wrote an order of service for this ceremony to clearly state the engagement of the congregation in the selection process; the depth of commitment and confidentiality being asked of the Search Committee members; the commitment of the congregation, including the children, to supporting them in their work; and the confidence the Standing Committee placed in them. The ceremony closed with the interim parish minister blessing the newly installed committee.

To guide the Stewardship Team, which consisted of the Standing Committee members and a few other congregational leaders, I prepared a quartile analysis of financial commitments. (See Wayne Clark's "Does Your Congregation Have a Healthy

Distribution of Financial Commitments?" on the UUA's congregational stewardship blog). The analysis confirmed that a large proportion of congregation members were contributing at the bottom quartile (59 percent versus the recommended 40 percent). I challenged the members of the Standing and Stewardship Committees to model giving from an attitude of both abundance and commitment to the congregation's future by increasing their own pledges by 30 percent. To their great credit, they collectively reached this goal. They planned circle suppers, at which one of them would lead a conversation with a group of congregants about a wider vision of stewardship. The president told me that "there was some criticism of this as some members felt that circle suppers should be social events and not a time to discuss stewardship"—stewardship at that time being almost universally understood as meaning "money." She continued, "However, going forward, I think that circle suppers could be an opportunity to discuss mission and vision."

The congregation did their best in this stewardship effort, and overall giving increased by approximately 12 percent. This was not quite enough to fund a full-time interim minister for the following year, but it was still a good start toward a new understanding of stewardship.

The congregation was rightly proud of two of its programs of outreach to the wider community. They had successfully held a spaghetti dinner for the hungry every Wednesday for some fourteen years. And a series of lectures by prominent speakers had run at the church every summer for more than forty years. Yet there was a sense that the congregation also longed for a deeper commitment to the wider Unitarian Universalist community, without knowing how to turn this longing into reality.

I preached about the six hundred Unitarian Universalists, including me, who had marched across the Edmund Pettus bridge fifty years after Unitarian Universalist Rev. James Reeb was murdered as a result of his commitment to walking in Selma with Dr. Martin Luther King Jr. in 1965. The congregation had not known his story, and they were deeply moved to hear of our denominational commitment both then and now. This history was also the subject of my next newsletter column.

I was able to connect congregational leaders with excellent workshops being offered by UUA regional staff, including one on multisite visioning and one on small and midsized congregations. The Standing Committee was coming to understand the value of creating a line item in the budget for such excellent training. The president agreed: "Having a budget to support this and experience in the value of such trainings will continue to serve the congregation."

As my ministerial colleague and I came to know this congregation and be known by them, we understood their concerns around conflict more deeply. We learned that they had no real experience of shared ministry. At least at first, they were somewhat skittish about both the term and the concept. It turned out that they had called three settled ministers in a row who tended to be authoritarian. They had experienced dreadful conflict between a minister emeritus and a newly settled minister, which the congregation had been inexorably drawn into. After twenty years of challenging relationships with ministers, they had had two years of interim ministry before calling their most recent settled minister. He was an extraordinary and well-loved pastoral presence. However, while a conflict management protocol existed now, nobody really knew what it was. I felt I needed to address the congregation's aversion to conflict and teach them that there are ways, compassionate ways, to work through difficult conversations.

So the following month I preached on compassionate communication, the work and theories of Marshall Rosenberg, demonstrating with a willing couple that there are compassionate ways to approach conflict that yield a far more affirming result than fight, flight, or freeze. My colleague and I both tried hard to model shared leadership, working with each other and with lay leaders to come to shared understandings from which to confidently lead the congregation.

My work with the Standing Committee in the last few months of my time there was to identify key areas of focus to be undertaken in the following interim year. In my final newsletter column, I described the insights the congregation and its leaders had given me into who they were, what they believed, and how they conducted their lives.

There are several reasons why the work my colleague and I did with this congregation was successful. I think it was a great advantage to the congregation to have both a parish minister (even at half-time) and a dedicated and experienced accredited interim minister leading the transition work. I know my new interim colleague believes that our shared ministry gave her an extraordinary introduction to transition work and Unitarian Universalist resources for ministers and congregations. I know I gained insights into the work I was focused on through hearing her perspective. I think our ability to serve well together as a team also helped model the whole idea of shared ministry for congregational leaders.

It must be said that my twenty-five-year friendship with my colleague helped us work as a team: We had great faith in each other. Our circumstances also allowed both of us to agree to part-time work, something not everyone can do. And I found it extremely rewarding to make a significant contribution to the work of a congregation in transition while still honoring my own awareness that I had recently retired and it was time for me to take life at a slower pace.

The congregation's president observed, "One challenge of this model is that it takes an extraordinary amount of time and energy from the leadership and the ministers. I don't think we were prepared for that (really, how could we be?), but I do think we rose to the occasion." She's quite correct; they did so admirably.

Clearly it was helpful that my colleague and I both lived within a reasonable commuting distance of the church so that no moving or travel expenses were incurred. She had a fair compensation professional expense budget and was a paid employee of the congregation. Since I was contracted as a consultant, I was effectively self-employed. The $2,000 budget line item I had contracted for included any expenses I might incur in creating workshops for the leaders or congregation, or in attending regional workshops with church leaders. Had I chosen to be an employee, I have learned, I would have had the right to delay my first mandatory withdrawal from my retirement fund, an option that others considering this work should bear in mind.

In the following year, even though leaders and congregants had worked hard to increase pledging, the congregation was still unable to offer a full-time interim position at a full fair compensation level and to cover a new minister's moving expenses. Therefore, the UUA transitions director approved exploring with the Interim Search Committee the possibility of our continuing to work with the congregation the following year. Ultimately we agreed that my colleague would continue as the interim parish minister, but with her hours increased to three-quarter-time, and I would continue as the transitions consulting minister, with my hours decreased to one-eighth-time. We removed preaching from my commitment; my key areas of focus were to be stewardship, updating the bylaws, and supporting the Ministerial Search Committee.

I believe we were far more effective that following year than we would have been had we not completed the first six months in jump-start mode. The president agrees. Continuing to serve allowed both the leadership and us to stay focused on expanding the work already done in communications, stewardship, and on connecting with the wider Unitarian Universalist community and on developing a much deeper understanding of shared ministry. Still, the boundaries we set on our activities in that following year meant that our work much more closely resembled an ordinary year of interim ministry. Had the congregation had the funds to offer fair compensation for full-time ministry, with moving expenses covered, I am confident an experienced interim minister could have served them very well.

Changing Work in a Changing World

KEITH KRON

■ ■ ▦ ■

As the Unitarian Universalist Association's Ministerial transitions director, I have a unique perspective on our religious movement. Every day I see up close congregations in need of a new minister. Some congregants are angry, some relieved. Some are sad, some determined. In nearly all such congregations, the wide array of feelings in the community creates an atmosphere of vulnerability and anxiety. And that's often what makes the process of transition so hard.

Congregants typically want to have a single story to help them understand what has happened and what will happen, one that features simple cause and effect, one that explains everything they need to know and will serve as a road map toward what lies ahead. But what happens is rarely attributable to one cause, one story. Instead congregations are compilations of stories interwoven over time, very often repeating themselves. And the congregations are often not aware of the patterns. Sometimes the stories are never spoken. Not knowing what the next story will be adds to the anxiety.

The anxiety plays out in various ways. Some congregations rush toward what they hope will be stability. Some congregational leaders try hard to manage as much as they can in order to control the anxiety. They try to hold the fort or force the group in a particular direction. Sometimes congregations just sit frozen in grief, often pretending they are not grieving.

Some congregations, however, take advantage of the opportunity that the transition presents. With the help of an interim minister, they discover that possibility can surpass fear. New stories, exciting stories, faithful stories emerge from their reflections, their conversations, their listening to both one another and their own dreams.

After serving as the Unitarian Universalist Association's transitions director for several years, I wanted to check out my own perceptions of how interim ministry has been evolving as both congregational and societal changes continue unabated. I decided to interview a number of experienced and currently serving interim ministers. I conducted these interviews in three group sessions. Altogether, fourteen interim ministers participated. They are: Nancy Arnold, Jennifer Brooks, Helen Carroll, Barbara Coeyman, Emily Melcher, Joel Miller, Mary Moore, Elaine Peresluha, Tracey Robinson-Harris, Don Rollins, Doug Wadkins, Marlene Walker, Sunshine Wolfe, and Gretchen Woods. This group includes men, women, trans people, people of color, white ministers, and bisexual, gay, lesbian, heterosexual, and older and newer ministers. They brought to our conversations the wealth of their experience and informed reflections about the congregations they have served. They have had a love for our faith that is unsurpassed by that of any people I have met. They see our congregations as giving us a real opportunity to make a difference in individuals' lives, in congregational life, and in the wider world.

During our conversations, I asked these interim ministers to focus on interim ministry as they experience it today, not simply as many remember it from one or two decades ago. As I both hoped and expected, our conversations dispelled the myth that all interim ministers and interim ministries are alike. There is no single story here. While the give-and-take of our conversations led us over a wide range of questions and contemplations, what stood out for me were the interim ministers' reflections on how their work has changed in the current world of changing congregational life, but also how in some ways the work of interim ministry has not changed at all.

What Has Not Changed

When the interim ministers described congregations at the beginning of a ministerial transition—in other words, at the time when they arrive to serve the congregation—they painted very much the same picture I see in my work with such congregations. The interim ministers typically find congregations much in need of grief work, although the congregations don't usually say so. In fact, the give-away is that the congregants are in a hurry to focus on the future. It is typical for them to want to move into the ministerial search process before they have done anything about coming to terms with their past. It is typical also for them to exhibit low tolerance for any changes the interim minister might initiate, particularly changes in worship. The interim ministers see this as indicative of a general wish to maintain the status quo, even though it means passing up opportunities that otherwise might be appealing.

The interim ministers find congregations in transition often have both low self-esteem and low self-awareness. Their low self-esteem is reflected in a common belief that no minister will want to be a candidate for their pulpit. The belief that they do not deserve a highly qualified minister plays out in their conviction that they cannot possibly raise the funds to pay for such a ministry. Congregations' low self-awareness typically plays out in their visions of themselves as they were in what they see as their "glory days." The interim ministers describe the ongoing challenge of bringing a church that is stuck in the 1970s or even the 1950s into the twenty-first century.

When I asked the interim ministers what were the easiest and the most difficult circumstances in which to pursue interim ministry, they generally agreed that the easiest might be the congregation that has just experienced a negotiated termination of a minister or some other kind of bad ending. Although this might be surprising, the truth is that such a congregation is likely to be broken open enough to be able to accept that things are in a sorry state and need attention. By way of contrast, the congregation that has just lost its much beloved former pastor is more likely to see no need for transitional work but instead to want to hurry up and find another minister as similar to the previous one as possible. The interim ministers agreed that the most difficult interim work is that following ministerial misconduct, sexual or otherwise, or following any major trauma.

What the experienced interim ministers stressed is how important it is not to begin a new interim ministry with a complicated program already set out in detail and not subject to revision. Instead the interim minister's first job is diagnostic—learning, not prescribing or even teaching. And the interim minister's ultimate job, with lots of participation by the congregation, may be to discern which practices and traditions need to be greatly modified or even let go and which are worth keeping. This has always been interim ministry's role and so it is still.

What Has Changed for the Better

In my group interviews, I was glad to hear the interim ministers agree that interim ministry has benefitted in recent years from some gradual but definite changes for the better. Long gone are the days when very many congregations needed to be convinced to hire an interim minister at all before proceeding to search for a called minister. Moreover, the norm, which used to be one year of interim ministry, has lengthened to two years and now, though rarely, three. Initially only congregations in special circumstances were believed to warrant two years of interim ministry. It has become more and more clear that the rare congregation is the one that doesn't exhibit any of the special circumstances, rather than the one that does. (See "The Temptation to Rush the Search.")

Also initially there was a widely held belief that large churches did not need an interim minister. There was often a succession plan in place whereby an associate minister would step up when the senior minister retired or otherwise moved on. But in recent years, interim ministry has become more of a norm even in large churches. This change has resulted in large measure from some old myths being put to rest. The stereotype used to be that interim ministers were not skilled in a particular kind of ministry but were instead damaged by unhappy experi-

ences as settled ministers, often had had negotiated terminations, and were merely marking time until they could retire.
They were assumed to have had little if any training in transitional ministry as a specialization, and it was expected that they
would merely serve as placeholders until new "real" ministers
could be called.

This stereotype has finally given way as interim training has
become more sophisticated and as more highly regarded ministers with experience in settled ministry have turned to interim
ministry as a career path that suits them and makes good use
of their skills. As the old stereotypes have died away and been
replaced by new realities, congregations in transition have
become far more receptive to interim ministry, less resistant
to the advice and counsel of interim ministers, less insistent
on quick fixes for their problems, more engaged as stakehold-
ers in analyzing their current situations, and more respectful
of interim ministers' expertise, skills, and insight. There is, of
course, much to applaud in this steadily changing congregational understanding and appreciation of interim ministry.

Changes in Congregational Life That Bring New Challenges for Interim Ministers

This bright picture of well-respected interim ministry is not
the whole story, however. During my interviews, the interim
ministers described several relatively new challenges that come
with changes in congregational life in an ever changing societal
context.

Technological Changes

Probably the main source of change in congregational life has
been increased reliance on technology. There are fewer face-
to-face meetings at church. People question whether even the
Board needs to meet face-to-face anymore. Committees that
meet essentially just to meet are quickly disappearing. Most
people don't read the newsletter these days, even an electronic
newsletter. In fact, high on the list of congregational challenges

is the need for new communication strategies. Congregational life is not nearly as Sunday centered, worship centered, or even building centered as it used to be.

Changes in Leadership and Governance

Congregational leaders tend to be older members, but they burn out even as they realize they are having trouble identifying what younger people need from the church. These older leaders are doers, some would say micro-managers, in a world that now wants them to be policy makers. They do not understand policy governance, and they are frustrated to discover there is not a cadre of volunteers available to take on the tasks of running the church. More and more, someone has to be paid to do tasks that volunteers used to do, and this means an increasing need for detailed job descriptions and personnel policies. It's hard to find anybody interested in learning about "leadership development." Leadership used to mean knowing what to do. Now it has come to mean being "adaptive," which entails not having all the answers but figuring out collectively with others what will revitalize the church.

Standing committees are disappearing, though some, especially those with older members, are hanging on for dear life, resisting anything like term limits. Typical among these are the finance committee, the endowment committee, and the aesthetics committee. It is much easier to recruit newer, younger members to serve on short-term task forces with a clear description of both the task and the desired outcome. The task is likely to be a service project, and it may well be focused on some need outside rather than inside of the church. Finally, people are looking for more meaningful work, not more meetings to attend.

Today's interim minister—in addition to helping the congregation complete the traditional interim tasks described in Part III of this book—needs to help it address these major changes in congregational life brought on by burgeoning technology and changing understandings of leadership and governance.

The Way Forward

As I drew my conversations with interim ministers to a close, I wanted to know what they believe lies ahead and whether they see reasons to be hopeful about interim ministry in the future. Clearly they are hopeful about their generally shared vision of the future of the church and the role of interim ministry in it. Above all, they are clear that the church of the future will be a missional church, focused on working for a better world, not focused merely on congregants' own personal needs. That does mean that more and more of church life will happen outside of any "bricks and mortar" church building and will happen every day of the week, not just on Sunday. They agree that if churches are to thrive, nothing, especially worship, dare be boring. But they also see plenty of evidence of people willing to work hard in new ways to put Unitarian Universalist values into action to change themselves, their congregations, and the world. And interim ministers can provide a great service by helping congregations discover new ways to do this. The congregations that make such discoveries during their interim years and act on them will clearly be the congregations most appealing to ministers in search.

Some congregations, it turns out, can reap great benefit from additional special care in preparation for interim ministry. Some are discovered to need additional special care following interim ministry. And you can also stay tuned for the further evolution of interim ministry that will inevitably come along in due time.

Afterword

BARBARA CHILD

■ ■ ▦ ■

I bought a door harp for the outside of my church study door, and then I discovered that when the door was open, someone who walked by was likely to stop and bounce the suspended wooden balls against the wires, one at a time, and smile at the music that came forth. If someone came into my study and we chose to close the door, our conversation waited until we had finished listening to the door harp's bouncing tones. Sometimes we closed the door again with a good thwack to get more sound out of the harp, and I confess that sometimes when I was alone in the study, I would give the door a little kick—not in anger, you understand, but because that was the way I could leave the door open and still hear the music of the door harp.

I searched out a door harp because I loved the jaunty sound of the one on a friend's front door. But I didn't appreciate its power until I began to notice its effect on my visitors and me. Whatever was on our minds, the door harp slowed us down and invited us to take a little time to enjoy its pure sound. It got lots more use if my door was open, so it encouraged me to keep my door open most of the time. If the door happened to be closed, the harp worked just fine as a doorbell, and was much more pleasant to listen to than a knock.

What makes music come from the door harp is the circular sound hole at its center. The music comes from the empty space. You can imagine how intrigued I was to discover Robert Dixon-

Kolar's essay on door harps, "As the Door Opens: When Music Arises from Emptiness," in the Winter 2001 issue of *Parabola*. The author points out that a door harp is a perfect instrument for a Taoist. Of course. According to the wisdom of Lao Tzu, in the *Tao Te Ching*,

> We shape clay into a pot,
> but it is the emptiness inside
> that holds whatever we want.

I was drawn to the door harp because as an interim minister, I was making an empty space for something—and someone— new to come into. The door harp seems the perfect symbol for ministry to people in liminal spaces, on thresholds, during interim times.

We hope the essays in this book have shown how congregations have a rare opportunity to take advantage of an open space, a breathing space during an interim period. This is a time to take stock of who they are now and how different they are from when they last called a minister, how their programs are faring, what worthy challenges they face, and how they are getting on together as a community. It is a time to do whatever needs doing to prepare to welcome a new called minister with enthusiasm for the possibilities of new paths, new ways, new ideas. The work of the *intentional* interim minister is not to serve as placeholder and supply preacher; it is to help the congregation make sure the next called minister is not an *unintentional* interim minister—that is, one who does not last long because the interim work was not done before the new called minister arrived.

In his essay "Circles," Ralph Waldo Emerson wrote, "People wish to be settled; only as far as they are unsettled is there any hope for them." Interim ministry invites congregations and interims to join together in sharing an exciting and fruitful time of being unsettled, in between called ministries.

What's to Love about Being an Interim Minister

Interim ministry was my plan B the year after I received my MDiv degree and preliminary fellowship as a Unitarian Universalist minister. I knew the church where I hoped to be called would be going into search the following year. And sure enough, the next year I got my plan A wish and served there for four fruitful years, all the while remembering that year of interim ministry, noticing the striking differences between interim and called ministry, and learning how much more suited I was to the former than the latter. The reasons for this include:

- The fast pace of interim ministry appealed to me with its invitation to "jump in with both feet" and the incentive it provided to learn a whole lot about a congregation in a hurry. In contrast, the pace of congregational life during ordinary times with a called minister was much too slow for me.

- Interim ministry put a premium on experimentation, trying new things, understanding mistakes as the way to learn more and learn it more quickly. In contrast, called ministry upheld values that favored precedent and continuity, and made it dangerously likely to do something a certain way because "that's the way we've always done it."

- Interim ministry encouraged the freedom to search out what was stuck and unstick it. It freed me from called ministry's pressure to follow a congregation's preconceived agenda.

- As an interim, I discovered it was quite all right to be a pain in the neck, at least to be perceived that way by some congregants. It was more than all right to engage in plain speaking and decline to participate as rescuer in some triangle with a self-identified victim who insisted somebody else was perpetrating no end of trouble. It was easier to keep myself differentiated and at some distance because I was hired by the Board with a contract for a fixed term, thus, in a sense, "pre-fired." As a called minister, on the other hand, with an indefinite term but always subject to the possibility of a congregational vote to terminate the relationship, I found that relational ministry created much more incentive to please and even appease people.

- I experienced the consultative quality of interim ministry as offering the opportunity to practice energetic and exuberant short-term ministry to congregational groups, where I could offer people good opportunities to work out the meaning and purpose of their lives in settings where they were invited to relate to each other beneath the surface. I was much more drawn to this kind of ministry to groups than to long-term ministry to individuals, so much of which has to happen one person at a time. I was, frankly, more interested in group dynamics than individual personalities, more sociologist than psychologist.

- Interim ministry taught me the essential value of being friendly to all but a friend to none, given my understanding that friendship includes mutual sharing of confidences, which is inappropriate in any minister-congregant relationship. Such a stance is more easily accepted by congregants when the minister is an interim. I could be myself without a lot of pushback from people wanting me to be their intimate friend. As an interim, I was always conscious of how important it was not to allow the congregation to get drawn into a relationship with me that would only lead them to another round of grieving when I left. Better that I leave with a few tin cans clanking along behind and congregants saying, in so many words, "Here's your hat. What's your hurry?" One congregation got the point so well and so delightfully that, on my last day with them, they presented me with a walking stick that had a bunch of real tin cans tied to it. The cans were brightly painted, and some had actual pictures of the building and congregants. I loved it, and it let my leaving be celebrated with lots of lovely shared laughter.

- As an interim, I came to value the benefits of having experience from inside many different congregations of different size, in different parts of the country, and with different congregational cultures. This appealed to me far more than the common ministerial aim to have only a few long-term pastorates. Indeed, I came to question the value of long-term pastorates for either the minister or the congregation.

- I came to love living a life that constantly insisted I test assumptions and try new things. I could no longer imagine living a life that would tempt me with comforts that would eventually leave me feeling stale.

- Finally, if the purpose of the church is to change lives, I believe interim ministry makes it easier to do that, because interims come to a congregation when the people are likely to be broken open by loss and its attendant grief or conflict or both, at a time when people are more inescapably real and thus more open to transformation.

In short, I count it an extraordinary stroke of luck that I experienced plan B for my professional life as a minister before plan A, and thus could truly discover the contrasts between interim and called ministry, and how much more suited I was to the former. In my life, for my life, it has made all the difference.

Some Moments That Make an Interim Minister Proud

Perhaps the best part about being an interim minister is those moments of pride in the work you have done in the congregation, when you see that they are beginning transformation, getting ready to embark on a new era with a new settled minister, and excited about the possibilities and adventure before them. For instance,

- You look around a room full of people who are speaking to each other in pairs during an initial stage of an Appreciative Inquiry project. They are each recalling a time at church when they were entirely engaged—as they are at this moment—and knew that this was the right church for them. And you know that by the time the Appreciative Inquiry project is completed some months later, this congregation will be putting some provocative proposals into action, getting a head start on bringing to fruition what they want more of, and also bringing forward the best of the past, which they want to be sure to keep. (See Diana Whitney and Amanda Trosten-Bloom's *The Power of Appreciate Inquiry: A Practical Guide to Positive Change* for more insight.)

- You walk into the room to begin the first session of a new-member series and see how many long-time members have taken up your invitation to come along. You know what you are offering them is a new and different look at Unitarian Universalism, with newcomers and stalwarts getting to know each other as well as the faith.

- You discover that, one by one, Board members are speaking out to the one among them who is routinely rude and disruptive, making it plain that this behavior is not acceptable to the rest of them. It has taken patience and persistence, but at last they are seeing that it is not true that "anything goes" if they are to have a healthy congregational community.

- You watch a Board reach the necessary but nonetheless painful agreement that a much-loved but incompetent staff member must be dismissed, even though they know the dismissal will cause them to be in hot water with some of their friends. Your work with them on the relationship between governance and ministry is bearing fruit. They have a new appreciation for what it means to fulfill their fiduciary obligations as Board members. (See Dan Hotchkiss, *Governance and Ministry: Rethinking Board Leadership.*)

- You watch a congregation for the first time in its known history work up real priorities for a stewardship campaign, insist on training for canvassers, and adopt a year-round stewardship calendar. And then you watch those decisions and choices bear fruit. (See Michael Durall's *Creating Congregations of Generous People* and *The Almost Church Revitalized: Envisioning the Future of Unitarian Universalism.*)

- You arrive at the moment when a long-entrenched Sunday Services Committee finally understands that they need to be open to working with the minister on worship services rather than claiming a certain number each month as "theirs" to do with as they please. (See Wayne B. Arnason and Kathleen Rolenz's *Worship That Works: Theory and Practice for Unitarian Universalists.*)

- You get to march in a local gay pride parade behind the denominational banner, with one end of it held up by a Board member of the congregation you are serving and the other end held up by a

Board member from the breakaway congregation that formed in the wake of the negotiated termination of the previous minister. When you arrived, these congregations were at war; this moment symbolizes truce—well, much more than truce: enthusiasm about working together for the greater good of the denominational presence in the entire metropolitan area.

- You watch with the ministerial settlement representative as your collaborative efforts bear fruit: The Board members have come to a shared understanding that undertaking a time-consuming and labor-intensive process for selecting Ministerial Search Committee members is worthwhile. It is worthwhile because it dramatically increases the odds that the committee members will have the trust of the entire congregation rather than being viewed as individually representing some particular interest such as religious education, social justice, or the Sunday services program.

- You are so proud you can hardly stand it when a congregation embraces its Ministerial Search Committee that has taken the courageous step of bringing forward no candidate rather than settling for a minister they really knew would not be an appropriate choice for the congregation. Even if you see yourself as more consultant than pastor, it is an honor then to serve as pastor and champion of that Search Committee. (For more about search committees and the search process, see "The Interim Minister's Role in Ministerial Search.")

- When the Search Committee does bring forth a candidate, you stay away during candidating week, but you are close enough in case things go awry on the final Sunday—that is, in case the vote is not high enough to result in a call, or in case the candidate for some reason does not accept the call. Should the president's phone call let you know of such an outcome, you'll be on your way to the church in seconds, ready to serve as pastor to Search Committee and congregation alike. But when the president calls to let you know the candidate has accepted the congregation's call, you rejoice. All your work and all their work has borne fruit, and it is quite all right to tease them that, from now on, they will not even notice you when you pass in the hallway.

The Invisible Signs over the Interim Minister's Desk

Throughout my interim ministries, I have had what I think of as invisible signs over my desk, constant reminders to myself to keep me sane and whole, and always focused on the called ministry next to come. One such invisible sign reads, "If I do this thing that I am contemplating doing—or if I do not do this thing that I am contemplating not doing—what effect is it likely to have on the next ministry?"

Another invisible sign, which has guided me in my life as well as my interim ministry, reads, "The idea is not to become comfortable but to remain relaxed in your discomfort." This was one of my great lessons from my first tai chi teacher, David Chapman at Long Wind Farm in East Thetford, Vermont. Dave got me to notice that I wobbled so much when I tried to stand on one foot because I clenched. If I relaxed—and if I thought of it less as a terrible failure when I toppled—I wobbled and toppled less.

Dave's lesson was amplified for me by Gil Rendle, then a senior consultant at the Alban Institute, when he was the major presenter at the annual continuing education seminar of the Unitarian Universalist Interim Ministry Guild. I told him my story about the door harp as my symbol for interim ministry. He reminded me that I did not serve a congregation as interim in order to make a space for somebody else to come along and become a new fixture, replacing the one who was previously affixed, even though temporarily so. The interim, he said, is there to help people learn to be agile (the opposite of fixed) and thus able to navigate not just one change—a change of ministers —but all the changes that life brings.

What a high calling! How much people need this agility! How much I need it too! And so I have always thought I teach myself while teaching others. Gil Rendle and Dave Chapman were surely in league with one another. When Dave Chapman said, "The idea is not to become comfortable; the idea is to become relaxed in your discomfort," he knew that was the way to stop wobbling and become agile. I believe he also knew it would keep you from shutting down.

Over my desk, I also have a couple of quite real and visible cartoons, just to keep my seriousness in perspective. One shows an executioner speaking to the prisoner about to be guillotined, saying, "Actually, my official job title is co-chairman of the Transition Team." The other cartoon shows a couple of cats in conversation behind an upholstered chair, the back of which has been torn to shreds. One cat is saying to the other, "I have a couple of other projects I'm excited about." Maybe, after all, these cartoons are there to remind me of some other people's impressions of interim ministry. Thus, when I finish chuckling, I need to remember the importance always of showing others what interim ministry actually is rather than what they might have been told it is by someone else.

That is in part why this book came to be. You who have been reading it might be an interim minister yourself, or you might be a minister interested to discern whether you would like to pursue interim ministry training and then take up this work. You might be a member of a Unitarian Universalist congregation, possibly a congregational leader in the process of deciding whether to apply for an interim to come when your called minister leaves. You might be a member of a congregational Board that has already signed an agreement with an interim to serve you for the next year or two; however, the interim has not yet arrived, or has only just arrived, and you wonder what lies ahead for you and the rest of your congregation. We think of this book as especially for all of you.

There is one more thing I have posted above my desk: a bookmark with Emily Dickinson's message, "I dwell in possibility." Beneath the words, a beautiful flower opens.

Resources

■ ■ ▨ ■

Adams, James Luther. *The Prophethood of All Believers.* George K. Beach, ed. Boston: Beacon Press, 1986.

Arnason, Wayne B., and Kathleen Rolenz. *Worship That Works: Theory and Practice for Unitarian Universalists.* Boston: Skinner House Books, 2007.

Baab, Lynne M. *The Power of Listening: Building Skills for Mission and Ministry.* Lanham, MD: Rowman & Littlefield, 2014.

Beaumont, Susan. "Core Competencies of Large Church Leadership": www.alban.org/conversation.aspx?id=7022.

Belote, Thom, ed. *The Growing Church: Keys to Congregational Vitality.* Boston: Skinner House Books, 2010.

Bendroth, Norman B. *Transitional Ministry Today: Successful Strategies for Churches and Pastors.* Lanham, MD: Rowman & Littlefield, 2015.

Branson, Mark Lau. *Memories, Hopes, and Conversations: Appreciative Inquiry and Congregational Change.* Herndon, VA: Alban Institute, 2004.

Bridges, William. *Managing Transitions: Making the Most of Change.* Second Ed. Cambridge, MA: Perseus Books, 2003.

————. *Transitions: Making Sense of Life's Changes: Strategies for Coping with the Difficult, Painful, and Confusing Times in Your Life.* Second Ed. Cambridge, MA: Da Capo Press, 2004.

Brown, Juanita, with David Isaacs and the World Café Community. *The World Café: Shaping Our Futures Through Conversations That Matter.* San Francisco: Berrett-Koehler Publishers, 2005.

Callahan, Kennon. *Twelve Keys to an Effective Church: Strong, Healthy Congregations Living in the Grace of God.* Second Ed. San Francisco: Jossey Bass, 2010.

Chait, Richard P., William P. Ryan, and Barbara E. Taylor. *Governance as Leadership: Reframing the Work of Nonprofit Boards.* Hoboken, NJ: John Wiley & Sons, 2005.

Chrodron, Pema. *Living Beautifully with Uncertainty and Change.* Boston: Shambhala Publications, 2013.

Cooperrider, David L., and Diana Whitney. *Appreciative Inquiry: A Positive Revolution in Change.* San Francisco: Berrett-Koehler Publishers, Inc., 2005.

Coutts, Peter. *Choosing Change: How to Motivate Churches to Face the Future.* Lanham, MD: Rowman & Littlefield, 2013.

Durall, Michael. *The Church We Yearn For: The Search for a New Minister as a Revolutionary Event in the Life and Times of Your Congregation.* Lakewood, CO: CommonWealth Consulting Group, 2012.

Freed, Rachael. "The Importance of Telling Our Stories," *Huffington Post*, November 15, 2010.

Friedman, Edwin H. *Friedman's Fables.* New York: Guilford Press, 1990.

————. *Generation to Generation: Family Process in Church and Synagogue.* New York: Guilford Press, 1985.

Harris, Robert A. *Entering Wonderland: A Toolkit for Pastors New to a Church.* Lanham, MD: Rowman & Littlefield, 2014.

Heifetz, Ronald, Alexander Grashow, and Marty Linsky. *The Practice of Adaptive Leadership: Tools and Tactics for Changing Your Organization and the World.* Boston: Harvard Business Press, 2009.

Heller, Anne Odin. *Churchworks: A Well-Body Book for Congregations.* Boston: Skinner House Books, 1999.

Herz, Walter P., ed. *Redeeming Time: Endowing Your Church with the Power of Covenant.* Boston: Skinner House Books, 1999.

Hotchkiss, Dan. *Governance and Ministry: Rethinking Board Leadership.* Second Ed. Lanham, MD: Rowman & Littlefield, 2016.

———. "Is It Wise to Hire Members?" *Congregations*, Summer 2005, No. 3. Alban Institute.

Jinkins, Michael, and Deborah Bradshaw Jinkins. *Power and Change in Parish Ministry: Reflections on the Cure of Souls.* Herndon, VA: Alban Institute, 1991.

Johnson, Barry. *Polarity Management: Identifying and Managing Unsolvable Problems.* Amherst, MA: HRD Press, 1996.

Kondrath, William M. *Congregational Resources for Facing Feelings.* Lanham, MD: Rowman & Littlefield, 2014.

———. *Facing Feelings in Faith Communities.* Lanham, MD: Rowman & Littlefield, 2013.

Latham, Robert T. *Moving On from Church Folly Lane: The Pastoral to Program Shift.* Tucson: Wheatmark, 2006.

Lawson, Kevin E., and Mick Boersma. *Associate Staff Ministry: Thriving Personally, Professionally, and Relationally.* Second Ed. Lanham, MD: Rowman & Littlefield, 2014.

Leas, Speed B. *Leadership & Conflict.* Nashville: Abingdon Press, 1986.

Lee Mun Wah, *The Art of Mindful Facilitation.* San Francisco: StirFry Seminars & Consulting, 2004.

Leu, Lucy. *Nonviolent Communication Companion Workbook: A Practical Guide for Individual, Group, or Classroom Study.* Nonviolent Communication Guides. Encinitas, CA: PuddleDancer Press, 2015.

Lott, David B., ed. *Conflict Management in Congregations.* Herndon, VA: Alban Institute, 2001.

Ludema, James D., Diana Whitney, Bernard J. Mohr, and Thomas J. Griffin. *The Appreciative Inquiry Summit: A Practitioner's Guide for Leading Large-Group Change.* San Francisco: Berrett-Koehler Publishers, 2003.

Mann, Alice. *The In-Between Church: Navigating Size Transitions in Congregations.* Herndon, VA: The Alban Institute, 1998.

———. *Raising the Roof: The Pastoral-to-Program Size Transition.* Herndon, VA: Alban Institute, 2001.

Mead, Loren B. *A Change of Pastors . . . and How It Affects Change in the Congregation.* Herndon, VA: Alban Institute, 2012.

Montgomery, Kathleen, ed. *Bless the Imperfect: Meditations for Congregational Leaders.* Boston: Skinner House Books, 2013.

Olsen, David C., and Nancy G. Devor. *Saying No to Say Yes: Everyday Boundaries and Pastoral Excellence.* Lanham, MD: Rowman & Littlefield, 2015.

Oswald, Roy M. "How to Minister Effectively in Family, Pastoral, Program, and Corporate Sized Churches": www.alban.org/conversation.aspx?id=1214.

Oswald, Roy, and Barry Johnson. *Managing Polarities in Congregations: Eight Keys for Thriving Faith Communities.* Herndon, VA: Alban Institute, 2009.

Owen-Towle, Tom. *Growing a Beloved Community: Twelve Hallmarks of a Healthy Congregation.* Boston: Skinner House Books, 2004.

Parsons, George, and Speed B. Leas. *Understanding Your Congregation as a System.* Herndon, VA: Alban Institute, 1993.

Rendle, Gil G. *Doing the Math of Mission: Fruits, Faithfulness, and Metrics.* Lanham, MD: Rowman & Littlefield, 2014.

Rendle, Gil, and Alice Mann. *Holy Conversations: Strategic Planning as a Spiritual Practice for Congregations.* Herndon, VA: Alban Institute, 2003.

Rendle, Gilbert R. *Behavioral Covenants in Congregations: A Handbook for Honoring Differences.* Herndon, VA: Alban Institute, 1998.

————. *Leading Change in the Congregation: Spiritual & Organizational Tools for Leaders.* Herndon, VA: Alban Institute, 1997.

Rosenberg, Marshall. *Living Nonviolent Communication: Practical Tools to Connect and Communicate Skillfully in Every Situation.* Boulder, CO: Sounds True, Inc., 2012.

————. *Nonviolent Communication: A Language of Life; Life-Changing Tools for Healthy Relationships.* Third Ed. Nonviolent Communication Guides. Encinitas, CA: PuddleDancer Press, 2015.

Rothauge, Arlin J. *Sizing Up a Congregation for New Member Ministry.* New York: The Episcopal Church Center, 1986.

Schaller, Lyle E. *Looking in the Mirror: Self-Appraisal in the Local Church.* Nashville: Abingdon Press, 1984.

————. *Strategies for Change.* Nashville: Abingdon Press, 1993.

Schwarz, Roger, Anne Davidson, Peg Carlson, and Sue McKinney. *The Skilled Facilitator Fieldbook: Tips, Tools, and Tested Methods for Consultants, Facilitators, Managers, Trainers, and Coaches.* San Francisco: Jossey-Bass, 2005.

Sellon, Mary K., and Daniel P. Smith. *Practicing Right Relationship: Skills for Deepening Purpose, Finding Fulfillment, and Increasing Effectiveness in Your Congregation.* Herndon, VA: Alban Institute, 2005.

Stafford, Gil W. *When Leadership and Spiritual Direction Meet: Stories and Reflections for Congregational Life.* Lanham, MD: Rowman & Littlefield, 2014.

Steinke, Peter L. *A Door Set Open: Grounding Change in Mission and Hope*. Herndon, VA: Alban Institute, 2010.

————. *Congregational Leadership in Anxious Times: Being Calm and Courageous No Matter What*. Herndon, VA: Alban Institute, 2006.

————. *Healthy Congregations: A Systems Approach*. Herndon, VA: Alban Institute, 1996.

————. *How Your Church Family Works: Understanding Congregations as Emotional Systems*. Herndon, VA: Alban Institute, 1993.

Thompson, George B., and Beverly Thompson. *Grace for the Journey: Practices and Possibilities for In-between Times*. Lanham, MD: Rowman & Littlefield, 2012.

Tran, Catherine C., and Sandra Hughes Boyd. *Spiritual Discovery: A Method for Discernment in Small Groups and Congregations*. Lanham, MD: Rowman & Littlefield, 2015.

Unitarian Universalist Association. "Disruptive Behavior Policies": www.uua.org/safe/44145.shtml.

————. "Safe Congregations": www.uua.org/safe/index.shtml.

————. *Interdependence: Renewing Congregational Polity: A Report by the Commission on Appraisal*. Boston: Unitarian Universalist Association, 1997.

Unitarian Universalist Interim Ministry Guild. *Janus Workbook*: www.uua.org/careers/ministers/interim/22352.shtml.

Whitney, Diana, Amanda Trosten-Bloom, Jay Cherney, and Ron Fry. *Appreciative Team Building: Positive Questions to Bring Out the Best of Your Team*. Lincoln, NE: iUniverse, Inc., 2004.

Whitney, Diana, and Amanda Trosten-Bloom. *The Power of Appreciative Inquiry: A Practical Guide to Positive Change*. Second Ed. San Francisco: Berrett-Koehler Publishers, 2010.

Wikstrom, Erik Walker, ed. *Serving with Grace: Lay Leadership as a Spiritual Practice.* Boston: Skinner House Books, 2010.

Wimberly, John W., Jr. *Mobilizing Congregations: How Teams Can Motivate Members and Get Things Done.* Lanham, MD: Rowman & Littlefield, 2015.

Yonkman, Todd Grant. *Reconstructing Church: Tools for Turning Your Congregation Around.* Lanham, MD: Rowman & Littlefield, 2014.

Websites

Daryl Conner's Blog: www.changethinking.net

Interim Ministry Network: www.imnedu.org

Side with Love: www.sidewithlove.org

UUA Transitions Office: www.uua.org/transitions

About the Contributors

■ ■ ▫ ■

ANDREA LA SONDE ANASTOS is a trained interim minister, with experience in dual-affiliated congregations. Now retired from parish ministry, she publishes spirituality and worship resources through her daily blog at immram-chara.net, offers spiritual direction and coaching, and is an almost full-time fiber artist.

NANCY BOWEN is the former regional staff team leader for the UUA's Pacific Western Region. She has worked as a regional staff member for the UUA for twenty-five years in both New England and the West. She helped implement the concept of developmental ministry in Boulder, Colorado. She is now retired and lives with her husband Howell Lind in New Mexico.

KAREN BRAMMER served as smaller congregation specialist for the UUA's Northern New England District until 2013. She has served as minister in Saco and Biddleford, Maine, and currently serves as part-time minister in Mohegan Lake, New York. She also serves as part-time manager for the UUA Green Sanctuary Program.

BARBARA CHILD, an accredited interim minister, retired from full-time ministry in 2010. Since then she has served as a ministerial settlement representative (the position now known as regional transitions coach), coaching congregations in transition and especially their ministerial search committees. She has served as good officer, ministering to ministers, and now serves on the UU Ministers Association's Good Officer Support Team, ministering to good officers. She also continues to serve as a short-term consultant to Unitarian Universalist congregations. She is the editor of *The Spirit That Moves: Readings and Rituals for Times of Change and Transition*, published by Skinner House Books. She lives in a log cabin in the woods in Brown County, Indiana.

NATHAN DETERING feels privileged to serve the Unitarian Universalist Area Church at First Parish in Sherborn, Massachusetts, where since 2003 the congregation and his ministry have thrived in part because of a strong two-year interim ministry prior to his settlement. He lives with his wife and two children in Holliston, Massachusetts.

FRAN DEW served as interim minister to congregations from coast to coast for her entire ministry. In retirement she is happily settled in the Midwest.

ROBERTA FINKELSTEIN is a lifelong Unitarian Universalist. In her twenty-five years of professional ministry she has served in consulting, settled, and new start positions. Most recently she has found her passion in transitional ministry; she has been an interim minister in five congregations and is currently exploring developmental ministry.

HEATHER LYNN HANSON has served Unitarian Universalist congregations from small fellowships to large well-resourced churches across the United States. Now retired and settled near family in Oregon, she enjoys singing in the choir and preaches occasionally in area Unitarian Universalist churches.

PAM BLEVINS HINKLE participated in an Appreciative Inquiry-based interim ministry process in a midsized congregation. A Unitarian Universalist since 1992, Pam is director of the Spirit & Place Festival in Indianapolis, Indiana, and she has served as the choir director for the Midwest Unitarian Universalist Summer Assembly since 1998.

OLIVIA HOLMES is an accredited interim minister who is pursuing short-term transitions consulting in her early retirement years, offering start-up, stewardship, Board retreat, and mission development workshops to congregations within both the Unitarian Universalist Association and the United Church of Christ. She has more than twenty-five years of experience as a UU parish minister and as director of international and interfaith relations for the UUA. She is a lifelong Unitarian Universalist.

EVAN KEELY is an accredited interim minister who has served Unitarian Universalist congregations from family-sized to corporate-sized, and from brand-new to centuries-old, in Maryland, Massachusetts, New Jersey, Pennsylvania, Texas, and Virginia.

MARGARET KEIP served the Unitarian Universalist Church of the Monterey Peninsula for twenty-five years with her co-minister husband, Fred. She went on to serve as interim minister to six congregations, all but one in the Pacific Western region. She is now contentedly retired in Grants Pass, Oregon.

DAVID KEYES consults with congregations on transitions, staff, governance, and fundraising. As an interim minister, he has served fourteen congregations.

MAUREEN KILLORAN is an accredited interim minister who has served Unitarian Universalist congregations in British Columbia, Oregon, North Carolina, Georgia, Pennsylvania, Maryland, Missouri, Texas, and Florida for more than thirty years. As an "organizational midwife," Maureen's greatest joy is seeing congregations claim their strengths and move toward greater health. She looks forward to an active and productive retirement in central Florida.

KEITH KRON is director of the Transitions Office for the UUA and has visited nearly five hundred congregations in his time working there. He enjoys learning about the enneagram, playing and coaching tennis, and collecting children's books (at 8,000 books and growing).

ROBERT T. LATHAM has been a Unitarian Universalist minister since 1969 and has served as an interim minister for ten years with medium- to large-sized congregations. He has also been the settled minister in four congregations, led a variety of specialized denominational ministry projects, and served as interim district executive. He presently heads a congregational consulting service.

ALISON MILLER is a minister who has had the experience of being called to a congregation following two years of interim ministry with two different ministers. She is a lifelong Unitarian Universalist who has served our faith in large and midsized congregations, at the UUA, on college campuses, and through interfaith community organizing efforts.

MARTHA L. MUNSON is a lifelong Unitarian Universalist and an accredited interim minister. She's served as a hospital chaplain, and in settled and interim capacities, in eight congregations in the U.S. and Canada.

JOHN NICHOLS is an accredited Unitarian Universalist interim minister, following a long career as a settled minister. His greatest achievement has been surviving cancer.

RICHARD A. NUGENT, currently employed by the Unitarian Universalist Association, served as interim minister to seven Unitarian Universalist congregations. Prior to entering the ministry, he worked for more than two decades as a political consultant, a staff member to two U.S. Senators, a lobbyist for the Epilepsy Foundation and the Unitarian Universalist Association, and the administrator of a health care reform project in Indonesia.

DEBORAH J. POPE-LANCE is a consultant to clergy, staff teams, and congregations and an author, speaker, and educator on ministerial ethics and practice and on interim ministry within a variety of faith communities and organizations, including the UUA, Andover Newton Theological School, the Alban Institute, and the Interim Ministry Network. She has served in parish, counseling, and interim ministries for more than thirty-five years. She currently maintains a clinical practice as a licensed marriage and family therapist in Natick, Massachusetts.

LISA PRESLEY has served as an interim minister, a called minister, and a member of an interim minister search committee. She now supports interims in her role as field staff with the MidAmerica Region. She strongly believes the interim time is a great liminal opportunity for congregations to reinvent themselves in positive ways.

SUZANNE REDFERN-CAMPBELL has served our denomination in both settled and transitional ministries since 1985, and she takes great joy in helping congregations become stronger, healthier, and more justice-oriented and mission-focused. She currently serves as developmental minister of the Unitarian Universalist Church of Las Cruces, New Mexico, where she shares a home with her husband Chuck and a mellow orange cat named Sunny.

ED ROCKMAN is a retired CPA and longtime active member of the Unitarian Universalist Church of the North Hills in Pittsburgh, Pennsylvania. He chaired the transition team that worked with the church's interim minister during its most recent and very successful interim ministry.

CARLTON ELLIOTT SMITH is an interim minister who has also served congregations as an assistant minister. A native of the South, he sees Unitarian Universalism as a good place to work on the salvation of his soul.

JUDITH WALKER-RIGGS is retired, following a career as both an interim and settled minister, and now acts as mentor to ministers. She also served a Unitarian congregation in England, where she temporarily acquired an English accent.

Index